The Bare-Sarked Warrior
A Brief Cultural History of Battlefield Exposure

MEDIEVAL AND RENAISSANCE
TEXTS AND STUDIES

VOLUME 451

The Bare-Sarked Warrior
A Brief Cultural History of Battlefield Exposure

Oren Falk

ARIZONA CENTER FOR MEDIEVAL
ACMRS
AND RENAISSANCE STUDIES

Tempe, Arizona
2015

THE ARIZONA CENTER FOR

MEDIEVAL &
RENAISSANCE

STUDIES

Published by ACMRS (Arizona Center for Medieval and Renaissance Studies), Tempe, Arizona.

Library of Congress Cataloging-in-Publication Data

Falk, Oren, 1969-
 The bare-sarked warrior : a brief cultural history of battlefield exposure / Oren Falk.
    pages cm. -- (Medieval and renaissance texts and studies ; Volume 451)
 Includes bibliographical references and index.
 ISBN 978-0-86698-502-4 (acid-free paper)
 1. Old Norse literature--History and criticism. 2. Women in literature.
 3. Women--Mythology. 4. Literature, Medieval--History and criticism.
 5. Literature and history. I. Title.
 PT7162.W6F35 2015
 839'.609322--dc23

                                                            2015013048

∞
This book is made to last. It is set in Adobe Caslon Pro,
smyth-sewn and printed on acid-free paper to library specifications.
Printed in the United States of America

TABLE OF CONTENTS

I. Preface

This book traces a peculiar microhistory: the career of a literary configuration, whose stable form endures across centuries, continents, and cultures, but is in each case modulated and firmly embedded within a particular society's history. Conceptually, the argument thus constantly looks in two directions: towards the timeless mechanisms of literary effect, on the one hand, and towards the specific contexts of historical circumstance, on the other. It is this interaction of the universal and the specific that I seek to chart.

This book is also astigmatic in terms of its intended audiences. The seven chapters of the main text aim to draw readers forward along a narrative track. They are largely free-standing and allow casual readers to bracket the more technical aspects dealt with in the notes. The intellectually curious and specialists in various aspects of the history I touch on can confirm the accuracy of my claims, retrace my argumentation, and weigh it against others' opinions by consulting the scholarly apparatus. Finally, a series of sidebars are designed to help non-specialist readers—which, in such a wide-ranging investigation, means every reader, at one point or another—orient themselves in the argument (Sidebars 1–4) or pursue some of its byways to greater depths (Sidebars 5–8).

Except as otherwise noted, translations throughout are my own; I have preserved the seemingly free alternation of tenses in Old Norse, and, to the extent possible, the orthography of editions and manuscripts cited (expanding, however, abbreviations). When writing in my own voice, I normalize Icelandic names and terms to thirteenth-century forms. Icelanders are referred to (and alphabetized in bibliographies) by proper name, not patronym. For languages I cannot myself read (Arabic, Breton, Gəʽəz, Greek, and Irish), I have relied on published translations, consulting dictionaries and scholars conversant with these languages whenever possible.

In many years' work on this topic, I have incurred innumerable debts. Many individual contributions are acknowledged in the notes below. I wish to thank especially Daniel Baraz, Natalie Zemon Davis, Roberta Frank, Andy Galloway, Walter Goffart, Jennifer Harris, David and Ian McDougall, Elizabeth Walgenbach, and my proverbially long-suffering family: Ruma and Raphael Falk, Hana and Dubi Levitte, Raya and Avisar Cohen, and Yael, Nomi and Daniella, *in sœtastu ljós augna minna*.

II. Introduction: First Contact

My sister's a hag of Hell! But of all our family I'm her last defender. She was fashioned of Erik's urgent clay, endowed with his reckless courage, and yet she was always a half—the violence of her father without his vision of justice. Even as a clawing, snarling teen-ager she craved acclaim, and her hunger grew with the years, but she was fated never to feast to repletion. If she'd been born with a phallus she might be sitting today in this high-seat. . . . Was it that baleful land that unbalanced her, the land that conquered both my brothers, or did she carry the flaw within her?

Leif Eriksson, in Irwin's *Gudrid's Saga* (1974: 234)

It's a story that's been told many times before: the proud dragon prows, cutting westward across a wine-dark sea; the fair-haired navigators, staring in amazement at Natives in their skin canoes; the tentative trading, the suspicions and brutalities, and finally the failure and eviction of Leifr the Lucky Eiríksson and his Norsemen from the New World paradise they had discovered, somewhere on the shores of what would not be known for five centuries yet as "America." By now, every schoolboy knows that Columbus came second; that Scandinavian sailors, reaching for an ultimate Viking Age achievement just as the Viking Age was drawing to a close, may claim credit for the first European crossing of the Atlantic; and that, at the auspiciously bilingual L'Anse aux Meadows on the northern edge of Newfoundland, archaeologists led by an Indiana-Jones-like Helge Ingstad have uncovered material confirmation of this unique Norse exploit, lying dormant in the soil since ca. 1000 AD. It is a rousing tale, tinged with tragedy: the anguish of daring explorers who reached their promised land but were prevented from establishing a permanent foothold in it, as well as the far darker one of the Native peoples who, this time around, were able to stave off the invaders. There are no winners in this story, only those who lost and those who would lose still more.[1]

---

[1] Of many excellent treatments of the Norse discovery and loss of America, perhaps the most accessible is Fitzhugh and Ward (2000). See also Ingstad (1985); Jones (1986); Wahlgren (1993); Wawn and Þórunn Sigurðardóttir (2001); Gísli Sigurðsson (2004: 253–302); Perkins (2004); and Wallace (2006). On the relations among Norsemen, Natives, and later settlers of America, see Mancini (2002: 885–87, esp. 886n48).

This book begins from a consideration of one tiny moment in this story of many-layered failure. It is an atypical moment, a local Norse triumph secured by the most unconventional means, and its enigma has attracted a good deal of scholarly (and not-so-scholarly) attention. None of the interpretations that have been ventured so far, it seems to me, quite fits together the pieces of this puzzle. In seeking a solution, I cast across vast stretches of time and space, sketching a vertiginous macro-context for this focused microhistory. In the process, I also recover a lost topos, a commonplace of the medieval (and, as I hope to show, in certain respects also pre- and post-medieval) imagination that has long escaped notice. Freydís Eiríksdóttir, the protagonist of this tale, emerges as one member of a far-flung sisterhood—far from the unique "hag of Hell" that Constance Irwin imagines her half-brother Leifr to have deemed her (see further Sidebar 1). Cracking Freydís's code casts new light not only on the botched Norse expedition to Vínland (as Leifr named his new-found land)[2] but also on a spectral host of other women—Hecuba, the Blessed Virgin, Marianne, and many others of lesser renown—who crowd in the shadows behind her. What begins as an effort to make sense of a one-off literary and historical curiosity, so remote and seemingly singular as to be nearly incomprehensible, ends up as an exploration of gender, power, and identity configurations shared and appropriated by many societies struggling to cope with extremes of violence.

The circumstances for the episode I analyse, the presence of Freydís at the forefront of the great exploratory venture that brought the Norse to Vínland and threw them into conflict with its Natives, are not in themselves surprising. Both texts and archaeology, for all the many points on which they diverge (most notably, the location of Leifr's Vínland itself), confirm the presence of women on the westerly voyages. Freydís, however, stands out among them. Where other women's roles are confined to suitably domestic pursuits—they bear children, spin wool, distribute drinks to guests[3]—Freydís is remarkable for her embroilment in that

---

[2] Since the toponym 'America' still lay centuries in the future, I apply 'Vínland' promiscuously to the entire area of Norse activity west of the Atlantic. In a narrow sense, Vínland is only one of three lands discovered beyond Greenland: *Helluland* (lit. 'Slab-land'), generally identified nowadays as Baffin Island; *Markland* ('Wood-land'), usually identified with present-day Labrador; and *Vínland* ('Wine-land'), a richer region somewhere to the south of the other two, which has yet to be convincingly pinpointed. See, most recently, Wallace (2006).

[3] On Norse child-rearing in the New World, see n24 in this chapter; on archaeological evidence for the production of textiles at L'Anse aux Meadows, see Wallace (2006: 68); on Norse women who bear milk to Native Americans, see *Grœnlendinga saga* cap. 6 (ÍF 4: 262; and cf. the traditional role of women as cup-bearers at Germanic feasts: Enright 1996; Kvilhaug 2004). One other traditional function women on the Vínland voyages fill is to serve as a cause of contention among men; see *Eiríks saga rauða* cap. 12 (ÍF 4: [*H*] 233, [*S*] 432) and cf. Jochens (2002). (See n13 in this chapter for an explanation of the sigla.)

1. Methodology: Prolonged literary echoes

Historians are generally accustomed to working with only two broad types of materials: *primary sources* are repositories of evidence, emanating from the greatest proximity attainable to the past on which the investigation focuses, while *secondary sources* provide interpretations, other scholars' accumulated efforts to make sense of the evidence. Over the course of the past century, historians have grown increasingly ecumenical and savvy in their definitions of primary and secondary sources. The former category now no longer includes only official records and eye-witness accounts—though these are certainly still prized—but also much farther removed and less obviously documentary genres, as well as conceptually more diverse, non-textual witnesses: private correspondence, programmatic manifestos, literary flights of fancy, and poetic reflexes may all be mined for evidence; so, too, can archaeological finds, architecture and landscapes, visual portrayals, even musical representations. Secondary literature, meanwhile, no longer means just the commentary of previous historians on the evidence at hand, but includes also the observations and analyses of scholars in many related fields—archaeology, again, but also sociology, anthropology, political science, and various material sciences, to name a few—as well as various theoretical apparatus proposed by sister disciplines, notably anthropology and literary studies.

Throughout my discussion in this book, however, I have occasional recourse to a third type of resource, not hitherto systematically tapped, to the best of my knowledge, in historical analysis: *modern authors' non-academic retellings*, in fiction and creative non-fiction, of the Vínland history and, specifically, of the episode at the heart of my investigation.[1] Many of the passages I draw on appear as epigraphs to individual chapters. These occasional quotations offer a kind of echo chamber, amplifying ideas that may be barely audible in the primary sources. Literary reflexes of the medieval evidence thus serve me in much the same way as visual images have traditionally served historians—often to the chagrin of art historians—to illuminate and punctuate an argument made primarily from the medieval texts themselves; but whereas iconography from the past should, properly, be treated as a primary source in its own right, medieval evidence imaginatively recast by a modern author functions differently.

Such modern reworkings offer valuable aid in analysing the primary sources in at least two ways. First, they recapitulate (or, occasionally, even preempt) scholarly theories, often articulating their underlying assumptions and (mis)conceptions more clearly than dry academic prose.[2] Second, with their

---

[1] I have offered a preliminary discussion of this new methodology in Falk (2011).

[2] In *Grœnlendinga saga* cap. 6, Guðríðr Þorbjarnardóttir meets a Native (?) woman who gives her name as Guðríðr, too (ÍF 4: 262–63); in the saga as it stands, the strange woman is the first speaker, but both Boyer (1976: 261–63) and Almqvist (2001: 26–27)

commonsensical filler—their own homegrown, popular hypotheses—fictional adaptations gloss over lacunae in the primary texts, as well as in the formal theories developed to explicate them. The comprehensive cohesion required of artistic renditions contrasts with the circumspection expected from academic analyses: the former do not have the liberty of admitting that some riddles cannot be solved.[3] Literary retellings thus offer a singular mixture of digested primary sources and modern interpretation, by both professional and amateur historians, often (especially in the less successful works) presented in a way that serves as a cautionary tale against the perils of anachronism: scholars too easily forget that the sources are never accessible to us in a primary state. Even when we read vellum manuscripts, we invariably superimpose modern filters on the medieval texts. Thus, for example, Jenny Jochens misremembers the saga narrative when she writes: "Freydís . . . pursues the invaders . . . they turn to confront her"—an inversion of the actual roles of pursuer and pursued recorded in the saga (cf. quotation at p. 12 below). Her slip seems telltale: the Hollywood-dominated modern ideal of epic heroism, disdainful of passive defence, intrudes on her recollection of the primary source.[4]

When dealing with a history like that of Vínland—especially apt to attract quacks, hacks, and earnest amateurs—the boundaries between serious scholarship and inspired frivolity are sometimes exceptionally difficult to draw. Many writers who choose to present themselves (and, in all likelihood, genuinely perceive themselves) as engaged in academic investigation do not, in fact, have the slightest grasp of the rudiments of critical methodology; still, their pronouncements often acquire the force of authority (as has happened, for instance, to the works of Henry Rowe Schoolcraft, Farley Mowat, or Frederick Pohl).[5]

---

suggest that the Native woman in fact imitated the introductory phrase she heard the Norse woman utter (see likewise Kolodny 2012: 66). I point out this example of art preempting scholarship in Falk (2004: 582). See also chapter II, n24 below.

[3] As Davis (1983: viii) and Bartlett (2004: 102) both point out.

[4] Jochens (1995: 77).

[5] Schoolcraft's claim to fame in Vínland circles is his account of a "formidable instrument, to which the name of balista may be applied," described to him by "[Chingwauk,] an Algonquin chief" and corroborated by images he discerned on the so-called Dighton Rock (1851–57: 1.85, 284); this instrument has been identified with a ballista-like weapon the *skrælingar* fire, according to *Eiríks saga rauða* cap. 11 (ÍF 4: [H] 228–29, [S] 429; see, e.g., Gathorne-Hardy 1921: 185–86; Gordon 1957: 219; Jones 1986: 133n17). If Schoolcraft's sources are not in themselves suspect enough (on Dighton Rock, see Brecher and Brecher 1958), nothing in his description (and in an accompanying illustration) in fact bears any resemblance to a missile weapon. On Schoolcraft, see further Kolodny 2012: 22–26, 121–24. Pohl, meanwhile, has identified the same saga missile weapon as "a white-faced hornets' nest" (1966: 150; see also 1972: 111–12). I have discussed these interpretations further in Falk (1998). For Mowat, see p. 51 below.

Conversely, some writers who self-consciously present non-scholarly interpretations (such as Constance Irwin or Nancy Marie Brown) offer, in fact, remarkably circumspect, rational, and occasionally shrewd readings. I do not contend that academic and imaginative treatments of the Vínland (or any other) history should be treated as equally authoritative, collapsing the distinction between the two modes completely. Rather, the porous nature of the boundary between scholarly analysis and popular retelling should itself be leveraged as a source of understanding.

most manly of all exploits: the labor of violence. That the Norse encounter with Natives rapidly devolved to bloodshed is, perhaps, also unsurprising; with post-1492 hindsight, we might even call such a trajectory inevitable. The majority of medieval Scandinavian texts, too, and especially the loquacious Icelandic sagas,[4] would lead us to expect from the Vínland explorers both proficiency at arms and an aggressive disposition. Yet most of the violence depicted in sagas tends to follow the familiar and ultimately cohesive pathways of feud. Antagonists on either side acknowledge their shared membership in a society that encompasses both, by whose unwritten rules both must abide; present enemies have been past allies and may yet expect to have friendly exchanges in the future, which creates strong incentives to follow the rules and wreak circumscribed havoc only.[5] In contrast, the clashes in Vínland fall into a menacing category of harm-mongering that pits against each other rivals unjoined by shared cultural discourse. This positioning of enemies across perceived societal margins dictates an insociable dynamic of

---

[4] There are many excellent introductions to the sagas and the issues involved in using them as historical sources. See esp. Meulengracht Sørensen (1993a), Miller (1990), and Byock (1988 and 2001), as well as Clover and Lindow (1985), Jónas Kristjánsson (1988), McTurk (2005), and Clunies Ross (2010). Attempts to distinguish among saga genres tend to generate much heat and little light. In general, when referencing 'sagas,' I have recourse to the so-called *Íslendingasögur* ("Sagas of Icelanders" or "Family Sagas") and *Sturlunga saga*, two sub-genres classified among the 'historical' sagas; occasionally, I also refer to *Fornaldarsögur* ("Sagas of Bygone Times") and *Riddarasögur* ("Chivalric Sagas"), sub-genres belonging to the 'legendary' sagas. The legendary material is sprawling, ill-defined, and poorly edited, so much less amenable to systematic study than the historical sagas; see Driscoll (2005), Glauser (2005), and Tulinius (2005).

[5] On feud as cohesive force, see primarily Black-Michaud (1975). Medieval Icelandic feuding customs are well-known nowadays, thanks to extensive (re)constructions by scholars such as Miller (1990), Byock (1982; 1988; 2001), and Meulengracht Sørensen (1993c). Medieval Icelanders presumably knew these feuding customs, too, although there is some controversy about the degree to which the sources available nowadays reflect their past lived reality.

strict exclusion.[6] The framework of feud acts as a safeguard against unchecked escalation; on the other hand, where combatants' codes for shaping their violence are incommensurable, risks multiply dramatically: destructive force unleashed when neither side can predict the other's actions is difficult to control.[7]

Still, as survivors look back on such violence, committing it to memory and imaginatively stylizing it in interpretative retrospect, brutalities begin to approximate familiar patterns and conform to secular myths. Such patterning contributes to internal social consolidation. When considered as an historiographic act—an attempt to interpret the past—the violent episode in which Freydís was involved begins to make sense, no matter how bewilderingly terrifying it might have been to anyone who lived through it. What had been experienced in real time as chaotic and perplexing becomes meaningful and predictable in hindsight.[8] The order imposed through narrative manipulation performs two simultaneous functions. On the one hand, it sharpens the boundaries between the social and the extra-social, reinforcing the exclusion of enemy Others: ambiguities are ironed out, potential pores plugged, and representations of violence, now pregnant with meaning, are directed to demarcating clearly the distinction between Us and Them. On the other hand, this new order insists on attributing to the clash with outsiders a primary domestic signification. The Others implicated must, by definition, be irreducibly foreign, but the role into which they are slotted is scripted purely in the narrating society's own symbolic language, played out according to its internal semiotic rules, and serves its Self-centered purposes only. No violence, certainly, is ever devoid of signification, but in accounts of exclusionary conflicts, elaborate, meaning-laden ceremony is especially close to the surface. The need to represent to social Selves a clash with inconceivable Otherness reduces opaque complexity to a set of theatrical gestures, designed

---

[6] On the dangerously vicious tenor of violence enacted between opponents who do not share cultural codes, see Clendinnen (1991), Gillingham (1992), and Halsall (1992).

[7] Elsewhere, I lay out a model for analysing violence along three principal axes, viz. power, signification, and risk. To analyse violence in instrumental terms, as an attempt to coerce others, is to focus on the dimension of power. To analyse it in symbolic terms, as an attempt to manipulate and project meanings, is to focus on the dimension of signification. Finally, to analyse it in cognitive terms, as an attempt to exercise agency despite an imperfect control over circumstances, is to focus on the dimension of risk. See further Falk (forthcoming).

[8] Cf. Morrison's discussion of myth: "empathies engrained by myth provide the moral cohesion of society. Initiation into its knowledge signals entrance into the network of obligations that binds individuals into community. . . . [M]yth ma[kes] sense of history. Myth [is] the context that [gives] meaning to [action], the game in which what might have been random events bec[o]me recognizable as ritualized play" (1992: 125, 189). See also Fischhoff (1980) and Kahneman (2011: 199–208).

to symbolize the Others' very Otherness.[9] Communicative aspects of the violent exchange, so ominously absent from actual confrontation, come alive in the retelling. Text, then, is able to extract meaningful ritual from senseless terror, subordinating the pell-mell of outgroup confrontation to structured ingroup tensions along lines of social (or narrative) hierarchy.

In such bids for intelligibility, gender metaphors are commonplace. Feminist semiotician Teresa de Lauretis proposes a bifurcating model of violence to explicate the work such metaphors carry out. In her analysis, men, real or metaphorical, confront each other as peers, and so their struggles ultimately resolve into a modus vivendi allowing social intercourse to go on; women, in contrast, are classified as categorically unequal, and so violence directed at them reinscribes the boundaries that exclude and subordinate them. Thus, while male-on-male violence creates, maintains, and proclaims reciprocity, male-on-female violence serves "to uphold the sexual oppression of women, or, better, to uphold the practices and institutions that produce 'woman' in terms of the sexual, and then oppression in terms of gender."[10] These convenient metaphors correspond, in fact, to the prevalent literal practice in Old Norse sources, which imagine the cohesive violence of feud to occur almost exclusively among men, but introduce women into accounts of conflict between irreconcilable imagined communities. The Vínland narrative thus transmutes a collision with distant, ethnic aliens into a more familiar friction with proximate, mysterious Woman. As in many other cultures, so also in medieval Scandinavia, the antithesis male/female was familiar, ready to hand, seemingly uncomplicated—yet clear-cut, radical, and ultimately irreducible. These characteristics made the gender antithesis an easily grasped representation of the unrepresentable.[11]

The episode I analyse draws on conventional gender imagery—securely anchored in a broad European context, but in certain respects specifically Norse—to craft a specialized literary topos. I coin the term "bare-sarked warrior" for this topos, with apologies to Snorri Sturluson. Snorri, a thirteenth-century

---

[9] On the indispensable rituals of violence, see, e.g., Coser (1956: 87–110), Davis (1973), Chagnon (1983: 170–77), and Nirenberg (1996). On the mechanisms of constituting Self and Other, see Ohle (1978).

[10] De Lauretis (1985a: 37); "the subject of violence," she adds, "is always, by definition, masculine; 'man' is by definition the subject of culture and of any social act. . . . [W]hat establishes the meaning of [any violent act is] the object on which or to which the violence is done . . . and that object is perceived or apprehended as either feminine or masculine" (1985a : 43, 42). On the usefulness of gender metaphors for resolving menacing opacity, cf. Douglas (1970). On the self-evidence of subjects' masculinity (and on the disturbing elision of metaphor and literal reality that this self-evidence begets), cf. MacKinnon: "'Human' and 'female' are mutually exclusive by definition" (1994: 184).

[11] Cf. Meulengracht Sørensen (1983: 20). On females as ultimate Others in Old Norse, see, e.g., Clunies Ross (1981), Linke (1996), and McKinnell (2005).

Icelandic scholar, suggested the etymology *berr serkr*, 'bare sarked [i.e., shirt-less],' for the native term *berserkr*, 'berserk warrior.' Although his etymology was false — berserks are evidently so named because they were thought to go into battle not bare-chested but wrapped in bear-skins[12] — it serves well to describe the literary concatenation I seek to isolate. The crucial formula locates an aggressor, unequivocally gendered as behavioral male, in precisely the textual space occupied by a victim, unequivocally sexed as biological female; alluding to a masculine enemy beyond society, this androgynous creature carries out a rite of reflexive violence before a male audience belonging to her own society. By couching her act in the (culture-specific) permissible language of women's intervention, she renders her gender transgression acceptable, channeling all censure (and aggression) towards the external enemy. Unlike normative male warriors, who go to battle clad in iron, this female warrior emphatically bares her body to all blows. Such women are not quite hermaphroditic; they do not in fact challenge a male prerogative to wield brute force. Rather, by dramatizing both the type of action required of their menfolk and the dire consequences for themselves, should they fail them, they rally the men to uphold a common cause.

Freydís's bare-sarked moment occurs in *Eiríks saga rauða* ("The Saga of Eiríkr the Red"), one of the so-called Vínland sagas that (together with *Grœnlendinga saga*, "The Greenlanders' Saga") comprise our main narrative sources for the Norse discovery voyages. These accounts are preserved in three medieval manuscripts (*Eiríks saga rauða* in two, *Grœnlendinga saga* in one), all fourteenth-century or later — copied, that is, three hundred years or more after the events they allegedly record.[13] As with most Icelandic sagas, we know precious little about the circumstances of the Vínland sagas' composition and recording; into this breach, hosts of speculations have marched. Until the 1950s, opinions about both sagas' relative and absolute dating (and, consequently, their interrelations and their relative weight as historical witnesses) varied widely, though most scholars were inclined to accept *Eiríks saga rauða* as older and more authoritative — a

---

[12] See *Ynglinga saga* cap. 6 (in *Heimskringla*, ÍF 26: 17) for Snorri's interpretation, followed, e.g., by Noreen (1932: 251–56), Holthausen (1948, s.v. "berserkr"), Kuhn (1968: 222), and Price (2002: 366); for the correct etymology, see de Vries (1962, s.v.) and von See (1961: 133–35).

[13] Two distinct versions of *Eiríks saga rauða* survive in medieval vellums, *Hauksbók* (AM 544 4to, henceforth *H*, dated ca. 1305 AD, ed. in ÍF 4: 195–237; see Gunnar Harðarson and Stefán Karlsson 1993) and *Skálholtsbók* (AM 557 4to, henceforth *S*, dated ca. 1420 AD, ed. in ÍF 4: 403–34); the latter manuscript, though younger, is thought to represent the archetype better than *H* (see Jansson 1944: 82). *Grœnlendinga saga* is reconstructed from two separate fragments, interpolated into a copy of *Óláfs saga Tryggvasonar en mesta* in the codex *Flateyjarbók* (dated ca. 1390 AD, ed. in ÍF 4: 241–69). Several post-medieval paper copies of both *Grœnlendinga saga* and *Eiríks saga rauða* are also extant; full variants printed in Rafn (1837). See Wahlgren (1993) for a serviceable overview in English.

position enshrined, for instance, in the standard critical edition's ordering of the texts. In 1956, Jón Jóhannesson's pathbreaking research altered the scholarly landscape, entrenching a new consensus view of *Grœnlendinga saga* as the older work and dating it tentatively to the very beginning of the thirteenth century (or perhaps even shortly before), while *Eiríks saga rauða* was relegated to the status of a secondary response and dated post-1264. This view prevailed until recently, when Ólafur Halldórsson, the most recent editor of *Eiríks saga rauða*, challenged it, offering instead a vision of the two sagas as independent reflexes of a shared oral tradition and dating both to the first decades of the thirteenth century.[14] Ólafur's authority has tended to elevate his opinion to the status of a new consensus: his "conclusions have not as yet been seriously challenged," writes one well-informed, if partisan, scholar.[15] As for an absolute dating, though a majority of scholars place both sagas early in the thirteenth century, possibilities ranging from the late twelfth to the late fourteenth century have been seriously entertained; "[t]he only certainties," as Helgi Þorláksson points out, planting his flag by the oldest extant manuscripts, "are that the existing *Eiríks saga rauða* is older than 1302–1310 and that *Grœnlendinga saga* is older than 1387." There is, in fact, some reason to suspect early datings of attempting to push the sagas' written composition as close as possible to a time when oral transmission of the Vínland discovery tales seems credible (cf. pp. 65–67 below): a fourteenth-century composition in the context of a local competition for prestige in some Icelandic district, as Helgi suggests, seems entirely plausible. I am, however, on the whole inclined to prefer Jón's arguments concerning the relative dating of the two sagas over Ólafur's suggestion of their contemporaneity or Helgi's more radical inversion, reinstating *Eiríks saga rauða* as the older of the two (see further n20 in this chapter).[16]

---

[14] See Jón Jóhannesson (1962–65) and Ólafur Halldórsson (in ÍF 4: 333–99, esp. 367–69, 391–95; and 2001). When ÍF 4 first appeared in 1935, it included editions of *Eiríks saga rauða* [*H*] and *Grœnlendinga saga* only; *Eiríks saga rauða* [*S*] was only added in a 1985 supplement. See n13 above.

[15] Gísli Sigurðsson (2004: 269; see also 265–66, 272); cf. Vésteinn Ólason (2001: 56–59), concluding: "Uansett alle spekulasjoner kan man konstatere at GS . . . er så gammel som fra omkring eller like etter 1200. Det er vel ikke utelukket at ER er omtrent like gammel, men det er en hypotese som hviler på et svakere grunnlag" [Disregarding all speculations, one can affirm that (*Grœnlendinga saga*) . . . is from about 1200 or shortly thereafter. That (*Eiríks saga rauða*) is about as old is not out of the question, but this is an hypothesis resting on a weaker foundation] (2001: 59).

[16] Helgi Þorláksson (2001: 66); cf. Perkins (2011: 3, 31) and Ólafur Halldórsson: "the only thing which we can say with complete certainty about the age of [*Grœnlendinga saga*] is that it was written before 1387" (2001: 43). Helgi also proposes reversing the sagas' order of composition, an argument I do not find persuasive. In his view, *Eiríks saga rauða* was written in connection with the establishment of a nunnery at Reynistaðr in northern Iceland in 1295, by an author sympathetic to the powerful chieftains Kolbeinn

As for content, the two sagas tell strikingly different versions of what is recognizably the same basic tale—transposing or attributing episodes to different cast members, adding or subtracting anecdotes, embellishing in divergent modes, but retaining a stable core: Norsemen came, they saw, they could not conquer. Many possible reasons have been adduced for their debacle. Both sagas agree that the belligerence of the Natives, whom the Norse called *skrælingar* (a derogatory term of obscure meaning), played some role in scuttling Norse settlement.[17] The arguably more historical *Grœnlendinga saga*, however, downplays the importance of Native resistance by splicing it with a storyline of internecine ill-will and murder, which gutted the tiny Norse colony. The saga identifies Freydís, a minor appendage to the illustrious lineage of the discoverers of Greenland and Vínland, as the scheming genius behind this treason, said to have masterminded a massacre and overseen its execution. Her motives appear as nothing but greed and a sheer delight in sowing mischief. When the Greenlanders, whom she had egged on, slay the Icelandic men but shrink from laying hands on the women, Freydís takes an axe and completes the gruesome work herself.[18] The saga reports that Leifr later found out about the atrocity, despite Freydís's efforts to conceal it. He would not punish his own kinswoman, but foretold that her descendants

---

and Björn at Auðkúla, while *Grœnlendinga saga* was composed sometime in the following half-century by an author allied with the chieftain Hrafn at nearby Glaumbœr, who is "unlikely to have been overjoyed at the developing links between Auðkúla and Reynistaðr" (2001: 70). A fourteenth-century dating is perhaps also supported by the romance features detected in these sagas (Kellogg 2001). All attempts to date the sagas from internal evidence are, as Ólafur Halldórsson freely acknowledges, exercises in clutching at straws (2001: 43); works such as Gísli Sigurðsson (2004) are particularly suspect of wishful thinking. Cf. Hallberg (1987: 79–80) and chapter V, n43 below.

[17] Favored etymologies connect *skrælingar* to Old Norse *skrælna* ('to wither, parch'—perhaps a reference to the Natives' tattooed or painted skin; Matthias Þórðarson 1930: 45–46), or to Norwegian *skrall* ('loud noise') or *skral* ('wretched'; De Costa 1901: 113n3; Jones 1986: 92–93n16). A link to Danish *skralle* ('rattle') has also been suggested (with reference to flail-like instruments the *skrælingar* wield; Vinding 1998: 100). De Costa (1901: 113n3) also toys with a charming emendation to **smællingar* [sic] ('small men').

[18] See *Grœnlendinga saga* cap. 7 (ÍF 4: 264–67). Several texts from ca. 1200 suggest that executing prisoners may have been a normative role for a medieval woman to play; see, e.g., Ambroise, *L'Estoire de la guerre sainte* ll. 3308–14 (1897: 89; echoed in the *Itinerarium peregrinorum* cap. 34, in Mayer 1962: 324); an even closer analogue is offered by the Hiberno-Norman *Song of Dermot* (ll. 1474–89, 1992: 98; cf. also ll. 1428–29, 1448–59, 1992: 96–98; and cf. ll. 1412–13, 1992: 94 with *Grœnlendinga saga* cap. 6, ÍF 4: 261–62, 263).

would amount to little—a prediction which the saga author, looking back from two or three centuries in the future, seems only too pleased to confirm.[19]

In *Eiríks saga rauða*, perhaps somewhat younger than *Grœnlendinga saga* and possibly written in polemical opposition to it—to set the historical record straight, as it were—the demise of Norse America is blamed unambiguously on the Vínland Natives alone.[20] The saga principally celebrates the saintly Guðríðr Þorbjarnardóttir, Eiríkr's adopted daughter, and her dashing husband, Þorfinnr *karlsefni* (whose byname fittingly means "The Stuff A Man Is Made Of"): he is credited with the lion's share of Vínland exploration, at Leifr's expense.[21] Here, too, Freydís appears briefly, but plays an entirely altered role; still, she is as unmistakably flinty as her *Grœnlendinga saga* avatar.[22] The author only recalls that Freydís had been a member of the expedition all along when a pitched battle against a horde of attacking *skrælingar* takes an ugly turn for Karlsefni's men:

---

[19] Though *Grœnlendinga saga* as a whole is generally thought to provide a more authentic historical witness than *Eiríks saga rauða* (see, e.g., Hovgaard 1914: 146; Jón Jóhannesson 1962–65; but cf. Jones 1986: 121–22), its Freydís narrative is often dismissed as dubious (see, e.g., Wahlgren 1969: 58–61; but cf. Hovgaard 1914: 144). On the narrative and ideological motivations for *Grœnlendinga saga*'s Freydís, see further Falk (forthcoming), cap. 4. On Freydís's progeny, cf. p. 122 and chapter VIII, n22 below.

[20] Arguments various scholars have adduced for a literary link between the two sagas strike me as more compelling than Ólafur Halldórsson's recent attempt to dissociate them (in ÍF 4: 377–90); see, e.g., Jón Jóhannesson (1962–65); Björn Þorsteinsson (1962–65); Magnus Magnusson and Hermann Pálsson (1965: 34); Wahlgren (1969); Ingstad (1985: 232–33); and Perkins (2011: 3–4n2). Such tongue-in-cheek homage as the placing of a landmark in *Grœnlendinga saga*, to be discovered already *in situ* in *Eiríks saga rauða*, suggest intertextuality: cf. *Grœnlendinga saga* cap. 4 (ÍF 4: 255) with *Eiríks saga rauða* cap. 8 (ÍF 4: [S] 423; cf. [H] 223). Similarly, the author of *Eiríks saga rauða* seems to devise Freydís's exploits as a means of redeeming her reputation (and that of Eiríkr the Red's lineage in general) from the tarnishing it had taken in *Grœnlendinga saga*; cf. Baumgartner (1993: 29–30) and Arnold (2006: 212–13; 2007: 133–34), who, following the same line of reasoning in reverse—Freydís's rampage is too shocking to have been made up—accept *Grœnlendinga saga*'s portrayal as more probably historical.

[21] Indeed, some critics (e.g., Halldór Hermannsson 1936: 27–29) argue that *Þorfinns saga Karlsefnis*, a title found in some manuscripts, is more appropriate than *Eiríks saga rauða*; see overview in Jansson (1944: 104–9). Ólafur Halldórsson suggests that *Guðríðar saga Þorbjarnardóttir* might have been an even more appropriate title (in ÍF 4: 340–41). Modern adaptations likewise often give precedence to Guðríðr herself; see, e.g., Hewlett (1918); Irwin (1974); Boyer (1976); Jónas Kristjánsson (1998); and Brown (2007).

[22] Cf. Hovgaard: "It is worth noting that the same woman who in one saga is represented as having saved the whole party by her valor, is in the other saga represented as treacherous and cruel, and as the instigator of crime. This points to strong partiality on the part of the authors of these sagas" (1914: 145). See also Barnes (2001: 29) and Sjoholm (2004).

A great terror seized Karlsefni and all his company, so that they desired nothing but to flee and get away up along the river, since it seemed to them that the Native forces were closing in on them from all sides, and they do not let up before they come to some cliffs, and there they offered stiff resistance.

Freydís came outside and saw that Karlsefni and his men were getting away, and called out: "Why do you run before these worthless men — such estimable men as you are — whom I'd have thought you could cut down like domesticated cattle? But if I had a weapon, I'd think that I should fight better than any of you." They gave no heed to her words.

Freydís wished to follow them but was slower because she was pregnant. Nevertheless, she went after them into the forest, but the *skrælingar* rush at her. She came upon a dead man: Þorbrandr Snorrason lay there, and a flat stone protruded from his head. [His] sword lay bare beside him. She picked it up and prepares to defend herself. Then the *skrælingar* came at her. She then drew [her] breast out from beneath [her] garment and slaps [it] with the bare sword. At this, the *skrælingar* were terrified and ran away to their ships and rowed off. Karlsefni and his men find her and praise her luck.[23]

The ink is hardly dry on this rather remarkable anecdote when the author turns to other matters, never to return to Freydís in this or any other saga. No explanation is offered for her behavior, nor for the dread she inspires in the Natives' breasts. Nor is anything told concerning a child, the issue of her pregnancy: a sharp contrast to the attention lavished on little Snorri, the first European boy born in the New World, to a proud Karlsefni and Guðríðr.[24] This silence has led some histo-

---

[23] *Eiríks saga rauða* cap. 11: "[S]ló ótta miklum á Karlsefni ok allt lið hans, svá at þá fýsti einskis annars en flýja ok halda undan upp með ánni, því at þeim þótti lið Skrælinga drífa at sér ǫllum megin, ok létta eigi fyrr en þeir koma til hamra nǫkkurra, ok veittu þar viðtǫku harða. Freydís kom út ok sá, at þeir Karlsefni heldu undan, ok kallaði: 'Hví renni þér undan þessum auvirðis-mǫnnum, svá gildir menn sem þér eruð, er mér þœtti sem þér mættið drepa niðr svá sem búfé? Ok ef ek hefða vápn, þœtti mér sem ek skylda betr berjask en einnhverr yðvar.' Þeir gáfu engan gaum hennar orðum. Freydís vildi fylgja þeim ok varð seinni, því at hon var eigi heil; gekk hon þó eftir þeim í skóginn, en Skrælingar sœkja at henni. Hon fann fyrir sér mann dauðan; þar var Þorbrandr Snorrason, ok stóð hellusteinn í hǫfði honum. Sverðit lá bert í hjá honum; tók hon þat upp ok býsk at verja sik. Þá kómu Skrælingar at henni; hon dró þá út brjóstit undan klæðunum ok slettir á beru sverðinu. Við þetta óttask Skrælingar ok hljópu undan á skip sín ok reru í brott. Þeir Karlsefni finna hana ok lofa happ hennar" (ÍF 4: [*H*] 229; cf. [*S*] 429–30). The text of *S* here appears somewhat defective; see Ólafur Halldórsson's notes and emendations (in ÍF 4: 429–30).

[24] See *Grænlendinga saga* cap. 6 (ÍF 4: 262) and *Eiríks saga rauða* cap. 12 (ÍF 4: [*H*] 233, [*S*] 432). Modern scholarship likewise pampers Snorri (see, e.g., Lodewyckx 1955: 183; Morison 1971–74: 1.54; Jones 1986: 135; Vinner 1993: 72; Schledermann 2000: 191; Linden 2004: 93), but mostly ignores Freydís's pregnancy; for exceptions, see Halldór

rians to the plausible conclusion that Freydís is an entirely fictional tissue, woven into the plot for color or narrative flow.[25]

But even if Leifr's historical half-sister was nothing like her saga name-sake—even if no illegitimate daughter of Eiríkr the Red ever drew breath—the strange antics of this fictive topless warrior raise clamorous questions regarding cultural expectations and norms in late medieval Iceland. Why does Freydís bare and beat her breast? Why do the Natives run off at this sight? What does the episode mean? Oddly, many critics—with two exceptions, discussed below—find the scene unworthy of comment and, as though exempting it from analysis, deal solely with its *Grœnlendinga saga* counterpart.[26] It seems safe to guess that their silence signals that they consider the *Eiríks saga rauða* episode incomprehensible rather than that its significance is for them self-evident. Some others, however, opt for the deceptively easy solution of historical translucence: "By uncovering her breast and striking it with her sword," Matthías Þórðarson reasons, "[Freydís] no doubt wished to indicate two things, that she was a woman and that she was unafraid and ready to protect herself with the sharp sword if attacked."[27] A

Hermannsson (1936: 22n2) and Wallace (2003: 380). Pohl (1966: 156), inspired no doubt by Freydís's enigmatic *ad hoc* pregnancy in *Eiríks saga rauða*, explains her murderous spree in *Grœnlendinga saga* as cover-up for cuckoldry of her husband, a theory which Scott (1958) imaginatively anticipates. Cf. also Iverslie (1912: 70).

[25] See, e.g., Thomas (1946–53: 318–21); Heller (1958: 69); Wahlgren (1969: 58–61); Ingstad (1985: 138, 212); Barnes (2001: 27); and Perkins (2011: 29). The name Freydís occurs nowhere else in the Old Norse corpus (Lind 1905–31: 1.283; cf. Perkins 2004: 47 and chapter VII, n44 below), which may further strengthen the hint that the character who bears it is cut from whole cloth; cf. what is manifestly a caricature of an exotic foreigner in *Grœnlendinga saga*, a German named Tyrkir [Turk / Trojan]. I am indebted to Orri Vésteinsson for this suggestion.

[26] As remarked also by Lodewyckx (1955: 184). See, e.g., Reeves (1890: 59); Gathorne-Hardy (1921: 127–30); Halldór Hermannsson (1936: 43–44); Thomas (1946–53: 318–21); Heller (1958: 69); Magnus Magnusson and Hermann Pálsson (1965: 38); Jesch (1991: 182–85); Clover (1993: 366–67); Vinner (1993: 72); Ebel (1994: 93); Høyersten (1998: 98–100); Hermann Pálsson (2000: 23); Jochens (2002: 146–47); Wallace (2006: 20, 22, 107; but cf. 79); and Somerville and McDonald (2010: 133–35). The same editorial impulse is evident in non-scholarly works, as well; e.g., Jensen, a retelling of the Vínland story aimed at young adults, expurgates the *Eiríks saga rauða* Freydís (though not the *Grœnlendinga saga* episode, 1979: 40–41; wanton violence is apparently less disturbing than inexplicable nudity). For the exceptions, see Stefán Einarsson (1939) and Wolf (1996), and see pp. 42, 94–95 below.

[27] Matthías Þórðarson (1930: 54). See also Holand (1940: 39); Jones (1986: 134); Duerr (1993: 35); Jochens (1996: 109); Vinding (1998: 95, 100); Barnes (2001: 30n80, citing Margaret Clunies Ross); and, imaginatively, Pedersen (1952: 74), Berry (1977: 178), and Jónas Kristjánsson (1998: 229). But cf. Nansen: "As it stands in the saga this incident is not very comprehensible" (1911: 2.11), and Hovgaard: "It is difficult on the whole to reconcile causes and effects in the description of the battle, and the tale is evidently much

Figure 1: *Freydís Eiríksdóttir: Heroine or Ogress? (1004)*
This life-sized silicone figure of Freydís is on display at the Saga Museum in Reykjavík, a private museum owned and operated by designer Ernst J. Backman and his
family. The Museum opened in 2002. It is notable that Freydís stands, sword in
hand and face contorted into a grimace, over the fallen body of Þorbrandr Snorrason; a blood-stained stone lies next to Þorbrandr's bashed skull. Since no figures

of *skrælingar* are on display, however, and since nothing in the catalogue description
(aside from the provocative caption byline, "ogress") refers to Freydís's manifestation
in *Grœnlendinga saga*, the diorama could be misunderstood to suggest that Þorbrandr
had been killed by Freydís. All other aspects of the physical diorama and accompanying text seems to refer to the *Eiríks saga rauða* image of Freydís.
© Saga Design

slightly different tack is adopted by the curators of a recent exhibition intended for a lay audience, who similarly assume historical transparency: "[Freydís's] bold gesture seems to have frightened the natives and they ran o[ff] terrified by what they apparently thought was an evil woman"[28] (see Fig. 1). Such explanations may have seemed straightforward enough to scholars a few decades ago, and still ring plausible in a popular context nowadays, but they must, on reflection, be rejected outright. Besides an unqualified concession of factual veracity to saga reportage, such interpretations presuppose full correspondence between signifier and signified: Freydís's gesturing needs to encode her message unambiguously and convey a single clear meaning to both culturally distal *skrælingar* and temporally remote historians (who, moreover, are wont to disagree on the specifics of its content). As an account of how communication works, this seems unlikely and unsatisfactory.

To avoid the fallacy of expecting gesture to map directly over meaning, attention must focus on the episode as textually re-presenting a performance event. Freydís acts out before an audience (or audiences) of spectators in Vínland, who, like her, are contained within the text; the saga, in turn, narrates this somatic spectacle, transforming it into a literary performance to be consumed by an extra-textual audience. No matter whether Freydís's action is approached from an interior or exterior perspective, as physical display (hers) or as verbal sign (the author's), the role she plays in this expository complex is clearly not that of an autonomous subject exercising unmediated agency, but rather that of a viewed object performing for others to contemplate. The simple fact that she disperses the *skrælingar* without striking a blow peremptorily rules out a purely instrumental interpretation: Freydís's violence hinges on perception, not on physical manipulation of her environment. Her audience are therefore pivotal for explicating her conduct: what might they have made of her gestures? What did she (or the saga author) likely seek to convey to these particular spectators?

Ultimately, of course, the intended audience are the saga's readers and listeners, and Freydís is piloted by a saga author's extradiegetic considerations. But an author's message may have been pitched at saga consumers in at least three distinct ways. The first is directly, meta-textually. Celebrating convention or parodying it are surefire modes of addressing an external audience directly, over the heads of intra-textual characters. Ironically, then, a focus on the direct impact the episode might have had on an actual, historical audience tends to minimize

---

distorted" (1914: 142). Similarly, Williamsen comments: "The *skrælingar* . . . seem inordinately skittish, running from loud noises and pregnant women" (2005: 468). Kolodny gives an overview of the confusion (2012: 88).

[28] Hlynur Páll Pálsson (2002: 15). The stated purpose of the museum's life-sized dioramas is "to exhibit a fragment of history in a unique way to foreign visitors and Icelandic elementary school children" (2002: 39). I am indebted to Águsta Hreinsdóttir for her assistance in obtaining images and information about the Saga Museum.

the historicity attributed to the narrative: to possess unmediated agency in the world, the text must substitute pronounced literary conventionality for self-contained realism.[29] The other two alternatives are for Freydís to have interacted with one or both of her audiences within the text—the *skrælingar* or Karlsefni and his men—to convey her message indirectly, through them, to the saga-consuming public. (The distinction among audiences should be understood as an analytic construct; I do not claim that the episode need be pitched at one audience level or another to the exclusion of others.)[30] In either of these latter cases, saga readers and listeners are assumed to have been able to recognize a resemblance between experienced, historical reality and narrated pseudo-reality. To interpret such indirect exposition correctly, we must assess how the verisimilar logic governing Freydís's display before either of her intra-textual audiences would have made it comprehensible and credible to medieval Icelanders.[31] I consider each of these three alternative frameworks in subsequent chapters.

In this book I propose, then, to make sense of Freydís's focused enigma by combining a close reading of text with a wide-ranging search for illuminating contexts. One must, on the one hand, attend closely to the saga's narrative construction and to the tendrils by which it reaches out to affect its intended consumers. On the other hand, if we treat Freydís as a *sui generis* phenomenon, we will have utterly missed the point. A narrowly text-focused reading would not merely fall short of interpreting this particular tale, it would also fumble the arguably more important task of using Freydís as a wedge for prying open a far more extensive tradition, that of all her sisters in topos. In the next chapter, I appose two cognate scenes—one textual and the other pictorial, one late-medieval and the other early-modern—to the Freydís anecdote. Analytically sublimating the bare-sarked warrior in this way from her immediate textual surroundings yields several benefits. For one, it places Freydís within a broadly European milieu, and crystallizes affinities that would otherwise have remained obscure; chapter 3

---

[29] Rimmon-Kenan has some evocative observations about the ability of literature to turn technical necessity into a virtue (1983: 119–20); see also Falk (forthcoming), Appendix. Cf. Meulengracht Sørensen: "The everyday world of ideas is not identical with the literary one, but the two stand in a particular relation to each other. . . . One of literature's most important tasks . . . is in effect to breach [the] bounds [everyday reality sets], so as to confirm the everyday norm by a breach at the imaginative level" (1983: 14–15).

[30] But cf. Buc (2001: 249–50).

[31] The methodology I propose is the inverse of the traditional division of labor in saga scholarship, which Meulengracht Sørensen criticizes: "Philological and literary study seeks the reality *in* the text. Historical and ethnological study seeks some kind of reality *behind* the text" (1993b: 172, his emphases). Cf. Rimmon-Kenan (1983: 17–18) on verisimilar causality on the level of the virtual reality posited by the text, opposed to teleological causality at the level of the narration itself. See also Rabinowitz's sophisticated model of author-audience communications (1977), marred, unfortunately, by untenable distinctions between 'history' and 'literature' as narrative modes (1977: 123).

explores two possible Norse matrices for her behavior that have not been noticed before, but whose relevance is brought out by juxtaposition with the non-Norse cognates. Correct labeling also helps rule out some explanations put forward in the past, as I show in chapters 4 and 6 especially. But most importantly, taking stock of the topos's breadth affords insight into the mechanics by which various cultures labor to convert inter-societal into intra-societal violence, taming the harmful force of risky confrontation with Others into the cohesive power of cultural articulation among Selves. Freydís, the sagas, medieval Norse society itself do not recede from view in this discussion, but assume the proportions, rather, of a mere case study—albeit a cardinal one, first among equals in its ability to exemplify and illuminate the widespread phenomenon of which it is an instant. Chapters 4, 5, and 6 focus closely on how this key transformative process, the alchemical internalizing of violence, works, contrasting the bare-sarked warrior with some parallel (and in all likelihood related) topoi. The final chapter relocates bare-sarked warriors to their original contexts, dwelling on the narrative and historical consequences of their conduct for their societies, their male interlocutors, and the women themselves. Freydís and her bare-sarked sisters shed light on how very difficult it is to look beyond the boundaries of one's culture and actually meet the Other: even when *skrælingar* or their ilk are encountered face to face, breast to breast, their historical reality and corporeal tangibility tend to evaporate under the imperative to appropriate them as signifiers, transmute them into the medium through which routine messages about societal norms can be relayed, reduce them to familiar foreigners with which the past might be made predictable again. Neither unique nor yet universal, Freydís beckons to us, a psychopomp on a tour of the seamier side of her own (and many another) culture's ideas about multiculturalism.

III. Dressing for Danger

> Privately they regarded her as a female berserk, but the praise came
> from the heart. She was tart-tongued, shrewish, wanton—and very brave.
> Today she stood as tall as a Valkyrie.
> Still, not every man pressed forward to praise her.
> She inherited her father's luck, one grumbled.
> She must have eaten daft-fish.
> Another held up his axe, shook his head at it and tossed it aside, then
> with a sly grin cupped his hands on his chest.
> But why? they asked one another. Why did the Skraelings run?
>
> Irwin, *Gudrid's Saga* (1974: 212)[1]

Considering the Freydís episode alongside two analogues, a fifteenth-century
Burgundian chronicle anecdote and a visual image from Revolutionary France,
facilitates analysis of the literary topos. There can hardly be a question of a genetic
link among the traditions of Iceland, Burgundy, and France; rather, I juxtapose
the three artifacts to elucidate their structural phenotype. The rhetorical gestures
by which the Icelandic text strives to reach its audience become easier to discern
when held up against analogous maneuvers performed by its topos peers (see further Sidebar 2).

The visual counterpart to the Freydís anecdote is a satirical print entitled
Grand débandement de l'armée anticonstitutionelle, which appeared in the Royalist press in February 1792, and is nowadays quite well-known again thanks to
Lynn Hunt's superlative analysis (see Fig. 2).[2] Bristling with innuendo (the verb
débander, e.g., means both 'to disperse' and 'to uncock,' whether a rifle or an
erection), the print shows a Revolutionary host confronting a detachment of the
Austrian army. A narrow watercourse separates the antagonists. The soldiers are
in the first convulsions of flight: muskets rattle to the ground, an officer's horse
rears, infantrymen scamper. What dismays them, however, is patently not the

---

[1] Cf. Vollmann (1990: 308); Clark (1994: 233). Irwin's references to eating "daft-
fish" and to discarding an axe seem to allude to *Eiríks saga rauða* capp. 8, 11 (ÍF 4: [*H*]
224, 230, [*S*] 425, 430) and *Grænlendinga saga* cap. 6 (ÍF 4: 263–64). On Freydís's luck,
see pp. 118–19 below.

[2] See Hunt (1992: 116–18). See also Hockman (1988: 213); Cameron (1991:
90–107); Grubitzsch and Bockholt (1991: 260–63).

Figure 2: *Grand débandement de l'armée anticonstitutionelle*, February 1792
Bibliothèque Nationale, Paris
From Cameron (1991: fig. 4.1)

sight of ill-armed Jacobins who advance against them from the margin, sporting morsels of phallic meat on the points of their pikes, but rather a front line of women who bare their bottoms at them. (The caption identifies these women as specific aristocrats, known for their egalitarian sympathies. It also refers to their rumps as "Villette," an explicitly sodomitic allusion.)[3] One brazen lady, identified as Théroigne de Méricourt, heads this female troop. She alone faces the Austrians (and the viewer), holding a rifle in her right hand and with her left raising her skirts to reveal what the caption cold-bloodedly calls *sa Republique*—"her

---

[3] The women are given (usually) transparent nicknames, for the most part offensive: Madame de Condorcet, e.g., is named "Condor," a carrion-eater but also a pun on *con d'or*; Théroigne de Méricourt is called "demoiselle Teroig**" [sic]. See Grubitzsch and Bockholt (1991: 500n63) and Cameron (1991: 92–93) for identifications. The caption explains that "elles se presentent aux troupes de l'Empereur . . . leur montrent leur *Villette*," a reference to the Marquis de Villette, known both as an advocate of women's rights and as a pederast; see Hunt (1992: 117) and cf. p. 111 below.

Republic," of course, but also "her public thing."[4] Unlike the Freydís episode, the Théroigne print makes no claim to factual historicity; the Austrian invasion it envisions was still some two months in the future at the time of its publication. Openly metaphorical, it is without the least pretense of realism, although the political persons and tensions it satirizes are real enough.

To appreciate the satirical thrust of the allegory, a few words are needed about its real-life figurehead. Born Anne-Josèphe Terwagne in the Walloon village of Marcourt, not far from Liège, this (then 27-year-old) beauty attained notoriety in the first months of the Revolution: the ironic, quasi-gentrified name the press bestowed on her is itself a testimony to her infamy. After some years of living "a *déclassé* existence . . . uneasily suspended between literary bohemianism, polite society and moral degradation," Théroigne fervently embraced the Revolutionary cause early in the summer of 1789.[5] She travelled to Paris and later to Versailles, attending the sessions of the National Assembly religiously. She took to dressing in a distinctive, masculine riding habit, and befriended numerous first- and second-string Revolutionary leaders, apparently expecting to be treated as an equal among the men. Small wonder that the Royalist press no sooner discovered her than it appointed her supreme icon of Revolutionary depravity: she was cast as a Penthesilea, a leader of mob violence; as a Jezebel, exerting unnatural political influence over men; as a whore, bed-fellow of any and all Revolutionaries.[6] During later years, Théroigne was to play a variety of

---

[4] Also a pun on *raie pubique* [pubic slit]. I am indebted to Walter Goffart for pointing out to me this wordplay.

[5] Roudinesco (1991: 9). I have educated myself concerning Théroigne's life and period primarily from secondary literature, spot-checking data and interpretation against the primary sources available to me. See esp. Lacour (1900: 93–314), Goldsmith (1935: 31–65), Grubitzsch (1989), Roudinesco (1991), and Grubitzsch and Bockholt (1991).

[6] Théroigne's initial notoriety stemmed from her alleged role in the *Journées d'octobre*, a riot in which she seems not to have been involved. During the night of 5–6 October 1789, a Parisian crowd besieged King Louis and his queen at Versailles. The situation bubbled perilously close but did not, eventually, boil over into a bloodbath: the king consented to return to Paris, in effect already a prisoner. The besiegers were National Guardsmen and a motley array of Parisian women. It was the latter who received credit — or blame — for overpowering the royal troops: "Les hommes ont pris la Bastille, et les femmes ont pris le Roi," writes Michelet (1847–53: 1.280; for extensive background and analysis, see Mathiez 1898–99). The Royalist press insisted on Théroigne's presence among these unruly women, though she probably only watched them go by from a street corner near her lodgings (Lacour 1900: 178–79; Goldsmith 1935: 45–46; Grubitzsch and Bockholt 1991: 86–88). Still, nothing so inert as fact could stop the pamphleteers, hell-bent on implicating her in every Revolutionary excess (and, with perfect symmetry, on besmirching every aspect of the Revolution by associating it with her). She was depicted alternately as riding in the vanguard, dressed as a man, pistols in belt and sabre in hand; as shrilling for the queen's blood, sitting astride a cannon; or as skulking through the

2. Methodology: Reconstructing a topos

Where points of contact can be detected among specific artifacts or between the cultures that produced them, the argument for a tradition shared by such artifacts (through 'genetic' diffusion or transmission) is fairly straightforward.[1] But when I speak of the bare-sarked warrior in terms of a topos, I do not imply any such shared heritage among its manifestations. How, then, is a topos to be identified and, once identified, used as a tool of analysis?

My methodology here relies, if somewhat reluctantly, on suggestions advanced by folklorists for the holistic reading of motif traditions. Such methods allow inference from one manifestation of a motif to another, even when no specific link can be established between the two. Such "romp[s] across time and space will no doubt scandalize specialists," concedes Nicole Belmont. Still, she defends the procedure, succinctly summarizing its rationale:

> [Weaving] this web . . . can allow [us] . . . to detect meanings hidden [in one instance] but revealed elsewhere. Building up such a web, which assumes diverse forms—myths, tales, legends, songs, idioms, rituals—around a motif is akin to the construction, or the reconstruction, of a metamythology, a 'paradigmatic' mythology. . . . Indeed, a motif is an ambivalent unity: it is a figure that is, at the same time, narratively specific enough to retain the stability which allows it to be recognized, and characterized by a certain irresolution which authorizes its reuse in different narrative contexts.[2]

I balk at Belmont's archetypal-sounding insistence on the existence of "*a universal discursive imaginary*"; the psychological assumptions behind such a claim are, at best, wholly speculative. As her discussion of blind motifs reveals, however, the methodology can have great heuristic utility in reconstructing possible

---

[1] See, e.g., Mundt (1993), for one attempt among many to chart such genetic links.

[2] Belmont: "Cette randonée à travers le temps et l'espace scandalisera sans doute les spécialistes de littérature orale soucieux, comme il se doit, d'inscrire les analyses dans un même contexte culturel. Cette mise en réseau . . . peut permettre . . . de lire des sens cachés ici mais qui se révèlent ailleurs. La construction d'un pareil réseau autour d'un motif, empruntant à des formes diverses—mythes, contes, légendes, chansons, pratiques langagières, rituels—est comme la construction, ou la reconstruction, d'une métamythologie ou d'une mythologie 'paradigmatique.'. . . C'est qu'en effet le motif est une unité ambivalente: il est une figure à la fois suffisamment spécifique narrativement parlant pour garder une stabilité qui en permet la reconnaissance, et pourvue d'un certain caractère d'indécision qui autorise son réemploi dans différents contextes narratifs" (1995: 183–84; cf. Lévi-Strauss 1963–76: 1.206-31, esp. 216-19, and Hill 2010, as well as Sourvinou-Inwood's dissenting view, 1991: 17–18).

contexts for fragments which do not otherwise make much sense.[3] Having proposed a configuration of unrelated artifacts as an associated "web," we may proceed *as if* they were linked and judge the validity of our assumption by the insight it yields. The test of the pudding, then, is in the eating, even if its recipe remains quite mysterious.

Folklorists usually speak, as Belmont does here, of motifs, whereas I refer in the course of my analysis chiefly to topoi; the terminological distinctions are quite fluid, and other terms, such as themes, are also sometimes introduced more-or-less interchangeably. In my usage, motifs are isolated images, which may be employed in varying narrative contexts, whereas topoi are enchained clusters of images which have their own, internal narrative coherence (though they, like motifs, can be further embedded within a variety of narrative constellations, of course). Thus Oedipus with his eyes gouged out, for instance, would be an example of a motif, while Oedipus's relations with his father and mother would be an example of a topos.

Data attrition is inevitable in all historical records; historians must thus reconstruct the past by proposing elements of a contextual webbing into which the surviving evidence fits. An imagined "paradigmatic mythology" can supply missing data reliably if (and only if) it correctly lumps together elements that are indeed specific enough, in narrative terms, to remain recognizable as manifestations of the same topos. My reconstruction proceeds, furthermore, on the assumption that such narratives can be discerned not only in strictly verbal retellings but even in other media; static visual representations, for instance, necessarily truncate the dynamic development of narrative, but they may well allude to it nonetheless.[4]

---

[3] Belmont: "en effet il existe '*un imaginaire discursif universel*'" (1995: 183, her emphasis; on blind motifs, see 184-85).

[4] Contrast King's reluctance to read images as no less narrative than texts: "What is specific to *anasyrmos* is that it is spontaneous, frontal, *temporary* and directional. . . . All visual images of *anasyrmos* are thus problematic, because by freezing the gesture in mid-performance they lose its particular characteristics" (1986: 63, emphasis mine). On *anasyrmos*, see chapter V, n11.

---

minor Revolutionary roles—a few of which actually approximated her earlier image in the Royalist gazettes. She spent most of 1791 in an Austrian prison, abducted by Imperial agents, but was released after an inconclusive trial. On her return to Paris (shortly before the publication of the print discussed here), she

---

Flanders regiment, bribing soldiers not to fire on the women (Goldsmith 1935: 43–46; Grubitzsch 1989: 92–94; Roudinesco 1991: 42–43, 67–68, 115, 170, 197, 200, 203–5; Grubitzsch and Bockholt 1991: 80–94. Schama 1989: 462–63 is eloquently uncritical).

advocated women's militarization; she may later have been personally involved in at least one political lynching, of one of the Royalist publicists chiefly responsible for slandering her. As the *Grand débandement* had predicted in libelous imagery, Théroigne's personal destiny became not merely inextricable from but synonymous with the fate of the Republic: things went rapidly downhill for Théroigne after the summer of 1793. I return to her later fate below (p. 120).[7]

The Freydís episode commemorates an occurrence several centuries in the past; the Théroigne print, in contrast, offers a cautionary prediction of how a future restorationist war might misfire. But—within their distinct media and different historical contexts, and despite some minor discrepancies[8]—both saga and caricature rely on a similar narrative template. Both envision a woman, solitary for all her more-or-less tenuous link with nearby allies,[9] who successfully routs a far superior enemy. In one hand she wields a weapon, while with the other she calls attention to an unequivocal attribute of her sex. The affinities of configuration further suggest that both the Old Norse text and the French print may address their audiences using closely comparable rhetorical channels.

A similar narrative pattern also governs an episode in a fifteenth-century Burgundian version of the *Annales normandes abrégées*.[10] The courts of northwest-

---

[7] See Goldsmith (1935: 48–65); Grubitzsch and Bockholt (1991: 208–470); and Roudinesco (1991: 51–156): "It was as if Théroigne was moving still closer to the simulacrum which had been devised to represent her" (1991: 101).

[8] The most salient discrepancies in detail, to which I return below, are the closer spatial association between Théroigne and her allies than between Freydís and hers, the threat of violence to herself implicit in Freydís's gesture (but absent from Théroigne's), and the specific physical emblems each unveils to demonstrate her sex. The saga and the print are also divided in their ideological attitudes towards their respective heroines.

[9] A solitary woman who faces down belligerent males is a saga commonplace; see, e.g., *Laxdœla saga* cap. 15 (ÍF 5, 1934: 33–36); *Gísla saga* capp. 21–22 (ÍF 6, 1943: 97–101); and *Grettis saga* capp. 52, 83 (ÍF 7, 1936: 166–72, 265–67). The French print, as noted, shows Théroigne as only one of several women. Her position in the center foreground, as well as her unique posture, clearly single her out, however. She subsumes the other women as body doubles of sorts, allowing the viewer to see her 'in the round' in a two-dimensional medium. These women also multiply the targets of the satirical broadside (cf. Grubitzsch and Bockholt: "Die Frauen stehen hier nicht als Individuen, sondern . . . als 'die wichtigsten Klatschweiber, die eine geistlose Rolle in der Revolution gespielt haben,'" 1991: 262).

[10] On the *Annales*, see Molinier's introduction (1882: i–lxxxv). Kervyn prints this anecdote (1879–80: 2.108–10) from Brussels Bibliothèque royale 11139 [shelf-marked 11138–39], dated ca. 1430–40 (1879–80: 1.xxxii–xxxiii; Marchal, 1842: 1.cclvi, 223; Van den Gheyn, 1901–48: 10.144; Dogaer and Debae, 1967: 127). Dismissive of this manuscript, Molinier (1882: xxx–lv) does not print this variant, which leads me to assume it is unique. See further chapter VI, n42 below. I am indebted to John Carmi Parsons for reference to this vignette.

ern Europe in the 1360s, which serve as the historical foil for this tale, were sites of cutthroat political and military maneuvering.[11] When Philippe de Rouvres, duke of Burgundy, died in 1361, his twelve-year-old widow Marguerite became an eminently marriageable pawn in the hands of her father Louis de Male, count of Flanders. Louis showed himself averse to contracting his daughter to an eager French suitor, Philippe *le hardi*, recent duke of Burgundy and brother to the king. By stringing Philippe along, Louis could play him off Edmund Langley—earl of Cambridge, Edward III's fifth son, and also a suitor for the girl's hand. Louis seems to have valued constructive ambiguity above all other options; he kept negotiations simmering for several years.[12] The uncertainty might have gone on for longer still, but in 1369 (as the *Annales* tell it), Marguerite d'Artois, Louis's mother, finally had enough of it. A Capetian herself, the countess may indeed have advocated closer ties with France. At this point in the narrative, her son is in Bruges, where he has just hosted a tournament attended by English, French, and Flemings. Following some ominous signs at the arena,[13] he sits in council to orchestrate his procrastination to the latest round of French suits, when his mother appears before him:

> Just as the discussion was about to begin, Madame d'Artois said to Louis, her son: "Dear son, you see that the king of France, who is nearby [at Tournay], has sent to you these great lords for [arranging] the marriage of your daughter, so that there may always be good affection and good allegiance between you and him, who is your lord, and as you are to hold the counties of Flanders, Nevers, Rethel, and (after my death) the county of

---

[11] The following historical synopsis is culled from Calmette (1962); Vaughan (1962); Seward (1978); and Nicholas (1992: 225–27).

[12] The reason usually cited for Louis's failure to marry Marguerite to Edmund is the hostility of the Avignon papacy: Urban V in 1365 refused to grant Edward III's request for a dispensation allowing the marriage (which would have been within the fourth degree of consanguinity), though he issued just such a dispensation in 1367 to Philippe, who "was almost as closely related to [the bride] as was Edmund" (Vaughan 1962: 5). Flemish politics seem to me more likely to have motivated Louis to keep the question of his daughter's marriage unresolved: as long as no decision was reached, he held on to a potential prize that could be dangled before both francophile and anglophile factions, both within his own realm and beyond it.

[13] Kervyn (1879–80: 2.109): "Et avint en celle journée que pluiseurs hours qui estoient fais autour de la place où on joustoit, fondirent, et y eut pluiseurs personnes tuées et blechiées, dont pluiseurs disoient que ce seroit aucuns signes et que il pourroit bien mesvenir au conte et au pays de Flandres pour ce que il ne vouloit mie marier sa fille à Phelippe, frère du roy de France" [And it happened on that day that many bleachers, which had been erected around the place of jousting, collapsed, and many people were killed and injured there; which, many said, was some sort of sign and that it could turn out badly for the count and for the country of Flanders because he did not in the least wish to marry his daughter to Philippe, the king of France's brother].

Artois from him; and [yet] I see that not for [any] petition nor for [any] request that these lords or I may make in the name of the king do you will to do anything."

And then the lady threw down her cloak, and opened her dress in front and took her right breast in her hand, and then said to her son: "As Countess of Artois, I beseech and command you to do the will of the king, who is your lord and mine; and behold my breast with which I nursed you, and none other of my children but you, and I vow to God that—if you do not do the will of the king and mine—I shall at once cut it off in defiance of you and throw it to the dogs, and you shall never enjoy [tenure of] the county of Artois."

This is more than Louis can stand; he falls to his knees, conceding to her: "Madam, you are my mother; act in this [matter] according to your pleasure."[14] The nuptials follow shortly.

About midway (chronologically) between Freydís and Théroigne, Lady Artois acts in a way that bears some resemblance to each, but also differs from both in significant detail. Like Freydís, Marguerite uses her exposed breast as a prop; the maternal, nurturing aspect of this secondary sex attribute is stressed (if only to be viciously undercut) in her verbal commentary, in preference to the openly ribald references of female flesh in the Théroigne print.[15] And, where the dangerous proximity of Freydís's blade to her body only alludes to self-mutilation, the countess's words announce it expressly. This similarity between the two women is even more pronounced if a seventeenth-century paper manuscript of *Eiríks saga rauða* is taken into consideration. This unique copy contains rubricated variant readings, whose ultimate source and age cannot be ascertained. One such rubric portrays Freydís as a veritable Amazon. The crucial passage here reads:

---

[14] Kervyn (1879–80: 2.109–10): "[E]t tant aprocha le traitié que madame d'Artois dist à Loys, son fils: 'Beau fils, vous véés que le roy de France qui est bien près de chy, a envoyé par-devers vous ces grans seigneurs pour le mariage de vostre fille, affin que tousjours il ait bonne amour et bonnes alliances entre vous et luy qui est vos sires, et se devés tenir les contés de Flandres, Nevers, Réthel et, après mon décès, le conté d'Artois tout de luy, et je voy que pour pryère, ne pour requeste que ces seigneurs, ne moy vous fachons ou nom du roy, vous ne voulés rien faire.' Et adont jetta la dame jus son mantel, et ouvry sa robe par-devant et prinst sa destre mamelle en sa main, et puis dist à son fils: 'Je, comme contesse d'Artois, vous prie et commande que vous fachiés le voulenté du roy qui est vos sires et li miens, et vecy me mamelle dont je vous alaitay, et plus de mes enfans ne alaitay que vous, et je promès à Dieu que, se vous ne faites le voulenté du roy et le mienne, que tantost je le copperay ou despit de vous et le jetteray aux chiens, et se ne joïrés jamais de le conté d'Artois.'. . . 'Madame, vous estes ma mère, faites ent à vostre bon plaisir.'" I am indebted to Alice Colby-Hall for reading over my translation.

[15] I do not, however, wish to suggest that the bosom's maternal and sexual registers are mutually exclusive (as is often done; cf. Bynum 1986: 85–88, a nuanced view); the two are, rather, entirely intertwined. See below, chapter VI, n18.

Hùn dró þá út bríóstið ùndan klæðúnúm . . . og skar það af sièr og grýttr eptir þeim, "She then pulled the breast out from beneath her garment . . . and chopped it off, and lobs [it] after them."[16] Marguerite does not quite go this far in violently instrumentalizing her bosom, but her stated intentions certainly do not fall short. Of the three women, she alone offers a verbal gloss on her somatic display. Perhaps she alone is at liberty to soliloquize because, unlike the other two, her performance is staged not before enemies facing her in open combat but before her closest kinsman, in the physically secure space of his council.[17]

Ranking intended audiences is entirely straightforward in this last case, and not merely because internal antagonists have been omitted: the dowager openly apostrophizes her [*b*]*eau fils*. Her primary audience is thus an intra-textual ally, whom she plies using several complementary tactics. First, as the term of endearment suggests, Marguerite's intervention pivots on emphasizing the bond between herself and her addressee, close on more levels than one ("the king . . . is your lord and mine"). This proximity guarrantees her right to a hearing, and only by emphasizing it can she then subvert it to full effect: "behold my breast with which I nursed you, and none other of my children but you"—but unless you humor me, "I shall at once cut it off in defiance of you and throw it to the dogs." The tangible intimacy of maternal bonding is in danger of destruction, the breast that fed her intimate addressee about to be fed to the dogs instead.[18] Such

---

[16] AM 770b 4to, 16[v]; printed by Rafn (1837: 154n7). Stefán Einarsson was the first to draw attention to this manuscript (1939). There is no ellipsis in the manuscript; the first half of the sentence appears in the body of the text, the remainder as a marginal addition. For the dating, see Kålund (1888–94: 2.190; cf. Rafn 1837: 81–82), but the marginalia (each clearly rubricated as a variant reading) must have been drawn from a lost original of indeterminable age. I am deeply indebted to Ólöf Benediktsdóttir for giving me access to photos of this manuscript.

[17] It may be noted in passing that, in retellings of the Freydís episode, her (in the saga, silent) pantomime tends to develop an accompanying soundtrack of war whoops; see, e.g., Morison: "she bared her breasts, slapped them with a sword, and screamed like a hellcat" (1971–74: 1.55). Cf., in fiction, Hewlett (1918: 251); Chapin (1934: 101), epigraph to chapter IV below; Pedersen (1952: 74); Scott (1958: 93–94), epigraph to chapter VIII below; Boyer (1976: 215); Berry (1977: 178); Vollmann (1990: 307–8), epigraph to chapter VII below; Jónas Kristjánsson (1998: 229).

[18] Medieval noblewomen did not normally breastfeed their own children, as incidentally attested by Albert the Great, who rhetorically asks the Virgin: "Quid est ergo, quod lactas puerum, o mundi domina? Cuilibet reginae huius mundi sufficit, quod filium a rege conceptum portat et parit, qui statim genitus amovetur a matre et nutrici traditur, onerumque et indignum nimis reputaretur, quod regina lactaret proprium filium" [How then is it, O mistress of the world, that you suckled the Child? For any queen of this world it is enough that she carries and bears a son begot by the king; who, as soon as he is born, is removed from the mother and given to a nurse. And it would be considered onerous and highly unseemly that a queen should suckle her own son] (*Homilie* 10, 1916:

a frightful image could well paint the countess herself in sordid hues — indeed, reference to Théroigne's *Republique* aims at just such condemnation by inversion of norms — but here it is turned not against the speaker but against a recalcitrant Louis. What his mother only hypothesizes, he has already committed, neglecting his obligations to family and feudal liege.

Marguerite's would-be transgressions, meanwhile, are aligned with the interests of Louis's overlord, thereby proclaiming their propriety: "do the king's will, and mine."[19] Invoking physical violence is another key aspect of the countess's tactic. Threatening to cut her son out of the will may seem like a prospect sufficiently terrifying to ensure compliance ("you shall never enjoy the county of Artois"), but rather than stop at this definite, measurable, utilitarian threat, Marguerite compounds it with the risky, symbolic atrocity of projected self-mutilation. Turning the knife on herself would certainly be dangerous for her, and although it might not damage Louis directly in quite so predictable a way as disinheriting him, damage him it would, raising the stakes for him in an open-ended way no definite threat could. Conversely, an uninherited county would remain quite abstract, whereas a mother's bloody breast would make for an immediate sensory spectacle. A final component in Marguerite's tactic is her orchestration of the dialogue with her son before an assembly of other allied observers within the text: she seeks not simply to appeal to Louis's sense of decency or to cajole him in private with threats material or maternal, but to humiliate him sensationally before his peers and subordinates. This is conditional humiliation, however: if Louis does not give in, she will renounce him and he will lose face as she publicly casts him into the outer Otherness — but if he relents, all will be forgiven. The elderly countess's blustering, then, is not literally a declaration of war, in defiance (*ou despit*) of the young count; it should rather be read as a last-ditch

---

47). Cf. also Wolfram von Eschenbach, *Parzival* 1.2.113 (1952: 1.194). Occasionally, the youngest child might be given its mother's breast rather than a wet nurse's; see (on Tuscany, where the data are good) Klapisch-Zuber (1983), Shahar (1992: 55–63, 68–71), Miles (2008: 36–37, 104–5), and (on our relative ignorance of Flemish practices) Nicholas (1985: 120); cf. Nip (1995: 210, 214, 216–17). Louis, however, was Marguerite's only child (Schwennicke 1980–2011: 2. table 8), so the contrast she draws between having personally nursed him and (by implication) having entrusted her other children to wet nurses is purely rhetorical.

[19] The overall effect of her appeal — the cause it is made in, the means by which it is attained, its success — seems intended to endorse the political values (and to contribute to the political education perpetuating these values) of an extra-textual fifteenth-century Burgundian court. It is easy enough to see, e.g., that allegiance to the Valois kings was constructed in this court as an uncontroversial default, from which only an unnatural count might deviate. The omens at the tournament stamp this political stance with narrative 'objectivity.'

plea for him to resume his prescribed social roles as faithful son (and scion to the French royal house) and obedient vassal.[20]

Triangulating Marguerite d'Artois and Théroigne de Méricourt with Freydís Eiríksdóttir allows us to begin picking out the essential characteristics of the bare-sarked warrior. Although not every feature is evident in each instance, and despite differences of emphasis in the presentation of particular facets, the topos as a whole appears both coherent and consistent. Across the various ideological landscapes, the positioning of the bare-sarked warrior vis-à-vis potential audiences emerges as one defining feature. The apposition of *ostentatio pudendorum* and a brandished weapon is another.[21] Finally, the bare-sarked warrior straddles a particular intersection of violent risk, menaced on one side by ruthless adversaries, and on the other by her own hand. I explore these characteristics further in the following chapters, beginning with the question of what terms the Icelandic cultural repertoire might have had to hand for classifying a rich ritual *mélange* such as these women enact.

---

[20] For a sensitive analysis of similar techniques for coercing consent, see Koziol (1992: esp. 245, 251–53).

[21] I use the term *ostentatio pudendorum* in acknowledgement, but also to broaden, Steinberg's coinage, *ostentatio genitalium*, which he uses to refer to the "ostensive unveiling of [Christ's] sex" (1996: 3).

IV. Help and Humiliation

> But Freydis, finding Thorward in the wood,
> wounded and cowed with fear, snatched up his sword
> and killed him with a stroke and faced the foe.
> She foamed with berserk rage, she stripped her shift,
> and waved her naked blade and slapped it hard
> against her great up-standing breasts and howled.
> Gest stood beside her grinning, and these two
> there turned the tide of battle for the Norse.
>
> Chapin, *Leifsaga* (1934: 101)[1]

A program of incitement through shaming, similar to the one detailed above for the late-medieval Burgundian chronicle, is well known in medieval Iceland, too. Aggressive female gesticulation and fighting words were institutionalized as *hvǫt*, 'whetting,' allowing Norse women to take part in public strife (see further Sidebar 3). Whetting women's function was to egg sluggish men into action. They would question men's *virðing*, 'worth,' with pointed words—as Freydís does by comparing Karlsefni's men unfavorably to *auvirðismenn*, 'men without *virðing*'—or through performative acts such as tossing a bloodstained cloak over the shoulders of their slain husband's kinsmen in order to fan the flames of smoldering feud.[2] The Norsemen in Vínland are engaged in no feud that Freydís might rekindle, but it might be argued that she whets her male allies to preempt a future injury. Slapping a sword to her naked flesh might mime the fate to which Karlsefni and his men have abandoned her, much like the symbolism behind the acts of German women, reported by Tacitus to have snatched victory from the jaws of defeat with their piteous pectoral displays: "It is recorded that some battle-lines, already falling back and buckling, have been reinvigorated by the constancy of women's pleading and [their] exposed breasts and bewailing of

---

[1] Thorward (Þorvarðr) is Freydís's husband; Gest (a *nom de guerre* for Thorgils, Leif Ericson's illegitimate son, 1934: 49–50, 80; cf. *Eiríks saga rauða* cap. 5, ÍF 4: [*H*] 209–10, [*S*] 414) is an invented character, based on a type common to many other sagas (cf., e.g., *Grettis saga* capp. 64–65, ÍF 7: 209–14).

[2] See *Brennu-Njáls saga* cap. 116 (ÍF 12: 291–92); richly discussed by Clover (1986b).

impending captivity."[3] Freydís's abusive speech complements the gesture, exhorting her compatriots to stand and fight like *gildir*, 'estimable'—rather than *geldir*, 'emasculated'?—men. If the *skrælingar*, in a variation on timeless lambs-to-the-slaughter similes, are reviled as less than human ("you could [have] cut [them] down like domesticated cattle"), the Norse men run the risk of being scaled still farther down the evolutionary ladder. (The point is neatly brought out in Henry Chapin's fictionalization, quoted in the epigraph above, where Freydis butchers her own "cow[ing]" husband before she turns her fury on the Natives.)

So, too, the scene depicted in the Théroigne print may be read as a *hvǫt* of sorts, though muffled by constraints of the form. The pictorial medium distils narrative to a single instant frozen in time, making the women's rebuke of their male allies difficult to pick out at first; rather, the obvious targets of the women's provocation are the Austrian soldiery. The Théroigne print thus offers, on the one hand, "self-criticism, depicting the counterrevolutionary army as cowardly" and, like the *skrælingar*, unmanly; the women's obscene exposure has a more pronouncedly *débandant* effect on this internal audience of their adversaries than in the Norse analogue, an effect underscored by images of chopped meats held aloft and of stiff weapons clattering to the ground. Still, compressed as it is, the French caricature in fact goes to remarkable lengths to ensure that no party emerge unscathed. The women themselves, in turn, are shamed by shamelessly revealing their privates; the bared bosom, fast becoming monopolized by Revolutionary iconography as a badge of heroic patriotism, is conspicuously absent from this depiction, which communicates hostility by recourse to a bare-skirted variation on the toplessness topos. That such gestures were firmly implanted in the discursive imagination of the period is confirmed by an incident from the summer of 1794 when, "at a sign from an old woman, the entire female audience [at a celebration of the Supreme Being] rose, turned their backs on the altar of liberty, and raised their skirts to express their feelings to the new deity. Confronted by the spectacle of serried rows of naked female backsides the celebrant was reduced to gibberish. Officialdom departed in unseemly haste with aspersions on its manhood made from all sides." Even if allegiances are reversed in this

---

[3] Tacitus, *Germania* 8.1: "Memoriae proditur quasdam acies inclinatas iam et labantes a feminis restitutas constantia precum et obiectu pectorum et monstrata comminus captivitate" (1938: unpaginated); cf. Lodewyckx (1955: 186) and Moreau (1951: 297), who suggests that Tacitus may have substituted pectoral for pubic exposure, for the sake of decency (1951: 291–92; cf. Bonner 1920: 258); see also chapter V, n11 below. Caesar, *Gallic Wars* 1.51, attributes to Germanic women similarly pathetic entreaties; cf. 7.48 (1917: 82, 450). Cf. also the tactic employed by the Batavian general Julius Civilis in Tacitus' *Histories* 4.18: "matrem suam sororesque, simul omnium coniuges parvosque liberos consistere a tergo iubet, hortamenta victoriae vel pulsis pudorem" [he ordered his own mother and sisters, as well as the wives and little children of all (his men), to stand at (the troops') back (as) encouragements to victory or disgrace to the fleeing] (1925–37: 2.34).

3. Background: Whetting women

Queen Skuld has plenty of grievances against her half-brother, King Hrólfr *kraki*, going back a generation or two. First, there's the genealogical mess. Their father, Helgi, raped Ólöf, Hrólfr's grandmother, then unwittingly committed incest with the daughter she bore, making him simultaneously Hrólfr's grandfather and father. Helgi went on to impregnate an elf-woman, siring Skuld. Then, Hrólfr tricked Skuld's husband, bending him into political vassalage; on top of that, Hrólfr's gambit slyly insinuated her husband's sexual subordination to him, too.[1] There is little love lost between the half-siblings, and Skuld seeks an opportunity to be avenged:

> Now it happened one time that Queen Skuld conversed with King Hjörvarðr, her husband, sighing heavily: "It doesn't sit well with me, that we two should pay tribute to King Hrólfr and be coerced by him, and it must no longer be [so], that you are his subordinate." Hjörvarðr says: "It would serve us best, as it does others, to endure it and leave everything be."
>
> "How little you stand up for yourself," she said, "that you're willing to suffer every kind of indignity done to you!" He said: "It isn't possible to contend with King Hrólfr, because no one dares take up a shield against him."
>
> "So little do you stand up for yourselves," said she, "for you have no guts: he who risks nothing never prevails. Now, it may not be known before it is tried, whether King Hrólfr or his champions might not be harmed."[2]

Skuld's dialogue with her husband exemplifies the Norse genre of *hvǫt*, the 'whetting' or incitement of a reluctant aggressor to action, usually by his nearest and dearest ally—a wife, a mother, or some other close relation—who claims to have his best interest at heart and so relentlessly prods him to live up to the

---

[1] See Phelpstead (2003: 12-14; cf. 8-9 [on Skuld's parentage], 19-20 [on her revenge]).

[2] *Hrólfs saga kraka* cap. 47: "Nú var eitthvert sinn, at Skuld drottning mælti við Hjörvarð konung, bónda sinn, með þungum anda: 'Þat fellr mér lítt, at vit skulum gjalda skatt Hrólfi konungi ok vera nauðþínd undir hann, ok skal þat ekki vera lengr, at þú sért undirmaðr hans.' Hjörvarðr segir: 'Þat mun oss bezt gegna sem öðrum at líða þat ok láta allt vera kyrrt.' 'Þat er lítill þú ert fyrir þér,' sagði hún, 'at þú vilt þola hvers kyns skammir, er þér eru gerðar.' Hann sagði: 'Þat er ekki möguligt at fást við Hrólf konung, því at engi þorir móti honum rönd at reisa.' 'Því eru þér svá litlir fyrir yðr,' sagði hún, 'at engi krellr er í yðr, ok hefir sá eigi jafnan, sem ekki hættir. Nú má slíkt eigi vita, fyrr en reynt er, hvárt Hróli konungi má ekki bella né köppum hans'" (FSN 1: 93).

role she has in mind for him.[3] As here, and as in most cultures where such discourse is institutionalized,[4] *hvǫt* becomes a vehicle for female participation in the political sphere, allowing women to express their opinions and influence the conduct of the full-fledged political players (by definition, men, as de Lauretis points out).[5] The shrill, small voice of women's agency is audible through the narrow aperture of whetting. It is an agency securely contained, however, both by being restricted to working within the conventions of the genre (as a form of intervention that presupposes the speaker's social inferiority) and by having its message confined to predetermined talking points (allowing women to call for men to exercise their agency through violence, but ruling out any nuance or variation). *Hvǫt* thus restricts women at least as much as it enables them.

---

[3] See Clover (1986b); Miller (1990: 212-14 and 2000: 239-40); Jesch (1991: 188-91); Jochens (1996: 162-203); Tolmie (2001: 1-7, 15-69); and cf. Meulengracht Sørensen (1983: esp. 21). Jóhanna Katrín Friðriksdóttir critically surveys much of the preceding scholarship (2010: 55-76, 198-200; cf. eadem 2013: 17-25, 87-88, an abbreviated version); I am indebted to the author for making her dissertation available to me.

[4] Cf. Geyer (1909) and Bloom (2007: 99-100); see also el-Baghdadi (2011: esp. 2:19-2:33).

[5] See de Lauretis (1985a: 42-43). Some men do goad other men, but circumstances in such cases often conspire to feminize the whetter, as, e.g., in an impotent old man's incitement of his son in *Þorsteins þáttr stangarhǫggs* (ÍF 11: 70; further examples in Miller 1990: 212; on the social emasculation of elderly men, see, e.g., Miller 1990: 209; but cf. Overing 1999). Similarly, in late-medieval England, scolding and, more generally, "illicit speech was so emphatically coded a feminine failing [that] men who spoke too much or in inappropriate contexts risked the charge of effeminacy" (Bardsley 2006: 104). Respectable men's *hvǫt* has a different tone, appealling "ikke så meget til følelser som til resonnement" [not so much to emotions as to reason], as Høyersten points out (1998: 95, citing *Brennu-Njáls saga* cap. 139, ÍF 12: 371-72).

---

case (and in other copycat incidents inspired by its success), with mooning serving here as a counterrevolutionary tactic, the idiom is unmistakably the same as that attributed to Théroigne and her companions.[4]

But above and beyond any formal restrictions, the political ideology underwriting the print sufficiently accounts for its reticence in depicting *hvǫt*. Intended

---

[4] Hockman (1988: 213); Hufton (1992: 118), who also notes that "[m]ontrer le cul aux gens as an expression of female scorn has a long history in France even before Zola enshrined the practice in *Germinal*. It was emphatically a technique of the working classes" (1992: 118–19). On the positive connotations of Marianne's bosom, see Trouillas (1988: 201–72, esp. 243–68), confirmed by Warner (1985: 290), who also richly complicates the picture (1985: 267–93 [cap. 12: "The Slipped Chiton"]); see also chapter V, n11 below on the autonomous development of a tradition of below-the-waist exposure.

for Royalist viewers, it seeks to elicit censure, not celebrate the women's triumph. Certainly, the imagery criticizes the useless Reactionary troops; certainly, it ridicules the Republican harpies.[5] But the butt of the satire are ultimately neither the women nor the Austrians but the grim *sans-culottes*. Disciplined women broadsiding the Imperial regulars, who ignominiously break rank, are in a sense their equals if not their betters; the male Revolutionaries, in contrast, are a ragtag crew of useless ruffians. The disembodied sausages they dangle could just as easily index their own emasculation as prophesy it for their enemies. The men are kept visible, if just barely, in the background, to be literally eclipsed by the women's bare bodies. The male Jacobins must thus be included in the picture for ideological reasons. What prevents the artist from representing physical distance between the female protagonists and their male allies (as in the Freydís episode) are mostly technical, iconographic constraints. The men need to be near enough for the women to overshadow them; the monumental proportions of the scene in relation to its frame (necessitated by the needs of caricature to minimize subtlety) also dictate cramped quarters all around. Thus also the channel separating Revolutionaries from Austrians is probably mandated by the iconographic need to draw a stark visual border between foes tightly confined inside the outer frame. Although the scene may be structurally homologuous to a Norse *hvǫt*, its meaning shifts from whetting encouragement to withering odium because the men's humiliation is made unconditional: showing women supplant them at their gender duties dishonors them irremediably. The viewing audience are never invited, as in the Icelandic and Burgundian analogues, to identify with the Revolutionary men. Improbable female-on-male violence spells the emasculation of a third party, the women's do-nothing male allies.

Political and pictorial constraints conspire to mute the whetting motif in the Théroigne print, but there can be little doubt that all three artifacts share the characteristics of *hvǫt* to varying degrees. Incitement is clearest in Marguerite's chastisement of her son; conversely, confrontation with extra-societal Others is least clearly in view here. The two narrative moves — candor regarding the provocation expressed in the woman's entreaty, equivocation regarding the presence of a threat from beyond society — are directly correlated: since *hvǫt* is a form of internal social regulation, it is most conspicuous where confrontation takes place within the community.[6]

---

[5] Though mocking the women, the print unquestionably also acknowledges their power; see Cameron (1991: 96).

[6] The de-emphasis on whetting in the Théroigne print is also correlated with increased, even exaggerated conventionality of portrayal, and with an emphasis on the caricature's direct address of external viewers. This correlation makes sense in terms of the model of audience levels outlined above, pp. 16–17. Clearly, though "[t]he notion that women should spur men to action pervaded revolutionary politics from its outbreak" (Desan 2004: 78; cf. 74–85), *hvǫt* was not regarded as a realistic option for French women

What sets the bare-sarked warrior apart from other whetting women, however, is that, at the same time that she provokes with scalding contempt, she must also plead for extraordinary help. The cataclysmic urgency of her distress licenses transgressive gender ambiguity.[7] In this respect, the Freydís episode stands halfway between the other two narratives: like the Théroigne print, it is concerned with showcasing a clash between two radically incompatible societies, but like the Marguerite anecdote, it also strives to keep attention (and, ultimately, even sympathy) focused on the railing woman's ingroup allies. In some particulars, Freydís's performance diverges from conventional *hvǫt*: the whetting-worthy audience of allies are a good distance away, while the antagonists, against whom the Norse men should be egged on, are perilously close at hand. Can her address be considered *hvǫt* when only her adversaries are really within earshot? Her action is also surprisingly efficacious, utterly overthrowing the Natives before Karlsefni and his men can so much as lift a finger.[8] In these respects, the Freydís episode more closely resembles a flyting—a Germanic genre of verbal abuse similar in most substantive features to whetting, but directed at enemies rather than at allies. Flyting may substitute rhetorical barbs for physical blows (Ward Parks calls this "ludic flyting"), or it may serve simply as a preliminary act, softening up targets with words before one proceeds to break their bones ("heroic flyting," in Parks's terminology). Some other characteristics of flyting—such as the feuding assumption of parity between the opponents, a reiterative structure, and focus on an addressee's past failings—are absent, however, from Freydís's performance.[9]

To date no critic has read the Freydís episode in terms of *hvǫt*,[10] perhaps because its transgressive audacity calls into question the very notion of gender distinction. Saga whettings are usually an opportunity for simple pronouncements

---

ca. 1800; see Warner (1985: 289) and Hunt (1992: 156–58) for notions of subdued female demeanor as 'natural.'

[7] Similarly, Coser notes that women, though generally less violent than men, play a relatively prominent part in revolutionary violence; "situations where the old norms have broken down differ significantly from normatively stable situations. . . . [Crises] allow underdogs to aspire to equal participation" (1966: 338). Cf. also Ness (2007: 87).

[8] Cf. Lodewyckx (1955: 186) and chapter VIII below.

[9] See Parks (2000), as well as Clover (1979 and 1980) and Smith (1981); contrast Swenson (1991). A link between *hvǫt* and flyting is seldom discussed (but see Clover 1980: 446n7). The generic differences are more situational than formal, however: opponents engaged in flyting are on roughly equal social footing (from a systemic perspective, though individually each endeavors to confer on the other an inferior status), whereas *hvǫt* presupposes acknowledgement of incommensurability by the (socially inferior) perptrator. Thus, flyting is to *hvǫt* rather as cohesive force is to exclusionary violence. See also Sidebar 3.

[10] Barnes (2001: 29) makes a passing allusion to Freydís as "whetter," but does not develop the point; see also Kolodny (2012: 87).

of role reversal: women talk in a decidedly *hvatr*, 'butch,' manner, denouncing the men they taunt as *blauðr*, 'sissy.'[11] Freydís could have stayed safely within gender bounds if she had merely berated Karlsefni's men, appealing to them to rescue her but herself remaining helplessly passive; Norse convention would have sanctioned using cutting words, even melodramatic props in such a plea. For all its bluster, *hvǫt* is securely feminized by its presupposition that women may initiate, direct, or accelerate the play of violence, but must yield its practice to the physical agency of men. This division of labor constructs gender firmly: women wield words, men perform deeds. Moreover, whether pure literary device or reflection of social fact, *hvǫt* probably struck medieval Icelanders as a realistic enough way for women to respond to crisis.[12] Women may call men women[13] or even style themselves men, as Freydís does here ("I'd think that I should fight better than any of you")[14]—but only so long as each sex is gendered either one way or the other at a time. Freydís, however, does not merely verbalize her contempt for her

---

[11] Clover (1993) discusses these (almost technical) terms of what she describes as a Norse conceptual "one-sex system," differentiating degrees of approximation to or distance from a *hvatr* (hyper-masculine) ideal and a *blauðr* (effeminate) degeneracy rather than between categorically distinct 'male' and 'female.' Her conclusion, that the Norse had no concept of gender as such, is overstated. To my mind she shows, rather, that gender and bravura were for the Norse inextricably intertwined (as they are, indeed, in the English terms 'butch' and 'sissy'). Cf. also Lewis (2000), Layher (2007: 189), and—for an analogous distinction between *virtus*, 'manliness,' and *mollities*, 'softness' (rather than between *vir*, 'man,' and *mulier*, 'woman') in Saxo's *Gesta Danorum*—Perron (2010); I am indebted to Shannon Lewis-Simpson for making a copy of her thesis available to me.

[12] Heller (1958: 98–122), Jesch (1991: 190), and Jochens (1996: 174–203) see saga *hvǫt* as mere literary convention; Clover (1986b: 180), Miller (1990: 212 and 2000: 239–40), and Meulengracht Sørensen (1993b: 179) argue in favor of its social plausibility; see also Jóhanna Katrín Friðriksdóttir (2010: 59–70; see also eadem 2013: 19–21). Steinvör's (only partially successful) egging of her husband Hálfdan in *Þórðar saga kakala* cap. 2 (in *Sturlunga saga* 1946: 2.6; see n14 in this chapter) illustrates realistically how *hvǫt*, even if essentially literary, may have worked (or failed to work) in actual practice; cf. Jóhanna Katrín Friðriksdóttir (2010: 57, 70).

[13] See, e.g., *Króka-Refs saga* cap. 3 (ÍF 14: 123): "Ávallt hrýss mér hugr við, er ek sé þik. . . . Væri þar betri dóttir" [It quite turns my stomach, when I see you. . . . A daughter would have been better]; cf. *Laxdœla saga* cap. 53 (ÍF 5: 162) and *Vatnsdœla saga* cap. 3 (ÍF 8: 8).

[14] Cf., e.g., *Þórðar saga kakala* cap. 2: "nú mun . . . svá fara, sem minnr er at sköpuðu, at ek mun taka vápnin ok viti, ef nökkurir menn vili fylgja mér" [now it will . . . happen so—which is hardly according to nature—that I shall take up weapons and see whether some men might follow me] (in *Sturlunga saga* 1946: 2.6); see also *Bróka*-Auðr, who rides out to attack the man she holds responsible for the slander that she dresses in men's clothing—"ok var hon þá at vísu í brókum" [and she certainly was in breeches (this time)!] (*Laxdœla saga* cap. 35, ÍF 5: 97, cf. 95–98; on this episode, see Wolf 1997c: 387–91, a reference for which I thank the press's anonymous Reader 1).

male allies: she picks up a dead man's sword "and prepares to defend herself," in effect assuming the persona of the fallen Þorbrandr Snorrason. That she then turns this sword on herself rather than heft it at the approaching *skrælingar* adds a further ironic (and destabilizing) kink to an already convoluted Möbius strip. Even women more liminal and transgressive than whetters—maiden warriors, for instance—appear able only to vacillate between gender roles; they seldom if ever confound them.[15]

Freydís's display mixes a *hvatr* resort to arms with the *blauðr* argument of her sex. The physical emblems of womanhood make Freydís an appropriate victim for exclusionary, male-on-female violence (in de Lauretis's typology). Bewilderingly, however, she is also dangerous enough to manfully perpetrate just such violence—putting the blade to her own flesh to underscore its femininity, putting the *skrælingar* to flight to accentuate their ethnic Otherness. In the face of the Natives' unsettling menace, subservient *hvǫt* welds with warriorlike flyting, making Freydís's behavior 'out of gender.'[16] *Eiríks saga rauða* grants her a greater degree of *hvatr* agency than any other saga allows to women who resort to *hvǫt*, while also ensuring that her *blauðr* physique is stated and restated, underlined with taps of the sword. Pregnant, disrobed, a helpless victim forsaken by male protectors, she is also, at the same time, the indomitable, armed virago who both

---

[15] See, e.g., Præstgaard-Andersen, who sees the eroticism of valkyries in armor as ambiguous but otherwise finds that warrior women "are under no circumstances able to play both [gender] roles at the same time" (2002: 314, cf. 293); Layher, carefully tracing the use of feminine and masculine pronouns to refer to such figures, concludes that "the maiden warrior assumes the male role when the patriarchal figure is absent or otherwise inhibited, [but resumes her femininity] when patriarchal authority is reestablished in the saga" (2007: 203). I am indebted to the press's anonymous Reader 2 for these references. In a seventh-century Anglo-Saxon context, Abels discusses Aldhelm's treatment of the Biblical Judith as "simultaneously a masculine warrior hero and a feminine seductress," pointing out that "Aldhelm was disturbed by the complexities of this image" (2006: 38, and cf. 36–39).

[16] Cf., imaginatively, Ballantyne: "Freydissa was one of those women who appear to have been born women by mistake—who are always chafing at their unfortunate fate, and endeavouring to emulate—even to overwhelm—men; in which latter effort they are too frequently successful. She was a tall elegant woman of about thirty years of age, with a decidedly handsome face, though somewhat sharp of feature. She possessed a powerful will, a shrill voice and a vigorous frame, and was afflicted with a short, violent temper. She was decidedly a masculine woman. We know not which is the more disagreeable of the two—a masculine woman or an effeminate man. But perhaps the most prominent feature in her character was her volubility when enraged,—the copiousness of her vocabulary and the tremendous force with which she shot forth her ideas and abuse in short abrupt sentences" (1872: 53–54).

menaces and defends this victim.[17] Attacker and attacked are conflated in the body of one and the same person, emanating and enduring its own violence.

The bare-sarked warrior is thus revealed (in samples from Norse America, Burgundian annals, and the Reactionary French press) as an androgynous figure, functioning to incite and motivate, not with the carrot of praise but with the stick of hectoring. Her primary audience are the recipients of her prickly encouragement, her intra-textual allies. Saga and chronicle prompt extra-textual readers and listeners to identify with these men; the Théroigne print—the better to suit its extra-textual, political goals and intra-textual, technical constraints—diverts viewers' sympathies away from her male allies. Within the Icelandic tradition, the bare-sarked warrior may be related to a better-known female figure, the whetter, who performs a largely identical function; so far, I have demonstrated no such links with other roles in the wider European tradition. Unlike other Norse whetters, however, Freydís and her sisters are not content to observe the bounds of gender, offering instead a subversive challenge to notions of *hvatr* masculinity and *blauðr* femininity. Freydís, Théroigne, and Marguerite are not like Tacitus' German wives, after all: the bare fact of their gendered bodies does not, on its own, suffice for fanning male aggression; they need the addition of a brandished weapon, besides. What they do, or threaten to do, to their tender flesh is as important as the reminders they supply of its appealing and vulnerable tenderness. Through the interplay of sex and gender in the construction of the bare-sarked warrior, through the violence she directs at herself yet mysteriously unleashes on her foes, she is somehow able to metamorphose the unbearable danger of the Other into manageable risk for the Self. The next three chapters thus focus on making sense of Freydís's nakedness and on her battlefield activities.

---

[17] Cf. Macdonald's sensitive analysis (1987: 44–46) of how Dio's portrait of Boadicea, in inverting Tacitus' scheme of male Roman violence against Briton women, nevertheless insists on the Briton leader's femininity: "in Dio it is the *Romans* who become the 'women.' They are not, however, women with the positive qualities that Tacitus attributed to Boadicea. . . . [I]t isn't quite the case that Boadicea becomes an 'honorary man'; it is rather that she loses the problematic *content* of her gender . . . but her femaleness remains as symbol" (1987: 45, emphases hers).

V. Magic and Mercy

At first Thorvard was as admiring as the others about his wife's courage, but as the talk continued, he became somewhat churlish and peeved. He was troubled that other men were talking openly about his wife's breast. Freydis wasn't at all embarrassed. On the contrary she was well pleased with herself. "What did you expect me to do?" she said to Thorvard. "Stand there and be murdered?" During the course of the discussions, Nagli said that before leaving Greenland, he had heard one of Thorfinn Karlsefni's men say that he had seen a skraeling woman in Hop bare her breast during battle to avoid being attacked. "That's very interesting," Freydis said. "But I never heard that tale myself."

"Even so, you might have heard the story from someone and forgotten," Thorvard insisted. He preferred to believe that the baring of a woman's breast was some sort of battle custom. He didn't want any of his men thinking his wife was wanton or loose.

Freydis thought baring her breast must have had something to do with being the daughter of Eirik the Red. She thought there was a fierceness in her that came from him, a willingness to do something rash when it was required. Freydis thought Thorvard would have preferred she not show her breast so that he could have saved her himself.

Clark, *Eiriksdottir* (1994: 233)[1]

For two schools of thought, the cardinal question in making sense of the strange episode in *Eiríks saga rauða* cap. 11 is why Freydís exposes herself. For both, the key to Freydís's conduct is her interaction with the *skrælingar*, the intra-textual antagonists who witness her display at close quarters. Both, accordingly, assume the realism of the account in *Eiríks saga rauða*, seeking to anchor it in historical fact rather than in literary technique. The glosses suggested for this encounter derive from its exotic cultural ensemble: on one side, a living embodiment of viking ferocity; on the other, a mysterious, prehistoric Maritime people. The focus on Freydís's incongruent attire, her enigmatic striptease before the

---

[1] Nagli is a made-up character. For the attribution of the gesture to a presumed Native battle custom, see pp. 50–51 below.

(presumed) primary audience of Natives, has led to interpretations of the episode as either a vestige of archaic Norse magic or an ethnographic record of cutting-edge cultural exchange (as Joan Clark's fictional Þorvarðr theorizes in the epigraph above).[2] Neither of these readings is sufficient; yet they serve me as convenient vehicles for accessing the important issues of gender and sex, of audience stratification, and of the play of violence within the topos.

According to the first school, the actions the saga attributes to Freydís should be read as dim literary echoes of ancient Norse battle magic, used to thwart opponents against whom conventional weapons fall short. Thus, for example, Stefán Einarsson, the first modern scholar to examine Freydís's breast-baring closely, believed that "[the author may] have seized upon a rationalized version of an ancient magic behaviour, whose significance he did not know."[3] Her violent pantomime, in his view, aims to manipulate power relations on a cosmic, not merely a social, scale. Much like a Canute commanding the tide to recede from his shoreline, Freydís seeks to impose her will on an inhuman adversary by following a protocol for communications with the supernatural; and like the Anglo-Danish emperor, she risks a humbling by inexorable fate.[4] This theory cites an evident Norse fear and contempt of *skrælingar*. Freydís herself deprecates them as men who fall below the status threshold or even as sub-humans (*búfé*). Elsewhere in Norse literature, *skrælingar* appear to be identified with trolls; in the Vínland cycle, they are easily duped during friendly bartering, but display a preternatural prowess as soon as fighting breaks out.[5] Against creatures like these

---

[2] Cf. Olender's comment on "two principal families" of interpretations of the ancient Greek legend of Baubo: "Either Baubo is seen to come from Elsewhere, and there is nothing Greek about her origins (this approach leads us on a 'world tour' of the *anasyrma*, and Baubo becomes a foreign servant imported into Greece). Or, on the other hand, Baubo becomes a sort of roundhouse, a center from which radiate various tracks conducting to 'general theories' of agro-mystical or magical obscenity" (1990: 93). On *anasyrma*, see further n11 in this chapter.

[3] Stefán Einarsson (1939: 256); similarly, Halldór Hermannsson (1936: 22); Jansson (1958: 539); Jones (1986: 134n18); cf. Busch's elaborate fictional account (1966: 188), drawing on a description of alleged pagan rites elsewhere in the Norse corpus ("Þrymskviða" 30, in Neckel 1962–68: 1.115). Similarly, witchcraft is sometimes ascribed to the *skrælingar*: see, e.g., Brøgger (1937: 146) and Thomas (1946–53: 320n33) on the oral tradition purportedly underlying *Grænlendinga saga*; cf. p. 65 below.

[4] Henry of Huntingdon, *Historia Anglorum* 6.17 (1996: 366-69) first tells the story of Canute's mock attempt to extend his authority over the rising tide (actually an *exemplum* of Christian humility).

[5] *Flóamanna saga* cap. 24 refers to (presumed) Eskimo women as "tröllkonur" [troll-wives] (ÍF 13: 290); *Historia Norwegie* 1 claims that the *skrælingar*, described as Stone Age hunters, do not bleed when injured, but that their blood gushes forth when they die (Ekrem and Mortensen 2003: 54). See also Native commercial gullibility and military magic in *Grænlendinga saga* capp. 4, 6 (ÍF 4: 256, 262–64) and *Eiríks saga rauða* capp. 11–12 (ÍF 4: [H] 228–33, [S] 428–32).

(the battle-magic hypothesis goes), a woman like Freydís, seething with archaic savagery, might well resort to pagan sorcery.

Throughout much of the world, displays of nudity, especially female nudity, are indeed a favored countermeasure to paranormal menace.[6] Medieval Europe has its share of such beliefs, conveniently exemplified by the famous sheela-na-gig, an architectural motif common on high- and late-medieval churchwalls; sheelas flaunt splayed vulvas (or sometimes other sexual attributes), often perching above doorways where they evidently serve as effective intruder repellent.[7] If the *skrælingar* possess a demonic capacity to terrify, Freydís may have just the gargoylian sexuality to stop them dead in their tracks.[8] Moreover, the Théroigne

---

[6] See Vorwahl (1933); Stefán Einarsson (1939: 252–56); Duerr (1993: 41–46); and, more generally on nudity as a measure of accessing the supernatural (principally in the ancient world), Heckenbach (1911). Contrast Weir and Jerman, who maintain that "in apotropaic magic it is usually the male sex organs which are invoked" (1986: 29), but do cite some evidence of female exposures (e.g., 1986: 146–47). Jochens's claim that Norsemen found female nudity universally frightening (1995: 76–77) may be dismissed.

[7] For overviews, see Andersen (1977); Weir and Jerman (1986); Kelly (1996); and cf. Easton (2008: 15–18). I extend the term sheela-na-gig from its traditional, confined reference ("[Anglo-Irish] carvings of naked females posed in a manner which displays and emphasises the genitalia," Kelly 1996: 5) to sexually explicit, mainly female sculptures throughout medieval Europe. Weir and Jerman find sheelas to have flourished from 1080 to 1250, peaking about 1150 (1986: 21; following Andersen 1977). They strive heroically to dissociate sheelas from pre-Christian Celtic (or other) religion and to minimize their tutelary function, arguing instead for a Romanesque origin in Classical sculptural motifs, reinterpreted to convey Gregorian Reformers' moralizing message (contrast Andersen 1977: 24, 133–38). Their rejection of an apotropaeic interpretation seems overstated, however, when one takes antecedents into consideration. Even when read through Ambrose's Christianizing lens, e.g., the image of St. Thecla, cowing a hungry lion by exposing herself, seems to confirm a tradition of apotropaeic genital display ("vitalia ipsa saevo [obtulit] leoni. . . . Cernere erat lingentem pedes bestiam cubitare humi, muto testificantem sono quod sacrum virginis corpus violare non posset" [she (exhibited) her abdomen to the savage lion. . . . The beast was (to be) seen, prostrate on the ground, licking (her) feet, mutely testifying that the holy virgin's body could not be violated], *De Virginibus* 2.3.19–20, 1948: 42). Exhibitionist, apparently apotropaeic figurines also survive from antiquity; see Montserrat (1996: 222, pl. 23; I am indebted to Elizabeth S. Bolman for calling this reference to my attention), Andersen (1977: fig. 92), and Weir and Jerman (1986: 111–14); Johns locates such images "virtually only in Roman Egypt," but finds possible analogues at Roman York (1982: 75; fig. 59). A sculpted stone from Trondheim Cathedral, dated ca. 1125–50, seems to depict two sheelas (Blindheim 1965: fig. 54).

[8] In his reinterpretation of the Vínland story, Pedersen depicts Freydís as a sheela: "I et nu rev hun sit tunge kjoleliv op fortil, så de vældige bryster sprang frem fra deres gemme. . . . Hun borede sine langfingre ind i øregangene og stak tommelfingrene ind i mundvigene og trak disse helt op imod ørerne, hun stak tungen langt ud af munden og vendte det hvide ud af øjnene. Det var et grufuldt syn! Halvnøgen og våbenløs løb hun således frem imod den hundredetallige fjende, udstødende hæse, uartikulerede kønshyl.

print, too, may echo a type of repulsive magic: the renowned eighteenth-century engraver Charles Eisen uses nearly identical (albeit more carefully sanitized) iconography to illustrate the La Fontaine fable "Le diable de Papefiguière," in which a woman scares away a devil by raising her skirts to him (see Fig. 3).[9] Earlier still, Machiavelli's fictionalized Caterina Sforza topples a rebel junta by resorting to the same technique—though, not surprisingly, Machiavelli rationalizes the efficacy of her gesture in terms of *Realpolitik*.[10] Such widespread analogues seem to

---

... Dette var stik imod alle krigskunstens regler!" [At once she tore open the front of her heavy bodice, so that the huge breasts sprang out into the open. . . . She poked her middle fingers into her ears and stuck her thumbs in the corners of her mouth, pulling them right up to her ears; she stuck her tongue a long way out of her mouth and rolled up the whites of her eyes. That was a ghastly sight! In this manner, half-naked and unarmed, she ran out among the hundreds of foes, emitting hoarse, unarticulated sexual howls. . . . This was utterly against all rules of the art of war!] (1952: 74). I am indebted to Rolf Stavnem for correcting an error in my translation.

[9] Andersen believes La Fontaine "no doubt incorporat[ed] folk tradition" (1977: 135; fig. 95) in his fabliau-like tale (1762: 2.149–56; 1961: 276–80), based on Rabelais' *Quart livre* 45–47 (1994: 642–48), who in turn refers to the ancient tale of Persian women exhorting their men to battle; see, e.g., Justin's account in his *Epitome* of Pompeius Trogus, 1.6.13–15 (1972: 9): "sublata veste obscena corporis ostendunt rogantes, num in uteros matrum vel uxorum uellent refugere" [lifting (their) garments, they displayed the shameful parts of (their) bodies, asking whether they wished to flee back into (their) mothers' or wives' wombs]; reproduced nearly verbatim by Orosius, *Adversus paganos* 1.19.9–10 (1882: 72), Frechulf of Lisieux, *Chronicon* 1.3.18 (*PL* 106: 991b), Ekkehard of Aura, *Chronicon* (*PL* 154: 548), and John of Salisbury, *Policraticus* 6.16 (1909: 2.44). Christine de Pizan locates the same story in an Ostrogothic context: *City of Ladies* 1.22 (1997: 140–42). Justin's Latin account is preceded in Greek by Nicolaus of Damascus, frag. 66 §43 (Jacoby 1925 [§90]: 369–70), Plutarch, "Mulierum virtutes" 5.246a-b (cf. "Lacaenarum apophthegmata" 241b, where the same tactic is attributed to an anonymous Spartan woman; both in *Moralia* 1927–69: 3.490–93 and 3.460–61, respectively), and Polyaenus (*Stratagems* 7.45.2, 1994: 2.702–5). See also further analogues in Much (1909: esp. 159, 160), Vorwahl (1933), Bruder (1974: 136-42), King (1986), and Duerr (1993: 36-71).

[10] See Machiavelli, *Discorsi* 3.6: when threatened that her children, whom the rebels held hostage, would be executed if she did not surrender, Sforza, "per mostrare che de' suoi figliuoli non si curava, mostrò loro le membra genitali dicendo che aveva ancora il modo a rifarne" [to show that she did not care about her children, exposed to them her genitalia, saying that she still had the form for making more] (1971–99: 1.2.1005); cf. *Istorie fiorentine* 8.34 (1971–99: 2.745), which repeats Sforza's defiant statement but omits the gesture. Hairston (2000), analysing the development of Machiavelli's accounts and setting them in a context of antecedent and derivative reports, demonstrates that this genital exposure has no basis in the historical Sforza's conduct; cf. Bausi (1991) and Freccero (1993). For another (unsuccessful) deployment of this gesture, see Procopius, *History of the Wars* 1.7.17–18 (1914–41: 1.55).

Figure 3: Charles Dominique Joseph Eisen, *The Devil Deterred*
Illustration for La Fontaine's "Le Diable de Papefiguiere" (1762: pl. opposite 2.149;
see also Salomons 1972: esp. 116–24)

lend credence to the hypothesis that Freydís, too, unleashes some eerie force on the *skrælingar*, overthrowing them with the magic of her nakedness.

The apotropaeic potential of exposure seems largely confined, however, to regions below the belt, as Eisen and Machiavelli exemplify; Classicists speak of a ritual "lifting of the garments to reveal the lower part of the body" as *anasyrma* or *anasyrmos*.[11] Théroigne, like most sheelas, bares her pudenda; the women who accompany her reveal their behinds. Keeping them more respectable company, Santa Claus's own mother slays a monster by displaying her pregnant belly to it: "she removes [her] mantle and shows the basilisk [her] naked abdomen; it is so startled by this sight that it falls down dead," reports one saga version.[12] Into the twentieth century, Finnish women might on occasion drive off prowling bears by raising their skirts at them.[13] Saga witches likewise occasionally denude themselves in battle, the sight of their bare bodies sufficing to dull enemy blades. And they, too, are in the habit of mooning, not flashing, their targets. As practiced by Norse witches, the gesture appears to be a vestige of a specific inversion ritual, perhaps linked with the notion of the evil eye (see further Sidebar 4).

Farther afield, Freydís's pectoral display may be matched with morphologically closer analogues, but these only reinforce an impression of qualitative difference between her actions and battle-magic nudity. When, in Ladislav Bielik's famous image of the doomed Prague Spring of 1968, a Czech protestor (in this case male) bares his breast at the Soviet tanks, his defiance is meant to shame the invaders by contrasting his naked helplessness to their armored might, not to send them shrieking in convulsive flight (see Fig. 4). There is irony here, and desperate courage, but no hint of sorcery. The Irish Cú Chulainn, in contrast, is under a taboo forbidding him from looking on naked women. The *Táin Bó Cúailnge* recounts how his uncle, forewarned of his battle-frenzy, sends a female

---

[11] King (1986: 60–61); see also Moreau (1951: 292–300); Bausi (1986); Olender (1990); Freccero (1993); Weber-Lehmann (2000); Hairston (2000: esp. 705–9); and Blackledge (2003: 6–34). The term is a modern coinage (King 1986: 63); King lists over a dozen instances in Classical literature (a few of which I touch on below), and provides references to ancient iconography. Loki's capers, making the giantess Skaði laugh by using his testicles to play tug-of-war with a goat (Snorri, *Edda: Skáldskaparmál* 1.2), may, as Moreau notes (1951: 294), also belong in this tradition.

[12] *Nikolaus Saga Erkibyskups II* cap. 15: "hon ber fra ser mottulinn ok synir basilisko beran kvidinn; bregdr honum sva vid þessa syn, at hann fellr daudr nidr" (Unger 1877: 2.61). Neither Unger (1877: 2.xvi) nor Widding (1961) identify a Latin source for this passage, possibly based (as capp. 13–14 definitely are) on Isidore of Seville's *Etymologies* 12.4.6–7 (1911.2: unpaginated); cf. also Isidore's *Mysticorum Expositiones . . . in Genesin* 5.7–8, where the *basiliscus* of Ps 90:13 is interpreted as sin and linked with women's travails in pregnancy (*PL* 83: 221b-c). Halldór Hermannsson was the first to suggest the relevance of the *Nikolaus Saga* passage for interpreting the Freydís episode (1936: 22n2).

[13] See Stefán Einarsson (1939: 255–56) and Pentikäinen (2007: 118–20; cf. 100, 118, 120 for reference to a woman's vulva by an ursine term).

4. Background: Bare-skirted witches

Witches are not especially common in the saga corpus, but they do recur with some frequency—and often, with buttocks bared for battle. So we hear, for instance, of a witch appropriately named Kerling ("Crone") who "had [pulled] the clothes up on her back, and [bent her] head down, and so saw the clouds from between her legs."[1] Most analyses of such conduct tend to emphasize only one component—turning one's back on an antagonist, exposing the privates, or the upside-down stare—to the exclusion of others. According to the most coherent interpretation proposed, the inverted stare from between one's legs, rump and genitals prominently displayed, has to do with proclaiming the witch's female (or effeminate) gender.[2] Similar gestures, clearly mocking and possibly also laced with magical residue, may be adduced from many different cultural contexts.[3] Ibn Faḍlān's description of a tenth-century Rūs chieftain's funeral may supply another hint to the resonance bared buttocks had for Norse notions of magic: "Then the deceased's next of kin . . . walked backwards, with the back of his neck to the ship . . . [with one] hand on his anus, being completely naked." Neil Price interprets the mourner's facing away from the burial ship and shielding his rectum as intended to protect all orifices from penetration by evil spirits.[4]

In the sagas and in most related examples, it is biological women who display their derrières with apparent sorcerous insouciance. The same posture, when assumed by biological men, has been interpreted as an (involuntary)

---

[1] *Þorskfirðinga saga* cap. 17: "[Kerling] hafði klæðin á baki sér uppi, en niðri höfuðit, ok sá svá skýin á milli fóta sér" (ÍF 13: 216); cf. *Landnámabók* cap. [H] 147, [S] 180 (ÍF 1: 222) and *Vatnsdæla saga* cap. 26 (ÍF 8: 69–70). A strikingly similar motif occurs in the *Gesta Herwardi* (Hardy and Martin 1888: 389, a text which arguably displays Norse features) and in later Germanic folklore (HWdA 4: 61–68; Feilberg 1901: 426–30; for an Icelandic example, see Jón Árnason 1862–64: 1.306).

[2] Pederson (1997); cf. Meulengracht Sørensen: "the practice of sorcery and sexual perversion [were] taken [to be] one and the same thing" (1983: 19), and contrast Ármann Jakobsson (2008: 55–63). For older interpretations, see Feilberg (1901); Kahle (1903); Pipping (1927: 27–29 and 1930); and Lundberg (1946: 130–31).

[3] See, e.g., Giovanni da Varazzano's 1524 report of Cape Breton Natives who scorn his men by baring their rumps at them (in Marshall 1996: 17), or various accounts of English rebels in 1549 baring their bottoms to devastating martial effect (in Stallybrass 1989: 53), as well as chapter IV, n4 above. Chaucer calls Alisoun's anus a "nether ye" in "The Miller's Tale," 3852 (1987a: 77), perhaps alluding to the evil eye. Cf. also Deonna (1914: 64–65); Johns (1982: 72–75, figs. 57–59; cf. fig. 51); DeForest (1993); Ajootian (1997: 230); and Burrow (2002: 44, 170n30).

[4] Montgomery (2000: 20); I am grateful to Russell Stepp and Shawkat Toorawa for bringing this translation to my attention. Price, personal communication (and cf. Montgomery 2000: 20n67).

admission of submission and emasculation.[5] But there may be more to cross-gendering than just degradation: some types of magic are restricted to a practitioner who is female, whether by biological sex or by ritual gendering.[6] If magical power inheres in bared female buttocks, some men might stoop to get it, at least as a last resort. Thus we hear that Haraldr *hárfagri*'s foes, fleeing before him during a naval engagement in the late 800s,

létu upp stjǫlu stúpa,	let [their] bums stick up,
stungu í kjǫl hǫfðum.	buried [their] heads in the keel.[7]

Clearly, the ninth-century poet here mocks their ignominious pose; but its associations might run deeper (or more polyvalently) than he consciously intended. Several verse allusions to female witches who disable men's 'blades,' a *double entendre* both literal and phallic, using an unspecified technique, suggest magical defense that could thwart physical attack no less than spiritual danger; at least one such verse implies that here, too, anal magic may have been imagined.[8] Haraldr's opponents may thus be conceding some dignity in order to adopt a magically appropriate defensive posture.

---

[5] See Clunies Ross (1973) and Meulengracht Sørensen (1983: 66–75).

[6] See, e.g., Price (2002: 210–17).

[7] Þórbjǫrn *hornklofi*, "Haraldskvæði" st. 10 (Skjd: B.1.23 = SPSMA 1.1: 104).

[8] See *Kormáks saga* cap. 23, v. 75 (ÍF 8: 290) and the discussion in Clunies Ross (1973: 91).

troop to intercept him. They bare their bosoms at Cú Chulainn; he covers his eyes and is wrestled to sanity.[14] Only manifestly non-combatant women can overpower the Irish superhero. The women identify themselves as "warriors," but

---

[14] *Táin*, ll. 803–15: "'A chariot-warrior is driving towards you!' cried the watchman in Emain Macha. 'He will shed the blood of every man in the fort unless heed be taken and naked women go out to meet him.' . . . Then the women-folk of Emain came forth to meet him . . . and they bared their breasts to him. 'These are the warriors who will encounter you today,' said [their leader]. He hid his face. Then the warriors of Emain seized him and cast him into a tub of cold water" (O'Rahilly's translation, 1976: 25, 147–48). The description makes it sound as if nude women are considered a general remedy against psychotic killers (as Cormier 1981 suggests, citing Plutarch, "Mulierum virtutes" 9.247f-248d, in *Moralia* 1927–69: 3.500–5; cf. Dirr 1920: 71–73, and Branigan and Vidal 2002), but Stefán Einarsson argues that this taboo is associated with Cú Chulainn alone (1939: 250–53). Cf. Skalla-Grímr Kveldúlfsson, Egill's feral father, who flies into a berserk rage at his son and nearly kills him, but is distracted by Egill's nurse; unlike the women who divert Cú Chulainn's wrath from his uncle, however, the nurse pays for the intervention with her own life (*Egils saga* cap. 40, ÍF 2: 101–2).

Figure 4: Ladislav Bielik, *The Bare-Chested Man in front of an Occupying Tank*
21 August 1968, Bratislava, Czechoslovakia
Reproduction courtesy of Peter Bielik

the appellation only pertains to them in mordant parody. Unlike Freydís, they do not snatch up swords to supplement their physique. Rather than align femininity with belligerence, the *Táin* episode contrasts uninhibited male destructiveness with unfettered female sexuality. Its gist (aside from finding an Achilles heel even for a hero like Cú Chulainn) seems to be that sex is not just an alternative but actually an antidote to violence — clearly a different message from that of the bare-sarked warrior.[15]

---

[15] *Pace* such readings as Brown (2007: 188). For further instances of this motif, see, e.g., Lactantius, *Divinarum institutionum* 1.20, telling how the women of Sparta, having just repelled a Messenian attack, are met by their husbands, who mistake them for the enemy: "[mulieres] cum viros suos cernerent parare se ad pugnam, quod putarent Messenios esse, corpora sua nudaverunt. Et illi uxoribus cognitis, & aspectu in libidinem concitati, sicuti erant armati, permisti sunt utique promiscue; nec enim vacabat discernere" [(The women,) when they saw their husbands prepare themselves for battle — because they thought them to be Messenian men — bared their bodies. And the latter, recognizing their wives and being stirred to passion by the sight, mingled with them — armed as they were — utterly indiscriminately, for there was no time to tell them apart] (1748: 1.62); Saxo, *Gesta* 7.LXVIIIa: "Borcarus, decussa Aluilde galea, mentique eius lenitate conspectus, animaduertit, osculis, non armis agendum esse, telorumque rigore deposito,

Interpretations of Freydís's *ostentatio pudendorum* as a half-remembered relic of Norse pagan rites thus have little to commend them. The other school that privileges the *skrælingar* as Freydís's audience takes a more ethnographic view, however, reasoning that Freydís's actions must mimic Native American practices.[16] Such a reading seizes on the patently non-utilitarian, symbolic nature of her behavior. It rationalizes the encounter by postulating prior contact between Norse and Natives, sufficient for the parties to have established a minimal inter-cultural pidgin. According to this view, Freydís must have been observant enough to take note of the *skrælingar's* body language and sophisticated enough to reproduce their dialect when addressing them: going topless into battle, it is conceded, may make poor sense in a European context, but Freydís is here assumed to have gone Native.

Supporters of this interpretation cite post-sixteenth-century incidents involving Beothuk women of Newfoundland, said to have bared their breasts at white men in an apparent plea to avoid being shot.[17] Nearly nothing is known of Beothuk prehistory. Inhabitants of Newfoundland in the 1500s, their extinction in the early 1800s has further shrouded them in mystery; this has only enhanced their ancestors' appeal as possible real-life models for saga *skrælingar*.[18] Yet, considerations both theoretical and practical make this ethnographic reading of Freydís's exposure unlikely. First, whereas Théroigne may be supposed to share a significant cultural vocabulary with the Austrian soldiery (and Marguerite, *a fortiori*, with her son), it is difficult to imagine the Norse mastering Native American argot sufficiently for Freydís to score a rhetorical coup in the local dialect.[19] Second, even if the possibility of inter-societal communications were

---

blandioribus hostem officiis attrectandam. Igitur Alf . . . [Aluildam] cupidius appre-hensam, uirilem cultum in muliebrem conuertere coegit; ex qua post modum filiam Guritham procreauit" [Having struck off Alvilda's helmet, Borcar, on seeing the smooth-ness of her chin, observed that they ought to deal in kisses, not blows, and—setting aside the harshness of spears—to lock their foe in a more tender grip. Therefore Alf . . . lov-ingly seizing Alvilda, forced her to change from men's clothes into women's; he later sired a daughter on her, Guritha] (1886: 229–30). Cf. Foote (1984: 75–76).

[16] See Mowat (1965: 257–60); Pohl (1966: 151); Jones (1986: 228n3); and Baitsholts (2003: 366–67). Cf. Stannard (1992: 132) and, in fiction, Clark (1994: 230–33), epigraph to this chapter. A variation is suggested in Vollmann's fictionalization (1990: 235).

[17] See Howley (1915: 93, 261) and Marshall (1996: 100, 163–64).

[18] On the Beothuk, see Marshall's remarkable study (1996). For identifications of proto-Beothuk with the *skrælingar*, see, e.g., Storm (1888: 361–62); Mowat (1965: 458–64); Ingstad (1985: 290–95); and Brown (2007: 190–91).

[19] Cf. *Grœnlendinga saga* cap. 6 (ÍF 4: 262–63) and *Eiríks saga rauða* capp. 10–11 (ÍF 4: [*H*] 227–28, [*S*] 428–29; see also cap. 12: [*H*] 233, [*S*] 432), where Norse and Natives are imagined to have got around the language barrier mostly by resort to non-verbal (and improbably self-explanatory) means of communication. The language barrier is often also thematized in fictional retellings; see Hewlett (1918: 241–44, 249–50); Chapin (1934:

granted, emphatic helplessness in the face of physical violence — so vital to the strategy attributed to the Beothuk women — is very much absent from Freydís's display. The precise nuances of meaning the Native women might have sought to convey cannot be recovered, but the idea seems clearly to have staked preserving their lives on highlighting their sex as, at a minimum, non-aggressive, and perhaps even as outright alluring. Like their Irish sisters taking on a barking mad Cú Chulainn (or a Czech civilian facing down the T-55s), they could only hope to counteract force of arms with displays of vulnerability. Nero's mother, the younger Agrippina, furnishes a poignant analogue. When approached by Nero's assassin, she instinctively responded in the same somatic idiom: "leaping up from her bed she tore open her clothing, exposing her abdomen, and cried out: 'Strike here, Anicetus, strike here, for this bore Nero!'" Her protest could not save her life, but the efficacy of her technique is nevertheless attested by her unnatural son's reaction to the news: "Nero, when informed that she was dead, would not believe it, since the deed was so monstrous that he was overwhelmed by incredulity. . . . So he laid bare her body, looked her all over and inspected her wounds, finally uttering a remark far more abominable even than the murder. His words were: 'I did not know I had so beautiful a mother.'"[20] In such tableaux, the frailty and (darkly sexy) penetrability of exposed female flesh are starkly juxtaposed with the unstoppable force of male arms and aggression.

Freydís, in contrast, exhibits no pacific, gendered passivity, nor yet readiness to volunteer her body as spoils of war. In order to read Freydís (or, for that matter, Théroigne or Madame d'Artois) as belonging to this genre of women whose nudity trumpets the meekness of their sex, the weapon in her hand must be excised. Finally, even if the Vínland Natives who underlie the literary *skrælingar* are indeed historically connected to the later inhabitants of Newfoundland, there is simply no evidence that "this gesture was in general use among the Beothuk," as Farley Mowat maintains. On the contrary, reports of indigenous toplessness remain isolated and contestible — and may, in fact, owe more to observers' education in the Classics than to empirical reportage.[21]

Indeed, the Old World motif of women who plead for quarter by baring their bosom at aggressive men is undeniably traditional: already Clytaemestra

---

100); Kamban (1936: 235–38); Scott (1958: 89–91); Busch (1966: 180–86); Irwin (1974: 200–2, 224); Boyer (1976: 161–63, 171–77, 207–10, 212–13); Berry (1977: 149–50, 158–59, 162); Vollmann (1990: 234–36, 249–50); and Elphinstone (2000: 200–8).

[20] Dio, *Histories* (Foster and Cary's translation, 1961–69: 8.64–7), 62.13.5–14.2; cf. Tacitus, *Annals* 14.8 (1925–37: 4.120), and Suetonius, *Nero* 34:1–4 (1997: 2.136–40).

[21] Mowat (1965: 257); likewise Baitsholts (2003: 366–67). Only two cases are recorded (references above, n17 in this chapter). One other Beothuk is reported to have begged for mercy by displaying her pregnant belly, in vain (see chapter VI, n20 below).

uses this device in her attempt to stay Orestes' avenging hand.[22] Her gambit hinges on reminding him of his filial duty—or, more generally, of a gendered division of labor, according to which women are to occupy a domestic, nurturing social sphere, entirely segregated from the violent exchanges of men. (Statistically speaking, we may note in passing, women who stake their survival on such pleading often fare poorly: Clytaemestra and the younger Agrippina die, the Beothuk women are likewise slain or taken captive.)[23] Tweaking the same set of conventions also allows for some significant variation: Helen's appeal to Menelaus at the sack of Troy, for example, reinforces the plea for mercy with an unequivocal insinuation of erotic rewards.[24] Hecuba, in contrast, bares her breast not to ward off an attack endangering her own person but in an effort to persuade Hector to save his.[25] The filial debt is here evoked not to assert female inviolability but to claim precedence for the reverence due to kin over an individual male's violent vocation. In all such examples, as also in the alleged Beothuk custom,

---

[22] See Aeschylus, *Choephori* 895–97 (1893: 127–28, 230–31), Euripides, *Electra* 1206–7 (1998: 282–85), idem, *Orestes* 526–28, 566–70, 839–43 (1987: 96–99, 118–19), and idem, *Phoenician Women* 1566–69 (1988: 148–51). Cf. Dracontius, *Orestis Tragœdia*, 739–45 (1905: 219).

[23] See also Polybius, *Histories* 2.56.7, 15.31.13 (1922–27: 1.376–77, 4.544–45), and further examples below. (A rare exception is Tonwenna in the Arthurian tradition; see references in chapter VI, n21 below.) Cf. scholarship on rape interdiction, which "shows that nonforceful verbal resistance [i.e., pleading] is an ineffective rape avoidance strategy" (Ullman 1997: 195); see also Bart and O'Brien (1985: 109–10); Rozee and Koss (2001), and Ullman (2007: 414–15).

[24] See Stesichorus, frag. 24 (Page 1962: 109 [§201]), Ibycus, frag. 15 (Page 1962: 153 [§296]), *Ilias Parva* frag. 19 (Davies 1988: 58), Aristophanes, *Lysistrata* 155–56 (1990: 32–33; cf. 162–63nn155–56 for references to early representations of the scene in iconography), and Euripides, *Andromache* 627–31 (1995: 330–31); cf. also Euripides, *Orestes* 1287 (1987: 146–47), and examples cited in n15 in this chapter. Caesar, *Gallic Wars* 7.47 (1917: 448), may impute a similar tactic to Gallic women pleading with the Roman soldiers who nearly overran Gergovia (cf. 2.13, 7.26, 7.48 [1917: 106–108, 418, 450]); so interpreted by Much (1909: 160) and Moreau (1951: 288–89). Cf. also Geyer (1909: 149–51, 154–55) and Sartori (1935).

[25] Homer, *Iliad* 22.79–84 (1999: 2.458–59). Cf. Ovid, *Metamorphoses* 10.391–93 (1916: 2.92): "instat [nutrix] canosque suos et inania nudans / ubera per cunas alimentaque prima precatur, / ut [Myrrha] sibi committat, quicquid dolet" [the (nurse) insists, baring her white (hair) and withered breasts, she begs by (the authority of) the cradle and the first suckling that (Myrrha) confide to her whatever ails (her)]; also Seneca, *Phaedra* 2.246–49 (1987: 58); and Pseudo-Seneca, *Hercules Oetaeus* 925–28 (in Seneca 1917: 2.262). Chariton, *Callirhoe* 3.5.5–6 (1995: 164–65), paraphrases Homer in apparent parody of the bathos of such supplication. Ryan (2002–3: 64) cites an Irish analogue.

men's violence is contrasted categorically with women's suasive gestures; never are gender lines blurred.[26]

These motifs retain currency into the Middle Ages, transmitted through such channels as Statius's first-century *Thebaid*, an enduringly popular school text. In this un-Sophoclean account of the misfortunes of the house of Oedipus, Jocasta survives long enough to interpose her body in (ultimately futile) efforts to stop her sons from killing each other: "Here I'll stand on the threshold of the gate, an unhappy portent reflecting [your] sin's enormity! Here, curse you, are the grizzled hairs, here the breasts which [you] must stomp, for [your] steed must course over [your] mother's womb!"[27] Such embodiments of the Classical archetype, though

---

[26] Other variations also occur, e.g.: (lamentation:) Hecuba and other Trojan women, awaiting transport to Greece: Seneca, *Troades* 88–91, 104–7, 113–14, 120–21 (1917: 1.130, 132); two women, pleading or more likely bewailing the Massacre of the Innocents: Egbert Psalter, Trier Stadtbibliothek MS 24 (ca. 983 AD), fol. 15ᵛ (Nordenfalk 1957: 119); (defiant resignation to inevitable death:) Polyxena, about to be sacrificed in reverence to Achilles: Euripides, *Hecuba* 557–65 (1995: 448–49; note that Polyxena here uses the gender-neutral *sternon*, not the feminine *mastos*, to indicate her breast), and Ovid, *Metamorphoses* 13.457–59 (1916: 2.260); cf. the rather bland comment Seneca puts into Phaedra's mouth at her suicide (*Phaedra* 1197: "mucrone pectus impium iusto patet" [(my) impious chest is justly laid open by the blade], 1987: 120), thrown into ironic relief by her earlier boast: "non, si per ignes ire et infesta agmina [me iubes], cuncter paratis ensibus pectus dare" [if (you order me to cross) through fires and enemy ranks, I would not hesitate to breast the drawn swords] (*Phaedra* 615–16, 1987: 80); (legitimation:) images of a goddess suckling a grown man have been interpreted as showing divine confirmation or conferral of a ruler's status ("On peut donc parler d'"allaitement de puissance',", Leclant 1960: 141; Orthmann 1969–70: 141), or, in connection with the tale of Heracles' adoption by Hera (Diodorus, *History* 4.39.2 [1933–67: 2.468–69]; cf. also 4.9.6–7 [1933–67: 2.370–71]), as gestures of adoption, initiation, resurrection and apotheosis (Renard 1964: 616; cf. Patterson Corrington 1989: 399–402). Cf. the polysemy of *anasyrma*, which has been plausibly interpreted in different contexts as meaning "'go away' (apotropaic), 'be fertile' (sympathetic) or 'would you like some of this?' (erotic)," and must communicate other meanings in still further contexts (King 1986: 63).

[27] Statius, *Thebaid* 11.339–42: "stabo ipso in limine porte / auspicium infelix scelerumque immanis imago. / haec tibi canities, haec sunt calcanda, nefande, / ubera, perque uterum sonipes hic matris agendus" (1928: 2.414); cf. her earlier intervention, 7.481–85: "venit [Iocasta] ante hostes, et pectore nudo / claustra adversa ferit tremulisque ululatibus orat / admitti: 'reserate viam! rogat impia belli / mater; in his aliquod ius exsecrabile castris / huic utero est'" [(Jocasta) comes before the enemy, and with bared chest rushes the barring gates, requests with tremulous wails to be admitted: "Make way!" demands the unholy mother of the war; "By this womb, (I have) some damned right (to come) in this camp"] (1928: 2.168). (Cf. the same motif, as developed earlier by Seneca: *Phoenissae*, esp. 401–14, 446–47, 535–42 [1917: 2.376–78, 380, 386]; and, for its later migration into an Arthurian orbit, chapter VI, n21 below.) Valerius Maximus alludes to the same convention in his account of the Roman general Coriolanus, spurned by his home city but

they have little to do with Beothuk customs, may in fact have played a linchpin role in the medieval genesis of the bare-sarked warrior, as will be discussed below. Women like Jocasta, admittedly still a far cry from bare-sarked warriors, could have familiarized medieval audiences with the figure of the bare-bosomed suppli- cant. The configuration of gender and violence in such scenes remains conservative; women's power is diametrically opposed to sabre-rattling—even, in medieval iter- ations, to the virtuous militancy of soldiers of Christ. Thus, Jerome, for example, in a letter that (on his own testimony) was favorably received during his lifetime and was later appropriated by several authors, among them the influential Peter the Cantor, exhorts his lax friend Heliodorus: "though, with dishevelled hair and torn clothes, [your] mother show you the breasts that nursed you . . . [you must] turn to the standard of the Cross."[28] Not even a maternal appeal may be allowed to super- sede the monastic calling (cf. Mt 10:37, 12:48). Such imagery doubtless rendered the meddlesome mother figure suspect in devout Christian eyes: while conceding Statius' point about the force of due *pietas*, Jerome's narrative paints the power of parental pleading as contrary to the obligatory progress Godwards.

Yet the ancient motif finds its most moving medieval expression in a con- text that simultaneously promotes the bare-bosomed supplicant as a role model and valorizes the appeal to consanguinity. This striking alchemy was only gradu- ally realized through association of the motif with the Virgin Mary (see further Sidebar 5). Already the Gospel (Lc 11:27) had paid affectionate attention to her breasts, as had early Christian poetry, without, however, ascribing to them any particular salvific faculty.[29] At the same time, belief in the potency of Mary's personal appeal on behalf of sinning Man is virtually as ancient: "You are able," an early Icelandic poet reminds her, "to win from the Ruler of 'the sun's mighty abode' [= Heaven] every merciful thing for men."[30] The Icelander was following

---

dissuaded from wreaking vengeance on it by his mother's pleas (*Memorable Doings and Sayings*, 5.4.1): "'expugnasti' inquit 'et vicisti iram meam, patria, precibus huius admotis, cuius utero quamvis merito mihi invisam dono'" ["You've overborne and conquered my wrath, fatherland," he said, "by interjecting the prayers of her, to whose womb I surrender you (justly hateful as you are to me!)"] (2000: 1.494).

[28] Jerome, *Epistola xiv* 2: "licet sparso crine et scissis vestibus, ubera quibus te nutri- erat, mater ostendat . . . ad vexillum crucis evola" (*PL* 22: 348). Jerome attests to Fabiola's having memorized this letter (*Epistola lxxvii* 9, *PL* 22: 697); for later medieval references to it, see, e.g., Peter the Cantor, *Verbum Abbreviatum* 71 (*PL* 205: 212a, 533c–d); Pseudo- Jerome, *Homilia ad monachos* (*PL* 30: 316d); Lupus of Olmedo, *Regula monachorum* 18 (*PL* 30: 363b); Othlo of St. Emmeram, *Vita Sancti Wolfkangi* 10 (*PL* 146: 400b); and Bernard of Clairvaux, *Epistola cccxxii* (*PL* 182: 527c).

[29] See, e.g., Bede, *Hymnus xi* (*PL* 99: 631c), and, on the motif of the nursing Virgin in early Christianity, Ronig (1974: 197–98).

[30] Gamli, "Harmsól" st. 59: "Hlut meguð hvern til gotna . . . miskunnar ramligs bús af ræsi rǫðuls . . . ǫðlask" (Skjd B.1.563 = SPSMA 7.1: 126), dated to the latter part of the twelfth century.

5. Interpretation: The bare-breasted virgin, whence and whither?

How, precisely, *Maria Mediatrix* came to bare her bosom in the course of supplication is a matter of some controversy. Hubert Schrade points to Christ's
ostentatio vulnerum, a motif developed in the eighth and ninth centuries, as
an antecedent to the Virgin's appeal; Caroline Walker Bynum's studies confirm the later medieval tendency to conflate Christ's wounds with the Virgin's
breast, but shed little light on how the associative link arose in the first place.[1]
Susan Marti and Daniela Mondini suggest a likely source of inspiration in
Jerome's letter to Heliodorus,[2] yet its distribution seems on the whole modest
(see chapter V, n28). Moreover, Jerome's condemnation of maternal pleading
makes it difficult to imagine how the gesture could have been grafted smoothly
onto the Virgin. Other scholars turn to Classical authors instead: Edward Stevens sees Ovid as the likely source, while Salvador Ryan proposes Valerius.[3]
Neither Myrrha's nurse in the *Metamorphoses* (see chapter V, n25) nor Coriolanus's mother in the *Memorable Doings and Sayings* (see chapter V, n27) is an
exceptionally good match to Mary, however. Instead, what they both demonstrate is that the motif was sufficiently commonplace to make other links
between antiquity and the Middle Ages plausible, perhaps even likelier. Given
the popularity and diffusion of Statius's *Thebaid* (above, p. 53) in the early Middle Ages, I am inclined to see it as the most probable source for the Virgin's
conduct. The earliest association I have found of Mary's intercessory power
with her womanly flesh occurs in an Old English homily of (probably) the
tenth century.[4] No direct source has been identified for the relevant portion of

---

[1] See Schrade (1930: 168–71), and cf. Bede, *Homilia ii* (*PL* 94: 141d-42b) and
Theodulf of Orleans, *Carmen* 6.11 (*PL* 105: 365a); Bynum (1986: 102–8 and 1987:
270–72) and Easton (2008: 3). For an illustration (datable to no later than the end of
the thirteenth century; Ronig 1974: 209), see "De sancta Cruce et Beata Maria V.," stt.
13–14: "Hic adhaerens pectori / Pascitur ab ubere; / Hic adfixus arbori / Pascit nos ex
vulnere" [Here, (Jesus,) clinging to (the Virgin's) chest, is fed by the breast; here, nailed
to the tree, (He) feeds us from (His) wound] (Dreves et al. 1886–1922: 54.203 [§132]).
[2] Marti and Mondini (1994: 80).
[3] See Stevens (1942) and Ryan (2002–3: 66). Cf. Stanford (1970: 32n66) and Gray
and Ryan (2007: 247), who find an echo of Plutarch (presumably via a Christian inter-
mediary) in the *Táin*'s account of Cú Chulainn (see chapter V, n14).
[4] Immenkötter maintains that "[d]ie Vorstellung [Christi und Mariä als Fürbit-
ter] geht auf Augustinus zurück," suggesting an association between Lc 11:27 and I
Io 2:1 at its source (1995: 173), but supplies no specific reference. I have been able to
find no evidence of such an association in the writings of Augustine. One variant of a
Greek *Apocalypse of Mary* includes an analogous rubric (§23: "Si ton fils ne t'écoute pas,
lui crient les pécheurs, montre-lui l'étable où tu l'as mis au monde, les seins qui l'ont
nourri, les bras qui l'ont tenu," in Pernot's paraphrase, 1900: 237; the version translated
in Rutherfurd 1897, based on an eleventh-century manuscript, does not contain this

this homily, which may illustrate, as Mary Clayton suggests, "a belief, unique in this form to Anglo-Saxon England," apparently "derive[d] ultimately from the *Apocalypse of Mary*"—another illustration, perhaps, of the creativity of the cultural margins (discussed below, pp. 76–77).[5]

If the origins of the bare-breasted Virgin are shrouded in mystery, her latter-day fate is no less curious: since the Reformation, she has descended into almost complete obscurity, even among Marian specialists.[6] This point is perhaps best illuminated by the periodic publication of studies that rediscover the topos every few years, each in turn more or less unaware of previous scholarship.[7] Barriers of language, discipline, and geographic focus are no doubt

---

appeal). Manuscript witnesses to this redaction are from the fifteenth and sixteenth century (Mimouni 1993: 121), but editors have suggested dates of composition ranging from the sixth to the ninth centuries; Mimouni, who admits that "[d]ans l'état actuel de la recherche, aucun élément ne permet de localiser de façon précise l'émergence de l'*Apocalypse grecque de la Vierge*," nonetheless favors dating the original to no later than the seventh century (1993: 124).

[5] See Vercelli *Homily xv*, ll. 142–49 (Scragg 1992: 259; for the failure to identify a source, 1992: xxxviii, 250); and Clayton (1990: 254–55, and cf. 1986: esp. 97–101). Cf. the roughly contemporary prologue to the Irish *Cáin Adamnáin* (discussed below, chapter VII, n36).

[6] Cf. the latter part of Steinberg's title: *The Sexuality of Christ in Renaissance Art and in Modern Oblivion* (1996, emphasis mine). The bare-bosomed Virgin appears in isolated instances in the late sixteenth and early seventeenth centuries (see, e.g., Knipping 1974: 2.263–76; Heal 2007: 229, a reference for which I am indebted to Duane Corpis), but medieval images (like that of the Munich Frauenkirche *Automatenuhr*, Fig. 6) were covered up by the sweep of post-Tridentine modesty (Schreiner 1994: 184). See also Koepplin: "Zur Zeit der Gegenref[ormation] verteidigte Molanus († 1585) das Bild der vor Chr[istum] die Brust entblößenden M[aria]. . . . Spätere aufgeklärte Zeiten fanden [dieses Bild] so 'geschmacklos,' daß dies wohl zur Dezimierung der Denkmäler beigetragen hat" (1970: 347); and cf. Künstle (1926–28: 1.550–51).

[7] Widding and Bekker-Nielsen expressly "appeal to those who have a better knowledge of mediaeval literature" for help in placing the motif (1961: 79). Fairly extensive references to preceding specialized studies can be found in Koepplin (1970; citing Perdrizet 1908, Künstle 1926–28, Panofsky 1927, the 1939–42 Dutch original of Knipping 1974, Frey 1952, Meiss 1954, Meier 1959, and Schiller 1968), Wenzel (1971; citing Perdrizet 1908, Panofsky 1927, and Meiss 1954), Körner (1988; citing Perdrizet 1908, Schiller 1968, and Seidel 1977), Frieß (1994; citing Perdrizet 1908, Meier 1959, and Körner 1988), Marti and Mondini (1994; citing Frey 1952, Seidel 1977, Miles 1986, and Dupeux 1991), Schreiner (1994; citing Perdrizet 1908, Seidel 1977, Miles 1986, Patterson Corrington 1989, and Marti and Mondini 1994), and Rubin (2009a; citing Marti and Mondini 1994, Ryan 2002–3, and Kauffmann 2003). In contrast, Meier (1959), Miles (1986 and 2008), Dupeux (1991), Whatley (2011), and, as far as I can tell, Berlin (2007) cite no antecedent specialized scholarship; likewise, Haastrup states that a fragmentary scene in Ballerup (which she wrongly regards as "enestående

responsible in large part for such failures of scholarly communication, though it is hard not to wonder whether present-day taboos (on Marian nudity, on heterodox theologies such as outlined in Sidebar 6 below, and so forth) might not also enter into play.[8]

---

i det danske område" [unique in the Danish sphere]) "kun i sin helhed kan tolkes ved hjælp af et kalkmaleri i Ungarn" [can only be fully interpreted with the help of a wallpainting in Hungary] (Haastrup and Egevang 1985–92: 4.§37). Intermediate positions are occupied by Frey (1952; citing only Panofsky 1927), Meiss (1954; citing only Panofsky 1927), Swartling (1963; citing only Perdrizet 1908 and Meiss 1954), Schiller (1968; citing only Panofsky 1927), Lane (1973; citing only Panofsky 1927 and Meiss 1954), Knipping (1974; citing only Panofsky 1927), Warner (1976, citing only Perdrizet 1908), Seidel (1977; citing only Perdrizet 1908), Lundén (1981; citing only Swartling 1963), Bynum (1986; citing only Lane 1973), Domínguez Rodríguez (1998; citing only Panofsky 1927), Kauffmann (2003; citing only Schreiner 1994), Williamson (2000; citing only Meiss 1954 and Lane 1973), Ryan (2002–3; citing only Perdrizet 1908), Gray and Ryan (2007; citing only Ryan 2002–3), and SPSMA 7.2 (660, citing only Lane 1973 and Williamson 2000).

[8] Cf. Bynum on the notion of Jesus as mother "arous[ing] distaste" in the 1950s and 60s (1982: 110).

---

in a tradition dating back at least to the eighth century, celebrating Mary's role as *Mediatrix*.[31] Only in the twelfth century, however—at about the time that milk relics began to proliferate and the *Maria lactans* motif to permeate Western iconography, while commentaries on the Canticle of Canticles identified its Bride with the Virgin[32]—do unambiguous associations between Mary's bosom and her role as intercessor first heave into view.[33] In the second quarter of the

[31] See Paul the Deacon, "Miraculum S Marie de Theophilo penitente," 12:32 (1908: 7); Warner (1976: 200, 203). "The Virgin . . . represented the acme of a mortal's intervention in heaven. She was invariably portrayed [in early Byzantine art] with Christ sitting on her lap. For her intercessions had the infallible efficacy of a blood-relative" (Brown 1973: 271); cf. Gripkey (1938).

[32] Bétérous (1975: 405) finds signs of veneration of the Virgin's milk already in the eleventh century (cf. Drews 1928: 160); by the twelfth, he counts 69 milk relics across Europe. Körner (1988: 56–57) and Williamson (2000) analyse the fast link between the *Maria lactans* and *Maria Mediatrix* motifs. Citing Carolingian precursors, Matter (1990: 151–77) singles out Honorius Augustodunensis's *Sigillum Beatæ Mariæ* (ca. 1100) as the first "fully realized . . . mariological reading of the Song of Songs" (1990: 155). Cf. Astell (1990: 43–44) and Schreiner (1994: 175–210, esp. 178–81).

[33] For the history of this motif, see Perdrizet (1908: 237–52); Panofsky (1927: 285–86, 302n75); Frey (1952: 117–20); and Seidel (1977). They treat almost solely the visual arts and the later, fourteenth- to seventeenth-century zenith of the motif; Warner (1976: 192–205 [cap. 13: "The Milk of Paradise"], useful despite some inaccuracies) and Marti

Figure 5: detail of *Mappa mundi*, Hereford Cathedral
ca. 1280–90 (see Harvey 1996: 2, 7–11, 54)
The Virgin addresses her Son (in the scroll adjacent to her): "Veici beu fiz mon piz.
de deinz la quele chare preistes. / E les mameleites. dont leit de uírgin queistes. / Eyez
merci de touz. si com uos memes deistes. / Ke moy ont serui. kant sauueresse me
feistes" [Behold, dear Son, my bosom, in which You assumed flesh, and the nipples
from which You sought a virgin's milk; have mercy on all (just as You Yourself have
pronounced) who have served me, for You have made me (their) Savioress].
© The Mappa Mundi Trust and Chapter of Hereford Cathedral

twelfth century, Ernaud of Bonneval writes the definitive script for her success:
"Mary [shows] Christ her torso and breasts; there can be no manner of refusal
where such monuments of pity and icons of charity cooperate and entreat more
mellifluously than any tongue." From the end of that century, this rubric (usually attributed to Ernaud's more famous friend and fellow Cistercian, Bernard of
Clairvaux) was frequently quoted in devotional texts and iconography.[34]

---

and Mondini (1994) supply a wider, and also somewhat earlier, context; see also Schreiner (1994: 173–210) and Rubin (2009a: 211–12). For an interesting late-medieval Icelandic analogue, see Hill (1992). See further Sidebar 5.

[34] Ernaud, *De laudibus B. Mariæ Virginis*: "Maria Christo pectus et ubera [ostendit];
nec potest ullo modo esse repulsa, ubi concurrunt et orant omni lingua disertius hæc cle-
mentiæ monumenta et charitatis insignia" (*PL* 189: 1726d); see Perdrizet (1908: 251–52).
On the misattribution to Bernard, see Seidel (1977: 73) and Dupeux (1991: 178); Schreiner (1994: 189–92) discusses the medieval fascination with "Bernhard als 'Zögling'

By imagining the relationship among God the Father, the Virgin Mary, and their Child Jesus in human family terms, Christian mythology was thus able to align traditional kinship values with its revolutionary ideals. Like Hecuba, Mary—universal mother of both God and men (as attested, for instance, by Anselm of Canterbury at the turn of the millennium: "the mother, I say, of Him Who alone delivers, [Who] alone damns, is our mother")—was unable to stop her boy from going to His death (Io 19:25).[35] Miraculously, she can nevertheless win quarter for her other, lesser sons by interceding with Him on their behalf, at the universal Last Judgment or in the hour of their individual deaths. By casting Mary in the traditional role of the bare-bosomed supplicant, this *interpretatio christiana* entirely subsumed the ancient prototype, simultaneously reenacting and reversing it.

The thirteenth century yields a cluster of bare-bosomed Mediatrices, both textual and visual, such as the supplicant Virgin on the upper border of the Hereford *mappa mundi* (see Fig. 5), and many others in a variety of media, genres, and languages.[36] But from the fourteenth century onwards, the topos

---

Marias" (1994: 191). Also twelfth-century are (homiletic:) Peter of Blois, *Sermo lxv* (*PL* 207: 773d); perhaps also §45 in Stiftsbibliothek Admont in Steiermark 638 (described in Mussafia 1886: 947; the manuscript, however, dates in part from the thirteenth century, Wichner 1888: 249); (poetry:) "Salve proles Davidis," ll. 22–23, 44–45: "Tua sunt ubera / vino redolentia . . . Nunc, o mater dei-hominis, / confer opem miseris" [Your breasts are fragrant as wine . . . now, O mother of God-(as)-man, grant relief to the wretched] (Mone 1854: 2.297 [§515]; Dreves et al. 1886–1922: 54.357–58 [§224], suggesting a probable late eleventh-century dating); and "O gloriosa femina," ll. 3–6 (Mone 1854: 2.129 [§420]; probable source of the vernacular "O gloriosa domina excelsa," n37 below).

[35] Anselm of Canterbury, *Oratio lii*: "Mater Dei est mater nostra . . . mater, inquam, ejus qui solus salvat, solus damnat, est mater nostra" [God's mother is our mother . . .] (*PL* 158: 957a).

[36] For some further thirteenth-century examples, see (homiletic:) BM Add. 15723: 87b (described in Ward 1883–93: 2.635); (poetry:) "Our Lady Help Us at Our Ending," ll. 3–4 (Brown 1932: 127; cf., with less of a salvational emphasis, "I Sing of One that is Matchless," ll. 21–22, Brown 1932: 55); Paris BN Fr. 2094: 164r-v (§9 in Kunstmann 1981: 83–84); Jacopone, "O Regina cortese," ll. 13–17 (1977: 42; cf. 1982: 69 and Underhill 1919: 250–53); idem, "Donna de Paradiso," ll. 46–47 (1977: 203; cf. 1982: 279 and Underhill 1919: 220–21); King Alfonso X's *Cantigas* 360, 422 (1986: 3.231, 349); st. 44 in a poem by Donnchadh Mór Ó Dálaigh (§25 in McKenna 1922: 49, 115), and Giolla Brighde, "Mary's Blessings," st. 36 (McKenna 1935–38: 1.194, 2.114; on both, see Ryan 2002–3: 60–62); (theater:) Gebhart (ca. 1906: 273) refers (without citing a source) to a thirteenth-century Umbrian Last Judgment play in which Mary intercedes for the damned by recalling her pregnancy and her breasts (a motif also used in Pseudo-Bartolo's *Processus Sathane* C.iiiir-v); (imagery:) a (now destroyed) mid-thirteenth-century mural in St. John's church, Winchester (Kline 2001: fig. 2.7); a miniature illustrating the Theophilus legend in the Lambeth Apocalypse, datable to ca. 1260–80 (Mettler et

truly takes off. Mary pleads with bared breasts in wall paintings and in lime-stone reliefs, on manuscript folia and on urban stages ("we encounter [this motif] in nearly every intercession scene in late-medieval plays," Theo Meier comments of medieval German drama), in plain-speaking sermons and popular songs, in Latin and in practically every vernacular.[37] This wide dissemination of the specific scene type must in large part be due to its inclusion in the vastly pop-ular *Speculum humanae salvationis*, a sprawling, typological world history, prob-ably compiled in the first quarter of the 1300s.[38] The *Speculum* retells the biblical

al. 1990: 46ᵛ, 318); a Last Judgment in the Gulbenkian Apocalypse, ca. 1270 (Morgan 1991: pl. 18); a Last Judgment in the Huth Psalter, ca. 1280 (Marti and Mondini 1994: fig. 47); Last Judgment scenes illustrating King Alfonso X's *Cantigas* 50 and 80 in the Códice rico, MS Escorial T.I.1, ante-1284 (Domínguez Rodríguez 1998: figs. 9–10).

[37] See Meier: "In beinahe allen Fürbittszenen der spätmittelalterlichen Spiele fin-den wir [dieses Motiv] wieder" (1959: 132). For some fourteenth-century examples, see (homiletic:) Wenzel (1989: 284–86); BM Harley 2851: 82ʳ⁻ᵛ (described in Ward 1883–93: 2.670); (imagery:) Stange (1934–61: 2. fig. 216); Warner (1976: fig. 48); Seidel (1977: figs. 25–26); Miles (1986: fig. 2); Marti and Mondini (1994: figs. 49, 51); Jetzler (1994a: Catalogue fig. 22); Immenkötter (1995: fig. 5); an individual judgment scene from Zse-liz, Hungary (Haastrup and Egevang 1985–92: 4.§37); a Last Judgment scene in St. Mary's church, Chalgrove (Kline 2001: fig. 2.8; see also Kauffmann 2003: 257); Kauff-mann (2003: fig. 154); (theater:) "L'Enfant donné au diable," ll. 1358–63 (§1 in Paris and Robert 1876–93: 1.49); "L'Evesque que l'arcediacre murtrit," ll. 802–17 (§3 in Paris and Robert 1876–93: 1.132–33); "Un prevost que Nostre Dame delivra," ll. 708–17, 772–78 (§14 in Paris and Robert 1876–93: 2.255, 257); (poetry:) *L'Advocacie Nostre-Dame* 73–88, 1411–24, 1458–67, 1476–81, 2259–63 (Davis, Akehurst, and Gros 2011: 4–6, 66–68, 70, 106; cf. 122); "O gloriosa domina excelsa," ll. 3–6 (Brown 1952: 53–54; cf. also a close variant in "Ave Maris Stella," ll. 19–22 [Brown 1952: 56]); "Quia Amore Langueo," ll. 54–61: "Thow sokyd my pappe, thow louyd man so; / Thow dyed for hym, myne hert he has. . . . [Man,] trust in me as I haue tolde. / Am nat I thy moder called?" [You sucked my pap, You loved Man so (that) You died for him: he has my heart. . . . (Man,) trust in me, as I have told (you to); am I not called your mother?] (Brown 1952: 235–36). See also Mech-thild of Magdeburg's *Das fließende Licht der Gottheit* 1.22, 2.3 (Neumann and Vollmann-Profe 1990–93: 1.18–19, 40), composed between 1250 and 1283 but only preserved in redactions of the mid-fourteenth century and later (see Neumann and Vollmann-Profe 1990–93: 1.xi–xix, 2.171–290).

[38] Nothing definite is known of the origin of this work. Henry (following Evelyn Sil-ber's unpublished Ph.D. Diss., *The Early Iconography of the Speculum Humanae Salvationis: The Italian Connection in the Fourteenth Century*, Cambridge 1982: 50–55, 309) dates it to 1286–1324, most likely ca. 1310–24 (1986: 10n2). She tentatively suggests a Dominican author (1986: 10n3), perhaps working in Bologna, though he hardly need be a native — "the [*Speculum*] certainly became more widely distributed in [transalpine] Europe than in the south" (1986: 10n4). Niesner concurs on the whole, but inclines towards a dating earlier within the suggested range (1995: 25). The oldest illuminated manuscript extant (also the oldest extant dual-language copy, in Latin and Middle High German), Codex Cremifa-nensis 243 (Neumüller 1997), is dated ca. 1325–30 (1997: 16–21).

story of Queen Esther's intercession for her people before King Ahasuerus as an antitype of the Virgin's intercession for Mankind: "In the preceding chapter we heard how Mary is our protectress . . . Now we shall hear how Mary shows her Son her torso and breasts. . . . Mary shows her Son the breasts with which she nursed Him. . . . How can there be any refusal here, where the entreaty is so very sweet?"[39] So indissolubly did the image of Mary, pleading with bared breast, and the hope for Man's salvation become linked that, at the beginning of the sixteenth century, the Munich cathedral was even outfitted with a mechanical clock whose Virgin bared her breast on the hour, imploring (alongside a Christ automaton pointing at his stigmata) an enthroned God the Father to resheathe the sword of His wrath (see Fig. 6 and Sidebar 5).

By the autumn of the Middle Ages (if not earlier), the bare-breasted Virgin also came to Iceland. Marian miracles of this type were known in Iceland by the fourteenth century at the latest, a textual tradition that appears to predate the earliest representations in continental Scandinavia, from the first half of the fifteenth century.[40] She survives in an Old Norse rendition of an English miracle, extant in several manuscripts. In this tale, Mary, down on her knees on behalf of a sinful abbot of Tavistock, bares her bosom to address Christ:

> "Do not oppose Your mother, who entreats You, for no necessity forced You to wish to have me as mother, but that You might justly grant mercy to sinning men. . . . Do not turn Your gaze from me; see here the womb that bore You, see the breasts that You sucked, see these arms that attended to

---

[39] *Speculum humanae salvationis* cap. 39: "In precedenti capitulo audimus quomodo maria est nostra defensatrix . . . Item audiamus quomodo . . . maria ostendit filio pectus et ubera. . . . María ostendit filio suo vbera quibus eum lactauit. . . . Quomodo posset ibi esse aliqua abnegatio / Vbi tam dulcissima est supplicatio?" (Neumüller 1997: 44ᵛ–45ʳ). (Niesner 1995: 117 transcribes the Middle High German verses.) The same folio (Neumüller 1997: 45ʳ) also bears an illumination captioned: "Maria ostendit filio suo ubera et orat pro populo" [Mary shows her Son her breasts and prays for the people]. Edgren (1993: 93–96) discusses the importance of this chapter of the *Speculum* in disseminating and popularizing the imagery of the bare-breasted Mediatrix.

[40] For the Icelandic textual tradition, see Widding and Bekker-Nielsen (1961: 77). For some continental iconography, see Kirke Såby, Denmark, dated ca. 1415 (see Mills 2004 [M-K 15–007]; cf. Marie Ma[gd]alene, ca. 1425–49 [M-K 17–009]; see also Haastrup and Egevang 1985–92: 4. §37 [Ballerup, dated 1425–50], which Mills 2004 erroneously dates ca. 1240 [M-K 04–005]). Most surviving exemplars are late fifteenth-century and later, from Denmark (see Banning 1976–82: 1.146, 149–51 [§§6.11, 6.22], listing some 15–17 examples; and Mills 2004, listing some 18 further distinct examples), Sweden and Finland (see Lundén 1981: 38–42, listing some eight examples; see also references in SPSMA 7.2: 660). Scant iconographic evidence from Iceland and Norway survives, and the only publications available to me are in any case too antiquated and popular to allow a close study of the artwork, which must await future research. On Marian devotion in skaldic verse, see Schottmann (1973).

Figure 6: Erasmus Grasser, *Intercession automaton*
ca. 1501, Munich Frauenkirche
Jesus and Mary interceding with God the Father.

The automaton's present-day mechanism.

© Peter Friess (photos by Walter Haberland)

You. Remember, my beloved Son, for whose sake You endured this fate. . . .
All of this fate You endured for the purpose that Your compassion might
justly help sinning men, on account of my prayers. . . . Hear, my Son, not
him but me."

Her supplication almost fails, but—forced at last to shift His wrathful focus
from the squalid client to his fast-talking lobbyist ("Hear . . . not him but
me")—Christ's sense of duty is bowed by *ad feminam* considerations:

Our Lord then said: "My sweet mother, what would you have Me do? What
this man asks, he ought not get, because an outrage may not get glory, nor
damnation [get] redemption, nor mortal perdition [get] succor. But on this
account—that, though Justice did not want to hear your prayer, Mercy
urged Me to grant you everything that you would ask—therefore I give
this man into your power, My dear mother. He shall now be yours: do with
him what seems to you good. He is now succored, not by My judgment but
by your gift."[41]

Through Mary's intercession, the abbot is granted a final, brief opportunity to
repent before he dies. The plot is comfortably stereotypical, closely resembling
both other Marian miracles and other renditions of the same tale in Latin and
in various vernaculars (though it is more verbose than most).[42] Moreover, even
though there is no hint of violence in this account, it bears an uncanny structural
resemblance to some bare-sarked warrior tales, where opposition is successfully
overcome through the leverage gained from exposure. Even some of the verbal

---

[41] *Maríu saga* §103: "'Gior eigi mot þinni modur, er þik bidr, þuiat engi bar þer
onnur naudzyn til, at þu villdir mik hafua til modur, vtan þv mættir þa rettliga veita
miskunn syndoggum monnum. . . . Vend æigi þinni asionv fra mer, se her þann kuid, er
þik bar, se þau briost, er þv saugt, se þessar hendr, er þer þionudv. Minz, minn sæti son,
hvers sakir er þv þoldir þessa luti. . . . Alla þessa luti þoldir þv til þess, at þin milldi metti
rettliga hialpa syndugum monnum fyrir min bæn. . . . Heyr, minn son, eigi hann, helldr
mik.'. . . Vorr herra sagdi þa: 'Min sæta modir, huat villtu at ek geri. Þat sem þessi madr
bidr, skal hann eigi fa, þviat eigi ma skommin fa dyrd, æigi fyrirdæming likn, æigi and-
latz tapanin hialp. En sakir þess at, þo at rettlétid villdi eigi heyra þina bæn, þa skylldir
miskunnin mik at veita þer allt þat, er þv villt bidia, ok þi gef ek, min kæra modir, þenna
mann i þitt valld, skal hann nv vera þinn, gior af honum, huat er þer þickir gott vera, er
hann nv hialpadr, eigi med minvm domi helldr med þinni giof'" (Unger 1871: 3.797–98).
On the manuscript tradition for this miracle, see Unger (1871: 3.789–800); Widding and
Bekker-Nielsen (1961).

[42] Widding and Bekker-Nielsen observe that this "is not one of the miracles of Our
Lady which had a universal fame" (1961: 76–77). The reservation only seems to hold true
for the circumstantial, historicizing details of the tale, however—the abbot's name, his
order, the diocese in which the miracle is said to take place, etc.—not for what I consider
its essentials, viz., the topos of bare-bosomed intercession. Cf. Wenzel (1971: esp. 81n1)
and Sidebar 5.

twitches match: "do with him what seems to you good," Christ tells His mother; "act in this [matter] according to your pleasure," Louis de Male says to his.

Bare-sarked warrior and bare-bosomed advocate are distinct figures, serving distinct functions. Nevertheless, the possibility that Mary's conduct as Mediatrix (and that of the long line of supplicants behind her) may have contributed to Freydís's battlefield behavior does warrant consideration—especially if the Vínland sagas have traditionally been dated too close to the lowest possible *terminus*. A dating in the early 1200s may reflect little more than scholars' desire to locate the sources as close as possible to the events they allegedly document—to give them, in other words, a stamp of approval as historical documents, at the expense of an appreciation for their literary achievements.[43] Conversely, a later dating would bring them squarely under the long shadow of the Virgin's tremendous popularity in late-medieval culture, making the probability of her influence on Freydís high indeed. Though Marian devotion, as discussed above, was already flourishing by ca. 1200, at the fourteenth- and fifteenth-century zenith of her cult, the Virgin effectively occupied the sublime summit of Christian veneration, coming within a hair's breadth (or closer) of actually surpassing the Trinity.[44] "God fed Man the fruits of paradise," concedes, for example, the fifteenth-century mystic Bernardino of Siena, "but the blessed Virgin fed Christ her most sacred milk, 'a breastful of heaven,' whose least drop outweighs all the fruit of the terrestrial paradise and of the entire world. . . . Thus, to [our] relief, one may say that on account of the blessed Virgin (even she whom God Himself made), He owes us more, in a way, than we owe Him."[45] For all its hyperbolic excess,

---

[43] See, e.g., Gísli Sigurðsson: "If the Vínland sagas contain any genuine information about past events, the only possible [source for] this information . . . is oral tradition, i.e., traditional tales and the memories of living people. . . . [The Vínland sagas are] clearly based on memories of former times passed down orally from generation to generation. . . . There can thus be little doubt that they contain genuine memories about actual people and events that took place around the year 1000" (2004: 268–69). Cf. Vésteinn Ólason (2001: 63), as well as chapter II, n16 above, n3 in this chapter, and chapter VIII, n2.

[44] Cf. Leach's bald words: "In an objective sense, as distinct from theoretical theology, it is the Virgin Mary, human mother of God, who is the principal object of devotion in the Catholic church" (1964: 50); cf. Ellington (2001: 109, slightly but significantly inflating the claim made by Oberman 1963: 312) and contrast Gripkey (1938). Graef (1963–65: 1.266–70) and Carroll (1986) review Mary's upwards mobility, in both the popular imagination and learned theology; Edgren (1993: 94–95) illustrates this development in Finnish church murals.

[45] Bernardino of Siena, *Opera* 61.1.11: "Deus nutrivit hominem de fructibus paradisi; sed beata Virgo nutrivit Christum de suo sacratissimo lacte, 'ubere de caelo pleno,' cuius minima stilla praevalet omnibus fructibus paradisi terrestris ac totius mundi. . . . [S]ic pro solatio dicere liceat, quod propter beatam Virginem, quam tamen ipse fecit Deus, quodammodo plus obligetur nobis quam nos sibi" (1950–65: 2.381); cf. King Alfonso X's *Cantiga* 138 (1986: 2.111–12). See also Graef's discussion of Bernardino (1963–65: 1.315–18).

Bernardino's Mariology reflects a widely shared view, already articulated by
the earliest period proposed for the penning of the Vínland narratives, of the
Virgin as calling the shots of saving grace. Though they stop short of gener-
alizing the Son's obligation towards His mother into a divine debt to humanity at large, more orthodox voices foreshadow Bernardino's view of Mary as
the surest guarantor of individual salvation. Early in the twelfth century, for
example, Guibert of Nogent says that "the mother's authority enjoins more
than it implores; I submit that He Who was undeniably once subject to her
cannot in any way deny her His eminence"; turning to address the Virgin herself, he adds: "it is altogether proper for you not to plead but to command."[46]
Guibert's contemporary Eadmer of Canterbury states matter-of-factly: "For
we have often seen and heard many people recall that good name, Mary,
during their trials, and immediately escape the evil of all [their] trials; deliv-
erance is sometimes quicker when her name is remembered than when the
name of her only-born Son, Lord Jesus, is invoked."[47] A century later, Richard of St Laurent likewise speaks of Mary as the acme of the intercessory
ideal: "[WHY MARY SHOULD BE REVERED,] NINETEENTH REASON: because,
for the salvation of her servants, she can not only supplicate with the Son
like other saints but also command Him by maternal authority. Therefore
we pray to her so: 'show yourself a mother,' meaning, supplicate for us with
the Son by [your] commanding and maternal authority."[48] Such voices would
have made it increasingly difficult for high-medieval authors—and Icelanders were as conversant with pan-European learned culture as any of their
contemporaries—to remain ignorant of the powerful image of the Virgin's

---

[46] Guibert of Nogent, *De laude Sanctæ Mariæ* cap. 9: "matris auctorita[s] . . . magis
jubeat quam exoret; ille qui quondam se ei fuisse non diffitetur subditum, non poterit,
securus dico, in omni re illi præstabilem negare seipsum. . . . tibi enim non orare, sed
ubique imperare præsto est" (*PL* 156: 564a, 577b). I am indebted to Hanna and Yossi
Roisman for their help in disentangling Guibert's Latin.

[47] Eadmer of Canterbury, *De excellentia Virginis Mariæ* cap. 6: "Sæpe quippe vidi-
mus et audivimus plurimes hominum in suis periculis recordari nominis istius bonæ
Mariæ, et omnis periculi malum illico evasisse. Velociorque est nonnunquam salus mem-
orato nomine ejus quam invocato nomine Domini Jesu unici filii ejus" (*PL* 159: 570a).

[48] Richard of St Laurent, *De Laudibus* 2.1.21: "[QUARE MARIÆ SERVIENDUM EST,
CAUSA D]ECIMA NONA: quia pro salute famulantium sibi, non solum potest Filio sup-
plicare sicut alii sancti, sed etiam potest auctoritate materna eidem imperare. Unde sic
oramus eam: 'Monstra te esse matrem:' quasi imperiose et materna auctoritate supplica
pro nobis Filio" (1890–99: 70, quoting "Ave Maris Stella," Dreves et al. 1886–1922: 2.39
[§29]). See also Williamson (2000: 49, 51) and cf. Couch (2006: 39).

intercessory might,[49] and would have inclined them to regard mortal women (Freydís, perhaps, among them) as imperfect reflections of the Marian ideal.

Like Hecuba, Jocasta, and other manifestations of the bare-bosomed supplicant—but unlike the bare-sarked warrior—Mary Mediatrix stakes her appeal on the contrast between her own emphatic tenderness and her addressee's hypermasculine severity: she and a grim Christ wage "a veritable battle of wills." To be sure, the ancient distinction between a vengeful Old Testament Father and His meek New Testament Son was never abandoned.[50] In that tradition, Christ's mildness is stressed to demarcate Him from a wrathful Father. But in the parallel tradition that casts Mary as Mercy incarnate, Christ inevitably tends to drift away from her, typing Him and the Father together as dispensers of stringent Justice (see further Sidebar 6). The sterner Christ's insistence on following the letter of divine law and the bitterer the initial dispute between Him and the Virgin, the more wondrous Mary's ultimate success. An increasingly confrontational scene type therefore emerges, with violence welling ever closer to the surface, a process I discuss in the next chapter. As such miracle stories become elaborated over time, they tend to deepen the divide between mother and Son, allowing Christ to resist Mary's entreaties for longer and with thinning patience, the more to glorify her eventual triumph.[51] It is a measure of the depth of Freydís's enigma that, even without Jesus as her foil, she proves no less efficacious than the Virgin mother.

The parallelism between Freydís and the Virgin is only partial, of course. Freydís fights for her own life (and perhaps, for the *ad hoc* foetus in her womb; cf. pp. 12 and 122); Mary intercedes for the souls of others. Freydís both endures and herself issues threats of violence, Mary does neither. Freydís is armed, approximating masculinity, whereas the Virgin wears the guise of *mater omnium*, perfecting femininity. The Virgin is already mother, Freydís only expecting. Still, there is enough overlap between the dynamics of their breast-barings to dispel any question of reading Freydís's exposure as a vestige of battle magic, be it Norse

---

[49] The precise degree of Icelanders' immersion in the Latin culture of the European Middle Ages, the routes by which knowledge of such culture reached them, and the modes in which it was incorporated into their own worldviews are still an area of active exploration, but there can be no doubt that Iceland was far from insular. For a recent contribution to the study of this problem, see, e.g., Anderson (2013); in broader terms, see Sverrir Tómasson (1988).

[50] Ryan (2002–3: 59). The tradition of the meek Christ continued to flourish well beyond the Middle Ages, in such popular motifs as the Man of Sorrows; see, e.g., Panofsky (1927) and Schrade (1930).

[51] See Graef (1963–65: 1.268), who observes how Richard of St. Laurent "actually reverses the roles of Christ and Mary when he applies to her Colossians 2.14—'Blotting out the handwriting of the decree that was against us'—which, he says, 'Mary did, her Son mediating' ('. . . quod fecit Maria Filio mediante')." Graef's reference is to *De Laudibus* 4.6.2 (1890–99: 187). Cf. Couch (2006).

6. Interpretation: Mercy triumphs over Justice?

In his mid-thirteenth-century Marial, Richard of St. Laurent gives a clear précis of the celestial political economy: "The kingdom of God is made up of two [parts], namely mercy and justice; and it is as if the Son of God has kept for Himself justice, or half the kingdom, [but] has conceded mercy as the other half to [His] mother."[1] This view is consistent with the tradition of bare-bosomed supplication I have traced, which typically features two protagonists: the Virgin and her Son. The internal logic of such a face-off inevitably emphasizes the harsh rationality of Christ's initial opposition to forgiveness, casting Him in the role of literalist judge bent on condemning the guilty. In contrast, Mary's position is explicitly unreasonable, urging an arbitrary bestowal of saving grace on undeserving sinners; she has, in Eamon Duffy's impish phrase, a "soft spot for worthless scoundrels."[2] Such narratives clearly champion the superiority of inconsistent mercy over manifest justice: "[This sinner] is now succored, not by My judgment but by your gift," as the Icelandic Christ tells His mother. Indeed, in the background of miracles like the abbot of Tavistock's reprieve, devils can occasionally be overheard to grumble at the subversion of due process: "Let us go before the true Judge, your Son," they challenge the Virgin, confident in their claim to a sinner's soul, only to rue their naïveté later: "Again we have been very foolish to leave it up to God. He is ever our enemy; on account of His mother, He dare do nothing else."[3] The attribution of such blatant miscarriage of justice to the Holy Family obviously did not sit well with some late-medieval thinkers; to counter claims such as these, presumably, the Franciscan Michel Menot thundered at his listeners on the eve of the Reformation: "Even if the Virgin Mary and all the saints should come, they would, upholding the law, not impede the soul from being carried off by demons."[4]

---

[1] Richard of St. Laurent , *De Laudibus* 6.13.3: "Regnum Dei consistit in duobus, scilicet in misericordia et justicia: et Filius Dei sibi quasi retinuit justiciam velut dimidiam partem regni, matri concessit misericordiam quasi dimidiam aliam partem" (1890–99: 355). See also Seidel (1977: 76).

[2] Duffy (2005: 629; cf. 187).

[3] "L'Enfant donné au diable" (§1 in Paris and Robert 1876–93: 1.1–56) : "Yrons nous devant le vray juge, / Vostre filz. . . . Encor sommes nous plus coquart / De nous en estre sur Dieu mis. / Il nous est touz jours ennemis; / Pour sa mére n'en ose el faire" (ll. 1259–60, 1380–83; 1876–93: 1.45, 49–50). Cf. Pseudo-Bartolo, *Processus Sathane*, C.ii^r. Contrast Gripkey (1938: 81, 85–89).

[4] Menot, "Dominica in sexagesima": "Nam si Virgo Maria et omnes sancti venirent, lege stante, non impedirent animam quin a demonibus importaretur" (Nève 1924: 21). Luther likewise objected to the lessons taught by such intercessory narratives: that Mary could usurp Christ's role as advocate for Mankind, and that Christ should inspire primal fear in believers' hearts; see Immenkötter (1995: 174) and Heal (2007: 55–56).

Such moral revulsion at the presentation of a Virgin indifferent to justice and, worse, a Christ devoid of natural mercy are perhaps responsible for some curious tunnel vision in modern scholarship on Marian intercession.[5] Those few scholars who have paid attention to Mary's bare-bosomed supplication (see Sidebar 5) have mostly fixed on the so-called 'double intercession' scene type, where Jesus and Mary stand side by side before God the Father, point to their insignia—stigmata and breast, respectively—and plead jointly for the salvation of humanity; Christ and the Virgin thus work in concert towards a common end. A related scene type strings out the intercessory chain, with the Virgin first pleading sinners' case before Christ, the Son then advocating before the Father.[6] Both scene types imply a very different (and much more comfortably orthodox) theology than that outlined above, allying mother and Son as harmonized spokespersons for compassion while casting the Father in the thankless role of strict, mechanical enforcer. It is possible that the three different scenarios—two in which Mary and Jesus cooperate to sway God, a third in which they are initially pitted as antagonists while the Father is effectively omitted altogether—developed in tandem with the distinction increasingly made in the later Middle Ages between an individual judgment at death, where Christ and the Virgin cooperate, and a universal Last Judgment, where Christ sits as judge while Mary, as advocate, opposes Him. The evidence adduced for such a trajectory of development remains thin and equivocal, however, and warrants no certainty until a more comprehensive study of the bare-bosomed supplicant Mary can be conducted.[7]

---

[5] Thus, e.g., Fulton, focusing on the Virgin's loyalty to those faithful to her, denies her "capriciousness" (2009: 287); Bynum seems closer to the mark (1982: 137).

[6] See, e.g., Meiss (1954); Lane (1973; but cf. next note); Bynum (1986: 106–8 and 1987: 272); Williamson (2000); Ellington (2001: 123–24); Berlin (2007); and Heal (2007: 33–34, 269). Bynum is actually misled into identifying the Last Judgment scene on the Hereford Map (Fig. 5) as a 'double intercession' (1986: 341n71). Frieß believes the scene type in which the Virgin first appeals to Christ (and He to God the Father) is older than the type in which both Mary and Jesus appeal directly to God the Father (1994: 544–45 and pll. 7–8).

[7] See Schreiner's suggestion (1994: 185; anticipated by Knipping 1974: 2.264–68 and Lane 1973: 20–25). On the distinction between judgments, see Jezler (1994b). In the Old Norse miracle, however, the sinning abbot of Tavistock is clearly facing individual, not universal, doom (see pp. 61 and 64 above).

or Native; the *skrælingar* can no more function as Freydís's primary audience than do the devils who gnash their teeth at the sight of Mary's immaculate intercession. The supposed Beothuk custom is likewise a red herring, except inasmuch as it points back to a tradition of European mediatrices—reinforcing, in the process, the sense that battlefield exposure may belong more to the realm of literary convention, apt to affect the extra-textual audience, than to that of historical verisimilitude. It remains to be seen, however, how a bare-bosomed supplicant might transmogrify into a bare-sarked warrior. The next chapter explores the permeable frontier between these two topoi.

VI. Women's Work

[A]vec son sein, une femme est plus redoutable qu'un homme, l'épée à la main.

Mlle Mars (?)[1]

Frustrating as Mary may find Christ's obduracy, nowhere in the medieval European tradition (as far as I have been able to discover) is the Son's juridical severity taken to such extremes that it provokes the Virgin to violence.[2] (On the contrary: in a related genre of miracle stories, Christ stoically tolerates sins against Himself, but finally flies into a white rage at a man who speaks blasphemously

---

[1] Attributed by Witkowski (1903: 11–12), who cites no source (and heavily emends the quotation); his reference is probably to the stage name of the comic actress Anne Françoise Hippolyte Boutet (1779–1847).

[2] Even when she moves her followers to violence (often, against Jews), the medieval sources insist that Mary's own hands remain unbloodied; see, e.g., Rubin (2009b: 45–77). Only in the early modern period do vengeful Virgins begin to appear with some frequency; see, e.g., Carroll (1992: 67–87) and Remensnyder (2014), and cf. Thomas (1971: 27, 70), but contrast Christian (1981: 33–42, 97–98); I am indebted to Duane Corpis for these references. Whether this periodization marks a difference in attitudes or merely in the density of the evidence remains to be investigated. If the medieval Mary exercised beatific restraint, however, the same cannot be said for mortal worshippers' manipulation of saints (including the Virgin), where nearly all means of cajoling assistance are fair, including even violence or the threat of violence; see, e.g., Caesarius of Heisterbach, *Dialogus Miraculorum* 7:45 (1851: 2.63–64); Jacobus (1851: 591–92); and cf. Geary (1979a: 110–15) and (1979b). Even non-Christians can coerce saintly help: e.g., a heathen African pirate (*viking[r]*) bullies St. Nicholas into repossessing for him some stolen goods: "þa tok hann svipu ok bardi likneskit; en er hann var modr af þvi, þa mællti hann: 'I elld mun ek þer kasta, ef þu gelldr mer eigi fe mitt.' En enn milldazti Nicholas leit miskunnar augum a likneski sitt, ok kom skyndiliga þangat, er þiofarnir skiptu feingi þvi . . ." [then he took a whip and beat the icon, and as he was mad about (the theft), he then declared: 'I will throw you in the fire, if you don't get me my money.' But most blessed Nicholas looked with merciful eyes on his icon and came swiftly to that place where the thieves were dividing the spoils . . .] (*Nikolaus Saga Erkibyskups I* cap. 13, in Unger 1877: 2.36).

of the Virgin's bosom.)[3] The Virgin's even temper is evident, for example, in the well-known intercession miracle of an Aquitainian youth who renounces God, though he maintains an unwavering devotion to Mary. Christ is so incensed that the Virgin's entreaties at first come to naught: "'Sweetest Son, have pity on this man,'" Caesarius of Heisterbach reports her plea. "The Child, however, did not reply to [His] mother, averting His face from her. When she again begged . . . He turned back to [His] mother, saying: 'This man denied me; what have I got to do with him?'" On hearing this refusal, the Virgin's "statue rose, placed the Child on the altar, and cast itself prostrate at His feet; [then] said: 'Son, I beg you to forgive him this sin on my account.' At once, the Infant, raising [His] mother, said to her: 'Mother, I have never been able to deny you anything, so on your account I forgive everything.'" Some versions of this dramatic miracle (such as the late fifteenth-century Finnish frescoes at Lohja) incorporate the motif of Marian breast baring, the better to emphasize the human intimacy between Virgin and Child on which the success of her pleading hinges.[4] But even where the Christ Child exhibits infantile petulance, the Virgin, in occidental accounts, is ever tender towards her Son.[5] That she should put Him over her knee remains, until the twentieth century, unthinkable (see Fig. 7); the Virgin gets her way by

---

[3] See, e.g., the thirteenth-century "Miracles of the Virgin" 22: "Nummularius quidam malignus fuit qui . . . per Christum et membra eius frequenter iurabat. Dum autem semel iuraret per ubera Beate Virginis . . . Christus qui iniurias suas patienter substinuit matris iniurias noluit substinere. Nam mox . . . divina ultione miserabiliter vitam finivit" [There was a certain wicked money-changer who . . . frequently swore by Christ and His members. One time, however, when he swore by the Blessed Virgin's breasts . . . Christ, Who patiently endured injuries to Himself, would not endure injuries to (His) mother. Thus (he) soon . . . ended his life miserably by divine vengeance] (Crane 1911: 265, and see analogues cited 265–66).

[4] Caesarius, *Dialogus* 2.12: "Dulcissime fili, miserere huic homini. Puer vero matri nil respondit, faciem ab ea avertens. Cumque iterum rogaret . . . matri dorsum vertit, dicens: Homo iste negavit me, quid ei faciam? Post haec verba imago surrexit, puerum super altare posuit, eiusque pedibus se prona prostravit. Et ait: Rogo, fili, ut propter me dimittas ei peccatum hoc. Mox infans matrem elevans, respondit illi: Mater, nunquam tibi aliquid negare potui, ecce propter te totum dimitto" (1851: 1.81). For the Lohja frescoes, see Edgren (1993: 66, 74, 106, figs. 19, 94). Erasmus in the sixteenth century attacked precisely such miracles; he has Mary mock the simplicity of those who "demanded everything from me alone, as if my Son were always a baby (because he is carved and painted as such at my bosom), still needing his mother's consent and not daring to deny a person's prayer" (cited by Heal 2007: 50).

[5] See, e.g., Thomas of Cantimpré's version of this tale in his *Bonum universale* 2.28: "cum puer quasi renitens vultum auerteret et mater econtra puerum in altera brachij parte transferret vt commodosius vultui eius vultum sue benignitatis ingereret" [when the Child, as though refusing, turned His face away, the mother, for her part, shifted the Child onto her other arm so that she might more easily press her kind face to His face] (ca. 1480: [68ᵛ] = 2.29.31, 1605: 312–13).

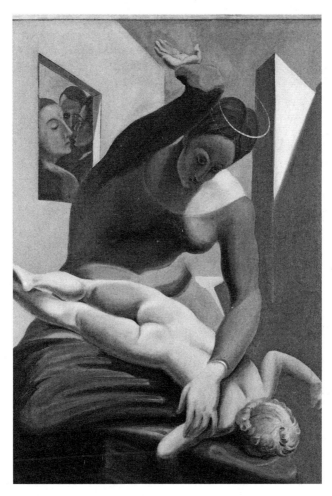

Figure 7: Max Ernst, *The Blessed Virgin Chastises the Infant Jesus Before Three Witnesses: A.B., P.E., and the Artist*

Oil on canvas, 1926, Museum Ludwig, Köln

"Most of us . . . are so accustomed to pictures of the Madonna and Child or of the Holy Family that we hardly notice the details. . . . [W]e tend to respond sentimentally if at all. . . . [W]e are not shocked. . . . It takes a jolt [such as the image above] to make us look carefully at how . . . artists depict family and child. . . . The picture brings home to us a profound truth. Not every aspect of family life is depicted in artistic renderings of the Holy Family. There are all sorts of homely scenes within which Jesus is not located, all sorts of childish actions that are not attributed to the baby God" (Bynum 1986: 79–80; cf. Horstmann 1875 for some medieval accounts of a naughty Jesus in His infancy).

pleading and cajoling ("Mother, I have never been able to deny you anything"), not by disciplinary or coercive violence.[6]

In the derivative oriental tradition, in contrast, relations within the divine family sometimes slip into open antagonism, before Justice at length yields to Mercy. In Arabic and Ethiopic variants of the same tale, the Virgin, as in the western archetype, responds to her Son's initial implacability by placing Him on the altar—but here, rather than simply genuflect in reverence, she threatens never to pick Him up again. What had been a gesture of supplication before the incarnate God becomes a mother's sinister design to abandon her baby.[7] But another fifteenth-century Ethiopian miracle takes this antagonism much farther, manifesting it in a form eerily cognate with the conduct of Freydís, Margueritte, and Théroigne. In this story, Christ persists in his refusal to forgive a sinning merchant, forcing Mary to resort to extreme measures:

> "O my Son, I beseech Thee to forgive the sin of this miserable man and sinner." And the Lord JESUS said unto her, "I will not forgive him because he denied Me and My angels." And when she heard this she wept bitterly, saying, "I beseech Thee, O my Son, to forgive this sinner his sin. I adjure Thee by my breasts which Thou hast sucked." And our Lord JESUS CHRIST said unto her, "I will not forgive this wicked man, for he denied Me and My angels, and rejected his baptism and his Christianity." And when she heard this, she stripped off her apparel, and said unto Him as she drew out her breasts, "If Thou wilt not forgive him for my sake, I will slit open my breasts and rip up my body." And when our Lord saw what she would do He rose up from His throne and sat in her bosom, and embraced her and kissed her,

---

[6] Perhaps the closest the Virgin comes in the western medieval imagination to outright violence directed at her Son is in speculation that she would have matched Abraham's cruel devotion, if necessary: "si non alius se obtulisset, virgo Maria tanto zelo amabat redemptionem generis humani, quod propriis manibus filium crucifixisset" [the Virgin Mary so ardently desired the salvation of humankind that, had no one else stepped up, she would have crucified her Son with her own hands] (Michel Menot, "Feria quarta post ramos palmarum," in Nève 1924: 453).

[7] Marian miracles were transmitted in the thirteenth century from Europe (via the Levant) to Egypt, and thence (in Arabic translation) to Ethiopia around the turn of the fifteenth century (Cerulli 1943: 529–35). On the Arabic variant of the Aquitainian youth's miracle, see Villecourt's comment: "[chez Caesarius,] la déposition de l'enfant Jésus des bras de sa mère sur l'autel n'est pas, comme dans l'arabe, un geste de menace, mais un simple acte préliminaire à un geste de supplication" (1924: 63). Cf. the Ethiopian adaptation: "'If Thou wilt not forgive him I will never again carry Thee in my arms, and I will never hold Thee in my bosom'; and she set Him down out of her arms onto the altar" (translation Budge's, §63 in 1933: 227–28). Cf. also King Alfonso X's *Cantiga* 164 (1986: 2.163–64).

and dried His mother's tears with His holy hair (?). And He said unto her, "Be not sad, O My Mother, I forgive him his sin for thy sake."[8]

At the far end of Christendom, the bare-sarked warrior finds her twin in the Abyssinian Virgin. In order to achieve her ends, the latter must egg her Son on, abusing Him, threatening to renounce Him, even menacing Him with the possibility of her own mastectomy. If even Christ is wont to forget His mission of delivering humanity from perdition until reminded by an explicit threat to His mother's human breasts, small wonder that Karlsefni and his men need to be kept on task by the drumming of steel against Freydís's bosom.

Unfortunately, as I am unable to read Gǝ'ǝz and Arabic, I cannot gauge how far removed the Ethiopic Mary is from her European prototype, nor analyse the algorithms that governed her transformation.[9] E.A. Wallis Budge's translation of Ethiopic miracle collections is expurgated; presumably, other unedited and untranslated tales may contain still more shocking material.[10] There is no reason to doubt that Ethiopian (and Arabic) narrative conventions influenced the African Marian corpus,[11] but one other tale hints that the violence inherent in

---

[8] §58 in Budge's translation (1933: 215–16). Budge dates the manuscript (BM Orient. 652) to the first third of the fifteenth century (1933: xxvii, xl). This miracle appears in at least one other manuscript (§110 in the codex Cerulli designates T, 1943: 25, 39, 44); an Arabic version is also preserved (§47 in Vat. Ar. 170; Cerulli 1943: 149, 153). Cf. the threefold pattern of repeated entreaties in another miracle (§29 in Budge 1933: 94–97; Getatchew notes it is the most popular Marian miracle in the Ethiopic tradition, 1992: 8n39): a cannibal twice refuses to give water to a thirsty man, but relents when the man invokes the Virgin. This proves the cannibal's salvation. (In a mid-fifteenth century elaboration of this story, Mary had earlier adjured Christ by her various attributes, including her breasts, to secure a general pardon for her devotees; see Getatchew 1992: 4–10, esp. 6–7.)

[9] See Baraz's pioneering study (1994). Cf. also Rubin (2009b: 20–21).

[10] Budge translates ca. one third of some 316 miracles extant in various manuscripts (1933: xxviii). He explains his selection criteria: "Many of the Miracles [a]re just silly stories, others ha[ve] little or no point in them, and some [a]re so 'naturalistic' as to be unprintable. . . . [M]any of the compositions given in [BM Orient. 652], and dignified with the name of 'Miracles,' are very poor things and have little or nothing of the miraculous about them. . . . Some few of these cannot be reproduced in this volume, for they deal with matters which, though commonly discussed with perfect freedom in Oriental works, are not openly talked of by Europeans" (1933: vi, xxix). In the effort to see past Budge, I have solicited help from medievalists specializing in Ethiopic and Coptic Church history; for their generosity with their time and learning, I am very grateful to Daniel Baraz, Elizabeth S. Bolman, Getatchew Haile, Steven Kaplan, Kirsten Pedersen, and Veronica Six.

[11] The topos of the mother who appeals to her son by reminding him of "my womb and my breasts which reared you," for instance, occurs elsewhere (Getatchew 2006: 2.6), and may be widespread in Ethiopian religious discourse. See also Chojnacki, who

breast-baring advocacy should, perhaps, be traced back to Europe. In this miracle, too, a threat of female self-mutilation and suicide drives the supplication. When the parents of a youth who had met a violent end discover his body, the mother in her anguish cries: "Alas, alas, my son! Alas, light of my eyes! Alas, joy of my heart! Here are the breasts that nursed you and the arms that swaddled you; it would have been far better for your mother to die than to live, and to have her limbs chopped off one by one and her flesh thrown to the dogs than to see you thus hung and suspended from a tree!"[12] There is no mistaking here the idiom of emotional blackmail to which Heliodorus's mother (and some Classical mothers before her) had resorted, but which in the medieval tradition is most typical of the tone the Virgin takes with her Son: "see here the womb that bore You, see the breasts You sucked, see these arms that attended to You." The suggestion of violence to the mother's body is likewise unmistakable (echoing Margueritte's threat to chop her breast into dog meat), and it, in turn, belongs to the European antecedant of this particular story—originally a miracle of St. James, not the Virgin—where the bereaved mother demands of the saint to revive her son: "Return [him to me], I ask, because you can; for if you do not do [it], I shall kill myself at once or have myself buried alive with [my son]."[13] In Latin, her wording may be less graphic than in Gəʿəz, but her tactic is identical: a bid to extract supernatural concessions by threatening grievous harm to herself. Through all the metamorphoses the story undergoes as it traverses traditions and continents, the mother's threat of self-immolation remains a constant.

Evoking the brute, coercive force inherent in maternal pleading seems to be the peculiar genius of the margins, however.[14] Whether through parallel

---

emphasizes the theological significance (based on "two apocryphal Eastern Christian texts . . . known to Ethiopians since the 14th century") attached to Mary's nursing of Jesus: "Sucking of the breast is a popular theme in Ethiopian [Marian] hymns: 'He who feeds all creation was suckled as a babe at thy breast' is mentioned in some form in all hymns of the Virgin" (1983: 78–79). Heldman (1994: 131) identifies the likely inspiration for Ethiopic images of the nursing Christ Child in thirteenth-century (and later) Italian and Byzantine art. Bolman notes that images of the nursing Virgin are frequent in early Coptic art (2005: 13).

[12] "Ahimè! Ahimè! figlio mio! Ahimè luce degli occhi miei! Ahimè gioia del mio cuore! Ahi le mammelle che ti nutrirono e le braccia che ti strinsero! Sarebbe stato meglio per tua madre morire che vive[r]e! E che le avessero recise le membra pezzo a pezzo ed avessero dato la sua carne ai cani anzichè vederti appeso ed impiccato così all'albero!" (Italian translation Cerulli's, 1943: 371).

[13] *Liber Sancti Jacobi* 2.3.142[v]: "Redde, inquam, quia potes: si enim non feceris, me statim interficiam, aut vivam cum [filio meo] sepeliri faciam" (Herbers and Santos Noia 1998: 162). Cf. Cerulli (1966: 122 [cf. 1943: 488–94]; 1969), tracing the transmission of other vehement or even violent miracles.

[14] Violence occasionally erupts also in some marginal occidental reflexes. In an early medieval sermon on the mother of the Maccabean martyrs, for instance, bare-breasted

evolution or by tapping into a common underlying tradition, Ethiopian miracle author and Icelandic saga writer (as, also, Marguerite's biographer and the French Reactionary printer) have produced characters whose behaviors are practically interchangeable. The possibility of (even indirect) cultural contact and borrowing between Scandinavia and Ethiopia during the Middle Ages may seem too remote to merit serious consideration; that it is just within the realm of the conceivable, however, may be hinted by Marianne Kalinke's discovery of overlap between a different saga topos and a tale contained in the *Thousand and One Nights* cycle. Kalinke is forced to conclude that "for lack of further evidence[,] the narrative paradigm [in the sagas] may be interpreted as an Icelandic realization and development of what is ultimately foreign, presumably oriental matter."[15] Such logic might be tentatively extended to suggest a common ancestry for the Norse and meridional iterations of the bare-sarked warrior, too (see further Sidebar 7).

Suggestive as the correspondences between Icelandic warrior woman and Ethiopic Mother of God are, any causal argument linking the two must (for now, at least) remain purely speculative. But more important, even, than any specific resemblance the Ethiopian Virgin bears to Freydís is her demonstration of how local literary reflexes can refashion imported motifs. "[F]rom the point of view of the experiencing social agent," anthropologist Kirsten Hastrup observes, "local relationships [necessarily] take precedence in the feel for community, quite irrespective of how many internationally produced items . . . people are exposed to." Cultures appropriate globally, in other words, but think and act locally.[16] Freydís may represent a naturalized Marian image, so to speak: she retains the core identity of violently manipulative advocate but carries the twin Icelandic passports of flyting and *hvǫt*.

---

supplication serves not to avert but to promote death: "Denudat ubera, ostendit cara filio nutrimenta. Fili, inquit, mi, noli defœdare coronam meam, et fraternam noli violare concordiam" [She bares her breasts, shows (her) son the beloved (sources of) nourishment. "Do not defile my crown, my son," she says, "and do not break faith with your brothers"]. The author does not hesitate to appropriate the Lucan rubric (11:27) which refers, originally, to Mary: "Beatus, inquit [David], venter qui vos portavit, et ubera quæ suxistis . . . septem vero martyrum Ecclesiæ de uno utero processerunt" [(David) said, "blessed the belly that bore you (pl.) and the breasts which you (pl.) have sucked" . . . for indeed, seven martyrs of the Church proceeded from a single womb] (Fulgentius, *Sermo lxix*, PL 65: 941c–42b). See also King Alfonso X's *Cantiga* 38, which imagines a Virgin so wrathful at a sinner that her eyes flash, her garment slips off her breasts, and she causes a host of "demões . . . come monteyros ben mandados" [demons like well-arrayed hunters] to punish the man (1986: 1.154–55; cf. the Virgin's violence towards a devil in *Cantiga* 47, 1986: 1.174, as well as in plastic art, Warner 1976: fig. 51).

¹⁵ Kalinke (1990: 106).

¹⁶ Hastrup (1998: 141). Cf. Geertz: "in order to have local effects . . . so-called outside factors . . . must first have local expressions" (1972: 325n12).

7. Interpretation: East meets West in the North?

Improbable as the possibility of cultural contact between Scandinavia and Ethiopia during the Middle Ages may seem, there are some tantalizing hints that it should not be ruled out entirely. The Near East, both Byzantine and Muslim, proved a powerful lodestone for both Scandinavian and African cultural entrepreneurs. Throughout its history, Ethiopian Christianity drew sustenance from the Coptic Church, and beyond it from the wider Mediterranean arena.[1] Norsemen, meanwhile, famously navigated to the Black Sea and beyond, leaving Viking Age graffiti in Constantinople, fighting under the banner of the Byzantine emperor, and going on pilgrimage to the Holy Land. Such contacts endured beyond the Viking Age: Near (and even Far) Eastern influences have been detected, for instance, in late-medieval legendary sagas.[2]

Norse and Ethiopic religiosity share some surprising peculiarities in the later Middle Ages. "A specific Norwegian form of religious deviation—the observation of Saturday as a holy day—can be dimly discerned from the 1430s until the 1550s or 1570s," remarks Ferdinand Næshagen. This practice, whose "prolonged existence and . . . geographic diffusion . . . argu[e] for its being widespread," has been interpreted as "an exaggerated worship of the Virgin Mary (whose day Saturday was)."[3] Næshagen adduces a twelfth-century Italian heresy as the "nearest parallel," offering no explanation for the 250-year gap between its occurrence in Italy and its reappearance in Norway.[4] Nearer in time, however, if not in space, are similar observances that gained currency in fourteenth- and fifteenth-century Ethiopia. In both Africa and Scandinavia, such devotions were often described (or disparaged) as Judaizing influence. In both instances, however, the rise of Sabbatarianism coincided with an efflorescence of the cult of the Virgin, making a Marian inspiration seem more likely.[5] The convergence of specific practices, timing, and underlying cause suggest

[1] See, e.g., Taddesse Tamrat (1972: 21–23, 29–31, 45–50, 70, 107–8, 245–67).

[2] See Kalinke (1990: 105–8); Mundt (1993). On runic graffiti in Hagia Sophia, see Knirk (1999) and Fischer (1999); cf. Jarring (1978). On Norsemen in the Byzantine Varangian Guard, see Ellis Davidson (1976: 177–246). On Norse pilgrims to the Kingdom of Jerusalem, see Kedar and Westergård-Nielsen (1978–79) and Hill (1983). Ciggaar provides a thorough, if old-fashioned, overview of Norse contacts with Byzantium (1996: 102–28).

[3] Næshagen (2000: 307); cf. Kolsrud (1910: 61–63). On Saturday as the Virgin's day, see Schreiber (1959: 208–11).

[4] Næshagen (2000: 307n53), referring to the Passagians, an obscure sect thought to have been active in Lombardy at the end of the twelfth century; see Wakefield and Evans (1969: 173–85 [esp. 181], 697–701).

[5] See, e.g., Ullendorff (1956: 243–45), Hammerschmidt (1963), and Getatchew Haile (1983: esp. 110–11). Adducing neither Jewish nor Marian links, Taddesse Tamrat does comment on "the controversy over the Sabbath [a]s only symptomatic of the divergencies in religious practice that had developed between the Alexandrian and

that the Norwegian and Ethiopian sects may both have derived from a common source.

Kirsten Pedersen, meanwhile, notes similarities between a specific type of Ethiopic religious hymn (*mälkĕ*), first recorded in the sixteenth century, and St. Brigitta of Sweden's orations, cataloguing and praising the body parts of Christ or Mary. She speculates a post-medieval contact via the missionary work of Iberian Jesuits, yet the Brigittine catalogues have clear medieval antecedents.[6] Eike Haberland's comments on a subterranean early-modern exchange may be cautiously extended to apply also to an earlier period:

> Seminal Western stimuli took root in Ethiopia much more often than anyone in Europe imagined. Although the purely spiritual influxes are not always easy to identify (unless they manifest themselves in, for example, theological polemical texts), still the correspondences 'discovered' in the last decade [1960s-70s] between European and Ethiopian painting, for instance, reveal these contacts most conspicuously. Who in Europe is aware that Italian painters were working in Ethiopia, or that European exemplars—from Flemish icons to copper engravings by Albrecht Dürer—were being copied in Ethiopia?[7]

Unquestionably, few in medieval Europe could have suspected that the baresarked warrior, exported from Europe in one direction as far as the shores of Vínland, would also be taken up half a world away by the Virgin in Ethiopia. That she nevertheless does turn up both here and there is a coincidence that cries out for further investigation.

Ethiopian Churches over the centuries," maintaining that "Zär'a-Ya'iqob (1434–68) understood the conflict in its true nature as a national movement" (1972: 219). The same emperor is also credited, somewhat hyperbolically, with "introducing the cult of the Mother of God into Ethiopia" (Hunt 2007: 414; cf. Getatchew Haile 1992).

[6] See Pedersen (1989, esp. 553 for parallels between Ethiopic and Brigittine praise of Mary's breasts and womb, and 558–59 for the proposed Jesuit introduction of Brigittine prayers which inspired *mälkĕ*), and cf., e.g., Honorius, *Sigillum* cap. 4 (*PL* 172: 505d-508b), and Richard of St. Laurent, *De Laudibus* 5.2 (1890–99: 279–319), both glossing the Canticle of Canticles. I am indebted to Kirsten Pedersen for discussing this topic with me and for making a copy of her article available to me.

[7] Haberland: "Befruchtende Stimuli des Abendlandes wurden in Äthiopien viel häufiger aufgenommen, als man in Europa ahnte. Sind die rein spirituellen Einflüsse—es sei denn, sie manifestierten sich z.B. in theologischen Streitschriften—nicht immer leicht zu identifizieren, so zeigen z.B. die in dem letzten Jahrzehnt 'entdeckten' Zusammenhänge zwischen europäischer und äthiopischer Malerei am augenfälligsten diese Kontakte. Wer ahnt in Europa, daß italienische Maler in Äthiopien wirkten oder daß europäische Vorbilder—von flämischen Ikonen bis hin zu Kupferstichen von Albrecht Dürer—in Äthiopien rezipiert wurden?" (1976: 1).

Beyond suggesting a literary source, the tradition of bare-bosomed supplicants sheds light on the bare-sarked warrior topos by highlighting the process through which social gender and biological sex are mashed up and molded
against each other as culture-specific variables. It reveals how the act of flashing
to signal helplessness is both socially and biologically feminized. Supplication, in
other words, is gendered feminine and associated with female sexual attributes,[17]
at the same time that femininity (of gender or sex) is characterized by curtailment
of physical and social agency, allowing such agency to be accessed only second-
hand via appeal to male arbiters and actors.[18] Furthermore, the fact that bare-
bosomed supplicants do not wield harmful force is revealing for why bare-sarked
warriors, in contrast, do. In the Western canon, most such supplicants—the
Virgin, Heliodorus's mother, even Hecuba on Troy's walls—neither inflict nor
are personally threatened with proximate physical violence. Even those who do
struggle to avert an immediate menace (Helen pleading with Menelaus, Clytaemestra parrying Orestes, Jocasta interjecting herself between Polynices and
Eteocles) offer only passive resistance. In none of these cases is the supplicant
woman assaulted by outgroup Others; the enormity of the attacks she sets her
breast against derives precisely from their rupture of intimate solidarities, what
Elisabeth Copet-Rougier calls the "*entre-soi*": husband threatens to kill wife, a
son his mother, or two brothers each other. An early fourteenth-century Picard
poem, *Tristan de Nanteuil*, succinctly captures this point: the eponymous hero's
grandmother, Aye, cross-dressed as a formidable knight, finds her grandson in
the forest, where he has been adopted by a she-deer. At sight of the knight, the

---

[17] Any fetishized emblem of femininity, not necessarily primary or secondary sex
attributes, may metonymize womanhood (cf. Miles 2008: 125). The sagas indicate, e.g.,
the gendering of particular articles of clothing: breeches are masculine, a low-cut shirt
or a silk cape is feminine (*Laxdæla saga* capp. 35, 34, ÍF 5: 97, 94; *Brennu-Njáls saga* cap.
123, ÍF 12: 313). In practice, the examples I have found in association with supplication
or whetting tend to focus on women's bosoms, pubes, or pregnant bellies. Tolmie points
out the utility of pregnancy for suggesting a woman's (indirect) violent potential: it is her
unborn child who "will avenge a wrong in the distant future" (2001: 4). Cf. Bloom: "[An]
IED is often disguised under a woman's clothing to make her appear pregnant. . . . The
advent of women suicide bombers has thus transformed the revolutionary womb into an
exploding one" (2007: 95).

[18] Male exposure, accordingly, signals aggression, not helplessness; see, e.g., Josephus, *Jewish Antiquities* 20.3.108 (1926–65: 10.58–59). Different female body parts,
moreover, effect different kinds of appeal: while reference to maternal bosoms or wombs
is useful for conciliatory supplication, reference to (more blatantly erotic?) pubes or rumps
appears to dominate appeals that rely on humiliation of the audience (or on magic) to
achieve their purpose. (Despite some scholars' efforts to distinguish sharply between
maternal and erotic significations—see, e.g., Cameron 1991: 98, and chapter VII, n45
below—the two aspects seem to me correlated: an exposed abdomen, e.g., can equally
signify a nurturing womb or a sexy vulva.)

infant is terrified, so Aye "showed him her breasts, by which his father was fed," causing him to calm down and fall asleep at her bosom.[19] Topless supplication is thus intended to restore ingroup harmony. Nudity, visually highlighting female sex, coordinates with pacific behavior—in Aye's case, a demonstrative lapse of her assumed militant masculinity—to defuse intramural strife.

When opposed to threats from beyond society, however (like the one the *skrælingar* pose to the Norsemen), physically female sexing must, in order to achieve its purpose, align with a type of behavior gendered masculine: a display of violence. Here, then, we move from the realm of the bare-bosomed supplicant to that of the bare-sarked warrior. Her violence targets the female perpetrator's own body in preference to her opponents'. Yet, somehow, this threat of self-mutilation, born of the alchemy of *hvatr* conduct and a *blauðr* physique, leaves the bare-sarked warrior herself unscathed while ushering the downfall of her foes.[20]

Three concluding examples may serve to emphasize the distinction between bare-bosomed supplicants and bare-sarked warriors, while also demonstrating some ebb and flow between the topoi. The sheer escalatory force of literary embellishment could tend to produce bare-sarked warriors out of pacific shirtless supplicants—a point strikingly borne out in a minor episode incorporated into the Arthurian prehistory of Britain. Here we find Tonwenna, mother of the legendary kings Brennius and Belinus, who mimics Jocasta's effort to prevent her sons from annihilating each other. She, in fact, succeeds where the latter had failed, thwarting her sons' internecine intents and goading them on to greater achievements. At the head of this Arthurian tradition, Geoffrey of Monmouth, writing perhaps ca. 1125, tells how Tonwenna clings to Belinus: "[She] locked her arms about his neck, showering longed-for kisses; having, moreover, bared

---

[19] Copet-Rougier (1986); Sinclair, 2533–47, at 2539: "Lui monstra ses mamelles dont son pere nourry" (1971: 151–52). The she-deer, which fosters the infant Tristan, is identified as *cerve*, a neologism used to distinguish it from a normal doe, *biche* (Sautman 2001: 229n61). On this outlandish *chanson de geste*, see further Sautman (2001: esp. 211–12). I am indebted to Kim Zarins for drawing my attention to this text.

[20] Of the cases so far discussed, the Beothuk women and Marguerite d'Artois would appear to be anomalous. The Native American women seem to enact an ingroup tactic in response to an outgroup threat. As I have suggested above, however, the authenticity of reports of their conduct is doubtful; an eighteenth-century account of the killing of a pregnant Beothuk illustrates how moralizing rhetoric overshadows ethnography: "Seeing before her none but men . . . she pointed with an air of most moving entreaty to her prominent belly. Could all nature have produced another pleader of such eloquence as the infant there concealed? But this appeal, Oh, shame to humanity! was alas! in vain; for an instant stab, that ripped open her womb, laid her at the feet of those cowardly ruffians" (Howley 1915: 34–35). The Countess of Artois, on the other hand, seems to use an outgroup tactic when dealing solely with members of her ingroup; this is indeed an anomaly, but one which can perhaps be accounted for by the peculiar political and literary circumstances of the Marguerite anecdote. See further n42 in this chapter.

her breasts, she addressed him in this manner, her speech rattled by interrupting sobs: 'Remember, son, remember these breasts which you sucked, and your mother's womb!'" A quarter century later, Geoffrey is closely followed by Wace, whose Toruuenne, still strictly supplicant, cries: "Recall, recall these breasts you see, which you suckled many times! Recall that you came out of this belly when you were born!" In the final development of this tradition, Laȝamon's Tonuenne (ca. 1200) recycles her predecessors' words, but embellishes just enough to come within hailing distance of the bare-sarked topos: "See here the breasts that you sucked with your lips! Behold here the woman who bore you into this world! Lo, here the womb in which you lay for so long! Lo, here that very body! Never do me this shame, that I should [be forced] by your action to stab myself with a dagger." Despite the absence of an outgroup enemy, this latter Tonuenne alludes briefly to the same bare-sarked option threatened by Countess Marguerite. Fueled by the hyperbolic momentum of ongoing narrative elaboration, the mother of the warring sons can imagine herself as resorting to violence, if only in passing. Her threat evokes no particular response, neither more nor less effective than the *blauðr* pleas of her predecessors. The success of her appeal obviates her hypothetical threat and ensures that she remain, in the end, a pacific supplicant.[21]

Tonwenna's status as queen is incidental to her intercession; her project hinges, rather, on her motherhood. But queens—intimately associated with the centers of temporal power, yet denied any formal part in that power—tend to get slotted into the role of mediators between society and the all-important center itself, their royal husbands.[22] The supplicant Virgin, for all her towering alone

---

[21] Geoffrey of Monmouth, *History of the Kings of Britain* 3.41: "brachia collo eius iniecit, desiderata basia ingeminans. Nudatis quoque uberibus, illum in hunc modum affata est, sermonem impediente singultu: 'Memento, fili, memento uberum istorum quae suxisti matrisque tuae uteri'" (2007: 55); Wace, *Roman de Brut* 2730–34: "Remembre tei, remembre tei / De cez mameles que tu veiz / Que tu alaitas mainte feiz; / Remembre tei que tu eissis / De cest ventre quant tu nasquis" (1999: 70); Laȝamon, *Brut* 2506–10: "Loka her þa tittes, þat þu suke mid þine lippes. / Lou war hire þa wifmon, þa þe a ðas weoreld i-bær. / Leo wær here þa wombe, þe þu læie inne swa longe. / Leo war here þa ilke likame, Ne do þu me neuere þane scome. / þat ich for þine þinge, mid sæxe me of-stinge" (1963–78: 1.130–31). I am indebted to Andy Galloway for drawing my attention to these texts.

[22] On interceding queens, see Strohm (1992), Huneycutt (1995), and esp. Parsons (1992: 65–68 and 1995), who discusses the ritual proximities between temporal queens and the Queen of Heaven (*pace* Miles 2008: 3). The longevity of this ritual is attested, e.g., by "The Story of Ill May-Day," a ballad set in the reign of Henry VIII, where "Queene Katherine . . . disrobde of rich attires, / with haire hangd downe, she sadly hies, / And of her gracious Lord requires / a boone, which hardly he denyes" (st. 11, Collier 1868: 99). In this context it is important to bear in mind that Freydís's status is as close to royalty as possible in the kingless Norse Atlantic. She is the daughter of Eiríkr the Red, discoverer of Greenland and its highest political authority, and the sister of Leifr, who discovered

above her sex, thus has earthly competition. In a supreme refinement of the ideal of female intercession, pregnancy comes to have emphatic utility in disposing the all-deciding monarch kindly towards his wife's pleas. The semantics of the pregnant queen are complex, and the reasons for her particular efficacy as intercessor manifold.[23] But among the components adding up to the queen's special status, there is no mistaking her waxing femininity. By the logic of marginalization, a woman's intercessory power stems from her very nature as woman—that is, as disempowered being—and so a physical condition which underlines her sex inevitably redoubles her gender.[24] When observing a meticulous protocol of address, a consort can obtain a special dispensation to perform the impossible: to intervene in the male public sphere, righting men's wrongs despite—or rather, thanks to—the very impropriety of her intervention.[25] Thus, the intercession of queens, which in the late Middle Ages grows in importance as a quasi-institutionalized detour around royal bureaucracy and acquires proportionate literary prominence, is also an example of the bare-bosomed supplication motif, even if royal pleaders typically emphasize their pregnant bellies in preference to baring their breasts. As with other supplicant women, an interceding queen's superabundant, overstated femininity is the key to her success.[26]

Vínland and staked a claim to it (cf. his insistence on retaining ownership of the huts he had built in Vínland, although he is willing to allow later explorers free use of the facilities; *Grœnlendinga saga* capp. 6, 7, ÍF 4: 261, 264).

[23] The queen bears, for one thing, manifest proof of her intimacy with the king (physically and, by extension, perhaps also politically), as well as of his virility and of her usefulness in ensuring continuity of government. She also embodies—in an entirely concrete sense—the king's most precious store of political capital; the heir she carries grants her extraordinary bargaining powers, which neither she nor those who apply to her for intercession are averse to deploying. Conscious manipulation of Marian echoes also enters into play.

[24] Cf. Strohm (1992: esp. 103–5); Parsons (1996: esp. 42–45); and Heal (2007: 269–70).

[25] As King astutely observes, "*Anasyrmos* by reproductive women says 'We are in place as women' [while] 'You are out of place as men'" (1986: 67). See also Hairston (2000: 694–97).

[26] See, e.g., the Middle English romance *Athelston*, where the principles governing stereotypical queenly intercession are honored in the breach: the eponymous king not only rejects the pleas of his wife, "before [him] come / Wiþ a chyld, douȝtyr or a sone" but actually kicks her in the belly, so that he "slowȝ þe chyld ryȝt in here wombe" (ll. 259–60, 283, Trounce 1951: 75). There is violence here, in word and deed, but it is his alone, and is harnessed to the romancier's purpose of characterizing Athelston as an unnatural tyrant (cf. King Alfonso X's *Cantiga* 105, 1986: 2.22). The queen, on the other hand, has failed to observe protocol, bringing disaster on herself by approaching the king in a way which implies her own agency—in effect, her masculinization. See further Rowe (1995) and Parsons (1996); cf. Farr: "in honorific contests a kick to the stomach of a pregnant woman (disturbingly, a far from uncommon gesture) is a blow to the family line, as may be a kick deliberately delivered to a male's genitals" (1988: 193); and cf. Clark (1994: 351).

Accordingly, when Froissart wishes to credit his patroness Philippa of Hain-
ault with dissuading Edward III from an ill-advised plan to execute some captive
burghers at Calais, early in the Hundred Years' War (1347), he conveniently if
unhistorically resorts to this motif: having "crossed the sea hither in great peril,"
the queen kneels before the king, "heavily pregnant," to plead for the men's lives.
A memorable, but inauthentic, image; Philippa gave birth fully nine months
later, so she could hardly have been great with child at the time of the event
recounted.[27] (A century and a half later, Caterina Sforza, the beleaguered Lady
of the Forlì, confirmed that agentive women were no less capable than retrospective chroniclers of fabricating pregnancy as an affective weapon: when her
enemies, who had already assassinated her husband the count, threatened to kill
her children, she claimed to be carrying another heir in her belly, coolly deflat-
ing their threat by rendering it politically pointless.)[28] The historical and literary context for Philippa's big-bellied intercession merits notice. While no bare-
sarked warrior, the English queen does subtly emphasize the hazardous Channel
crossing she had endured, and also perhaps the rugged conditions in Edward's
frontline headquarters, vulnerable to French counter-strikes.[29] Historical circumstances thus ratchet the humdrum literary drama of intercession up a notch
by adding an aroma of risk. The adversity of the Hundred Years' War, far more
intense than the workaday rivalry of domestic chivalric scuffles,[30] is here tenu-
ously linked with the queen's pregnant body in a way which hints at an escalation
in the pursuit of foreign animosities. Such a level of acrimony could even make
the bare-sarked warrior topos appropriate to the conflict.

This potential is realized in the mid-fourteenth-century Picard poem *Les
Vœux du héron*, "The Vows of the Heron," set at the English court on the eve
of the war (1338). Unlike Froissart, the anonymous poet is not kindly disposed
towards his imagined Philippa (who here remains unnamed). His interest in the

---

[27] *Chroniques* 1.66.312: "apassai[t] le mer par deçà en grant peril . . . durement
enchainte" (1869–1975: 4.62). For close readings of the intercession at Calais, see Strohm
(1992) and Parsons (1996), and, in a very different vein, Moeglin (1994). This part of
the *Chroniques*, mostly a revision of Le Bel's (Luce, in Froissart 1869–1975: 4.xxv n1),
was written in the 1360s. Le Bel, writing in 1358 (Viard and Déprez, in Le Bel 1904–5:
1.xvj), records Philippa's intercession in similar terms, but says nothing about the circumstances in which it is made (81, 1904–5: 2.166–67 and 2.167n1). Packe conjectures that,
during the siege of Calais, Edward III was more interested in his mistress than in his
wife, though he accepts the latter's alleged pregnancy at face value (1983: 169–78).

[28] See sources cited in chapter V, n10 above, and for accounts of Sforza's fabricated
pregnancy, esp. Hairston (2000: 694–701).

[29] Philippe VI did, in fact, deploy a substantial, if ineffective, army in an attempt to
dislodge the English besiegers; see Burne (1955: 214–16) and Packe (1983: 168–69). On
Edward III's "elaborate headquarters . . . methodically [constructed –] a nice example of
town planning," see Burne (1955: 212, 209–10).

[30] See Strickland (1996) and Kaeuper (1999).

queen is passing only, however; the poem's chief villain is the vindictive French exile Robert d'Artois. In imitation of other vowing poems (*gabs*), he kills a heron and dresses it as a baiting-dish, hoping to brew strife between Philippe VI and Edward III, respectively his past and present liege lords.[31] Gliding from diner to diner, Artois extracts from them a set of jingoistic vows which, with the historical hindsight the poet evidently possessed, can be seen to have found ironic fulfilment in the subsequent fighting. Thus the *conte* Salebrin (Earl of Salisbury), who in 1333 had lost an eye in a tournament, boasts he will campaign with only one eye open, while another lord, Jehans de Biaumont (Beaumont [or: Hainault]), who in 1346 would defect to Philippe, vows to serve Edward—unless the king of France order him to switch sides.[32] The poem reaches its emotional climax when Artois kneels before the queen and asks for her vow. "Never you speak to me of it," she demurs; "a lady cannot make a vow when she has a lord." But when the king grants her freedom to swear as she will ("whatever you pledge, my body will discharge; however much it can render, my body will labor for it"),[33] she says:

> I know well, for a while now,
> That I am great with child; my body has sensed it.
> It has not been long since it stirred inside my body.
> And I vow and promise to God Who created me –
> Who was born of the Virgin (whose body was not spoiled)

---

[31] Dronke mentions various proverbial characteristics of the heron, some of which (e.g., gluttony, ingenuity in hunting) seem relevant (1984: esp. 54–55); DeMarco highlights the bird's alleged cowardice (1997: 50). On the genre of the *gab*, see Grigsby and Lacy (1992: 2–7); Grigsby (2000: esp. 65–98); and Bellon-Méguelle (2008: esp. 497–501). *Hœnsa-Þóris saga* cap. 12 (ÍF 3: 34) supplies a saga analogue. For analyses and background on the *Vœux du héron*, see Whiting (1945), Grigsby (2000: 213–27), and DeMarco (1997: 15–63).

[32] For Salisbury's vow, see *Vœux du héron* (167–204); for his 1333 mishap, see Le Bel 22 (1904–5: 1.110–11); see also Whiting (1945: 269) and Grigsby and Lacy (1992: 11–12). For Beaumont's vow, see *Vœux du héron* (378–96); for his defection, see Whiting (1945: 274–77) and Grigsby and Lacy (1992: 14–15). Cf. Grigsby, who laments that "[t]he poem's intimate links to history become more and more an interference with its literary, or fictional, setting," hindering its interpretation "under the aspect of diegesis" (2000: 226). Bellon-Méguelle, speaking of a related poem, *Les Vœux du paon*, seems to me closer to the mark: "Grâce à l'établissement d'un protocole d'affrontement unanimement accepté, la guerre est ritualisée. Par sa codification et sa dimension spectaculaire, elle ressemble au tournoi et semble ne devoir être menée que pour divertir la société aristocratique. Tournant en dérision l'écriture épique, [l'auteur] en désamorce la portée pathétique" (2008: 350).

[33] *Vœux du héron* (406–7, 413–14): "[O]r ne m'en parlés ja. / Dame ne peut vouer puis qu'elle signeur a. . . . De quanques voerés, mes cors l'acquitera / Mes que finer en puisse, mes cors s'en penera!" See ll. 399–427 for Artois's goading of the queen.

And Who died on the cross (they crucified Him) –
That the foetus will not issue from my body
Until you will have led me to the country abroad
To pursue the vow that your body has vowed.
And if it still wants to issue when it is uncalled for,
With a great carving knife I will slay my body:
Thus will my soul be lost and the foetus will perish.[34]

Visibly shaken, Edward promptly calls off the vowing game. The poem closes by telling how he nevertheless complied with the queen's oath, taking her with his invading army to bear a son, Lÿon (Lionel), at Antwerp.[35] "Before the [vows] are all fulfilled," however, the poet sagaciously cautions, "many a gentleman will die for it, and many a good knight will cry out, lamenting, and many a gentlewoman will fall to the ground, wretched."[36]

Like Our Lady, the *Vœux du héron* queen uses her pregnancy as political propellant for the king with whom she intercedes to do the right thing. Her body, like the Virgin's, shall remain inviolate—if her lord, like Louis de Male, submits to her will. The queen juxtaposes Mary's ever-intact hymen with her own impending disembowelment.[37] The queen's elision of herself with Mary and her invocation of Edward by his unborn child align her with other pacific, interceding queens. But her goal is hardly conciliatory, and her method no less *hvǫt* than supplication. The situation the poem captures is that of a rhetorical arms-race spinning out of control: although there is no linear escalation in the severity of the oaths—perhaps precisely because even the most gruesome boasts have failed to set a rhythm of mounting bloody-mouthedness[38]—the queen is called upon to

---

[34] *Vœux du héron* (416–27): "Je sai bien que piecha / Que sui grosse d'enfant, que mon corps sentu l'a. / Encore n'a li gaires qu'en men corps se tourna. / Et je veue et promech a Dieu qui me crea, / Qui nasqui de la Vierge que ses corps n'enpira, / Et qui morut en crois, on le crucefia, / Que je li fruis de mon corps n'istera / Si m'en arés menee ou païs dela / Pour avanchir le veu que vo corps voué a. / Et s'il en voelt isir quant besoins n'en sera, / D'un grant coutel d'achier li miens corps s'ochira: / S'ara m'ame perdue et li fruis perira."

[35] Like Froissart, the *Vœux du héron* poet takes some liberties with the timetable of Philippa's gestation. In the poem, set in September 1338 (*Vœux du héron* 1–5), Philippa says she only recently felt the quickening; the real Lionel of Antwerp was born 29 November 1338 (Grigsby and Lacy 1992: 63). Cf. Parsons (1996: 50).

[36] *Vœux du héron* (439–41): "Ains que soient tout fait maint preudomme en mora, / Et maint boin chevalier dolant s'en clamera, / Et mainte preudefemme pour lasse s'en terra."

[37] On the paradoxical investment of late medieval queens with both Marian maternity and virginity, see Parsons (1995: esp. 153–54); cf. Clayton for Anglo-Saxon queens' association with Mary (1990: 164–65).

[38] *Pace* the progression apparently implied in Parsons's estimation that the knights' vows are "patently over the top" (1996: 49; cf. DeMarco 1997: 44–45, 58), a perception Grigsby and Lacy at times also seem to share (e.g., 1992: 13–15). Contrast, e.g., Wautier

jostle her husband and his knights into assuming full-blown macho personae, and this she does by stressing her own femininity.[39] At the same time, she assumes a *hvatr* demeanor, echoing the violence of an oath Jehan de Faukemont (Valkenberg) had made earlier in the poem: "I would spare neither minster nor altar, pregnant woman nor child whom I might encounter, neither kinsman nor friend, however much he loved me, if only he wanted to resist King Edward." Coming from Valkenberg, this sacrilegious ferocity had been applauded by one and all.[40] Now, however, the queen matches him word for word: like him, she will not shrink from violating [*f*]*emme grosse n'enfant* and is even willing to lose her soul (as surely he must, if he withholds his wrath from *ne moustier ne autel*) in her over-zealous soldiery. The grim irony which stuns Edward is that this unflinching commitment to securing a military objective, merely an overabundance of basically desirable *esprit de corps* in the berserk Valkenberg, is utterly inappropriate for the queen. Moreover, the entire barrage of threats, which Valkenberg had dispersed liberally over many targets, focuses in her case on only herself and the embryo inside her, further intensifying its ferocity.

---

de Manny: "sera de par moy . . . ochise la gent gisant [le] geule bee" [by (my hand) shall . . . the people be slain, stretched out with gaping maws] (*Vœux du héron* 243–44) with the vow following it, that of the *conte* Derbi [Earl of Derby]: "j'ai en men ceur voué, / Tant cherqueray le conte que je l'arai trouvé. . . . Et s'il ne vient a mi par tres grant poesté, / Par le foy que je doy Edouart le menbré, / Que [je] si pres de lui arai le feu bouté / Que bien sera par lui veü et esgardé" [I have vowed in my heart that I will look for the count (Louis of Flanders) until I have found him. . . . And if he does not counter me with very great force, by the fidelity that I owe to the hardy Edward, so near him will I strike a fire that it will be easily seen and noticed by him] (*Vœux du héron* 271–78). Even if the notion of setting a fire only sufficient to attract attention is taken as heroic litotes (cf. *Sturlu saga* cap. 10, in *Sturlunga saga*, 1946: 1.75: "Þá mælti Einarr, áðr þeir riðu at bænum: 'Nú væra ek á þat viljaðr, at vér eldim þeim ósparliga í Hvammi í nótt ok mætti þeir reka minni til kvámu várrar'" [Then Einarr declared, before they rode up to the farm: "What I'd like now is that we light them up unsparingly at Hvammr tonight, (so that) they'd have something to remember our coming by"]), Derby's commitment to proceed only so long as he is not opposed *par tres grant poesté* is underwhelming.

[39] Not only the reference to her unborn child but also the obeisance to her husband's authority, immediately preceding her outrageous vow, help feminize the *Vœux du héron* queen. Repeated references to the speaker's body may also draw attention to her corporeality, emphasizing her pregnancy, her biological sex, and the concreteness of her threat. (Grigsby rejects any emphasis on corporeality, noting that "*le mien cors* . . . mean[s] simply 'myself.'" He does concede that "this Old French expression . . . is a favored one in [the *Vœux du héron*]"—cf. Edward's turn of phrase at 413–14, cited above—but evidently attaches no importance to this prominence; 2000: 220.)

[40] *Vœux du héron* (341–44): "si n'espargneroie ne moustier ne autel, / Femme grosse n'enfant que peüsse trouver, / Ne parent ne ami, tant me peüst amer, / Pour tant que il vausist roy Edouart grever"; cf. ll. 21–25, and, for the cheers Valkenberg elicits, ll. 347–48. On the ferocity of the historical Valkenberg, see Whiting (1945: 272–73).

Though she stays fully clothed, and even enjoys a dainty dish in the safety of court, the *Vœux du héron* queen thus also qualifies as a bare-sarked warrior, or at any rate, like the counter-revolutionary printer's Théroigne, as a hostile parody of one. The earlier satires of Salisbury and Beaumont indicate that the poet anticipates an extra-textual audience attuned to topical allusion; the record of the real Valkenberg (noted for his brutality in the war) would have alerted this audience to the dead earnest in which his vow is made, and, by association, to the weight the queen's oath carries. With neither *skrælingar* nor French troops on hand to menace her physically, the queen takes on their role of would-be executioner in the very words that cast her as would-be victim and as Valkenberg's equal in violence. Her usurpation of masculine gender roles is all the more stinging for its mock deference to her husband's sovereignty.[41] Belligerently critical of English warmongering, the poet's attribution of gender transgression to his unnamed queen serves, in Patricia DeMarco's words, as a "vehicle of defamiliarization," capping his dramatization of English barbarity. By suggesting that Edward III's court regard the French with the ferocity appropriate to ethnic Others, the poet hurls this verdict back on them, manifesting to his audience the Otherness of the English.[42]

---

[41] Parsons notes that Aristotelian views on the roles of men and women in conception made even a woman's claim to the power to give life, let alone to terminate a pregnancy, a usurpation of her husband's prerogatives (1996: 51, 60n32). Through complementary reasoning, misshapen births were attributed to mothers' harmful thoughts; see Huet (1993: e.g., 21).

[42] DeMarco (1997: 59). The rhetorical escalation in the portrayal of the enemy during the Hundred Years' War, to which the *Vœux du héron* vividly attests, goes some way towards explaining the charged political ambience which may have enabled a redactor of the *Annales normandes abrégées* to embellish them with a bare-sarked warrior. Even if it does not explicitly depict an extra-societal enemy, the Marguerite anecdote seems to tap the same visceral attitudes addressed by the *Vœux du héron*. Political fears and hatreds were esp. pronounced in the 1430s—the era of Jeanne d'Arc and the treaty of Arras—and esp. in Burgundy, which allied itself with France in 1435; see Seward (1978: 188–90, 196, 225–34; for a Flemish connection, going back to the 1360s, see 1978: 105, 181). Moreover, the *Vœux du héron* may be the direct literary inspiration for the Marguerite anecdote, which occurs in only one manuscript, Brussels BR 11139 (ca. 1430–40); it is bound together with Brussels BR 11138, containing a version of the *Vœux du héron*, a coincidence that seems to have escaped notice to date. The two texts are also juxtaposed in Paris BN Fr. 9222 and in Brussels BR 10434 [shelf-marked 10432–35]; see Grigsby and Lacy (1992: 20–21), Straub (1995: 111–13, 129–30), and Van den Bergen-Pantens and Verweij (2009). See, however, Molinier (1882: xlviii-xlix n2) and Straub (1995: 111n29) on a possible confusion between Brussels BR 11138–39 and Brussels BR 10432–35. Grigsby and Lacy erroneously date the former to the late 1300s, though its version of the *Annales* continues to 1408 (1992: 20); they describe its version of the *Vœux du héron* (which they print in an appendix, 1992: 67–96) as a "maverick . . . boldly rearranged, perhaps with several manuscripts in front of the redactor" (1992: 24). I hope to investigate the contents and compilation of these various manuscripts in a future study.

Why does Freydís bare her breast, then? Bare-sarked warriors, like supplicant women, need to establish their *blauðr* credentials; exhibitionism is a convenient shorthand proclaiming womanly vulnerability. The preference for breasts and swollen bellies as emblems of such vulnerability may not be accidental: less offensive than the demon-repelling and deserter-mocking vulva, these physical attributes are no less effective as advertisements of their barer's sex.[43] The elderly Marguerite d'Artois—like Tonwenna and the Virgin Mary but unlike her younger, fertile sisters in fourteenth-century England and turn-of-the-millennium Vínland—is not provided with a convenient belly she can promenade, so she must make do with a reminder of lactations past in order to move her obstinate son.[44] Such female insignia strike just the right note, highlighting the very femininity that these women's hyper-aggressive appropriation of *hvatr* savagery renounces. But what, then, of their violence? In the next chapter, I swing back to this second half of the formula, the brandished weapon that establishes these bare-sarked women as warriors.

---

[43] It is left to social misfits like Théroigne, target of the printer's political antipathy, to shamelessly display their pudenda.

[44] Cf. Hairston (2000: 707n55), who speculates that the effectiveness of genital exposure "derives from the power of fertile women," and is thus anomalous when practiced by a post-menopausal woman.

VII. Pain and Pornography

"Where are you going, you cowards?" shouted Freydis. — No one paid any attention to her, Thorvard least of all. — As for the Skrælings, they laughed a brazen yelping laugh when they saw her, and called her *Kestijui'skw* [Bondsmaid]. — "Oh, you'd like me to take my shirt off, would you?" shrieked Freydis. "I'll show you, you savage thralls, you Hel-meat!" — She began to clamber over the wall of the palisade. . . . For all her girth of belly, Freydis was very fit and strong. She ran to where Thorbrand Snorrason lay dead and snatched up his sword. As the Skrælings ran towards her, she tore a great rip in her shirt with her hand and pulled one of her breasts out and began whacking it with the sword, yelling, "Is that what you want to see, thralls? Ha, ha — have none of you dogs seen a bitch? Look how I gash myself now with this sword! See the blood, you thralls? See my BLACK HANDS? See me touching myself with them? You'd better start running, thralls, or I'm going to touch you with them, too, and you'll all drop dead. Here I come!"

Vollmann, *The Ice Shirt* (1990: 307–8)[1]

If baring her breast grounds Freydís in physical femininity, the sword she swings stamps her with transient, behavioral masculinity. Again, some previous theories for explaining her conduct serve me as convenient signposts, even if these hypotheses must ultimately be sifted and discarded. Here, too, the tradition of interpretations follows two divergent modes. One set of interpretations focuses on the violent message that the whirling blade conveys to the *skrælingar*, the intra-textual, antagonistic audience; such readings emphasize historical realism. Interpretations in the alternative mode highlight the violence Freydís directs at her own body; assuming this violence to be a literary trope, this type of analysis glosses her performance as a meta-textual address of the external audience. As I have suggested above, Freydís's action apostrophizes primarily her own allies. By underestimating this additional intra-textual audience, interpretations in either mode are at best incomplete.

---

[1] In Vollmann's account, Freydis's black hands mark her allegiance to an autochthonous Greenland demon who had possessed her. Cf. Berry (1977: 177–78).

Norse women are popularly perceived as uncommonly fierce: real-life templates for mythology's shield-maidens.[2] This perception has led some readers, even if they concede that *Eiríks saga rauða*'s Freydís episode may be unhistorical, to treat Freydís's martial crust as essentially unproblematic, a reflex of valkyrie valor or berserk rage (even though only male *berserkir* are securely attested elsewhere).[3] Other sagas do furnish further samples of warlike women, but Freydís's battleaxe personality, her astounding battlefield success, and the particulars of her combat routine all serve not so much to bring her in line with saga tradition as to set her apart from bellicose Nordic ladies elsewhere in the historic saga corpus. Despite their fierce reputation, such women's actual capacity for violence is embarrassingly modest. They typically either remain unarmed, which rather limits their lethal potential,[4] or are simply pathetic in their martial ineptitude.[5] One thinks, say, of Gísli's brave wife Auðr, able only to bloody the nose of a

---

[2] Clover (1986a) presents a strong case for historical Norse women's participation in deeds of arms. Cf. Præstgaard Andersen (1982), and contrast Price (2002: 331–32).

[3] See Stefán Einarsson (1939: 255) and von See (1961: 130). Þórr once speaks of having fought "[b]rúðir berserk[j]a" ("Hárbarðsljóð," 37, in Neckel and Kuhn 1962–68: 1.84), which could mean "female *berserkir*," or alternatively, "the wives of *berserkir*"; his interlocutor, in any event, immediately takes this anecdote as reflecting badly on him: "Klæki vanntu þá, Þórr, er þú á kon[u]m barðir" [You won disgrace there, Þórr, since you fight against women] (st. 38, 1.84). It may not be taken for granted that the savage attributes of *berserkir* were readily transferable to female figures. For comparisons of Freydís to *berserkir*, valkyries, or both, see Stefán Einarsson (1939: 250) and Wahlgren (1986: 95) [*berserkir*], as well as Jones's passing reference to "Freydis's valkyrie-bosom" (1986: 134); and, in fiction, Désy's Freydis Karlsevni: "Je suis une Walkyrie; des femmes, je possède le sein, des hommes, je tiens l'épée. Des deux, j'ai le courage" (1990: 91); Chapin (1934: 101), epigraph to chapter IV above; Kamban: "i dette Øjeblik [var Freydis] helt og fuldt en nordisk Valkyrie" [in that instant (Freydis was) altogether a Norse valkyrie] (1936: 244); Irwin (1974: 212), epigraph to chapter III above; and Boyer: "Valkyrier-like . . . [w]ith the rage of a berserker" (1976: 215).

[4] Unarmed women do show notable fighting spirit at times (e.g., *Gísla saga* cap. 35, ÍF 6: 112; *Vápnfirðinga saga* cap. 18, ÍF 11: 62; *Sturlu saga* capp. 8, 11, in *Sturlunga saga* 1946: 1.72, 77), even to the point of pinning armed men as others stab them (*Íslendinga saga* cap. 2, in *Sturlunga saga* 1946: 1.229–30). But unarmed women are never themselves lethal combatants, naturally.

[5] For women who fail to wield weapons effectively, see, e.g., *Eyrbyggja saga* cap. 13 (ÍF 4: 23–24); *Gísla saga* cap. 37 (ÍF 6: 116–17); *Harðar saga* cap. 38 (ÍF 13: 90); *Sturlu Saga* cap. 31 (in *Sturlunga saga* 1946: 1.109); as well as examples cited in nn8–9 below. For successful exceptions to this rule, see Saxo, *Gesta* 5.xlva [Gunvara], 10.xcviib [Thyra] (1886: 149, 326); *Hervarar saga ok Heiðreks* capp. 4, 5 (FSN 2: 11, 23); *Illuga saga Gríðarfóstra* cap. 4 (FSN 3: 420); *Færeyinga saga* cap. 38 (ÍF 25: 82–83); and, after a fashion, *Vatnsdœla saga* cap. 44 (ÍF 8: 118), where a woman pretends to wield an axe in order to create the diversion necessary to cover a hunted man's escape (alluded to also in *Hallfreðar saga* cap. 10, ÍF 8: 190).

bounty hunter pursuing her husband with a swing of her purse,[6] or of her name-sake, *Bróka*-Auðr, who somehow botches the simple task of skewering a sleeping ex-husband in his bed.[7] Their sisters in the legendary sagas, where fantastic yarns abound, fare no better; some, the so-called maiden kings (*meykóngar*), aspire to govern as men, but the sagas pussyfoot around the question of their military prowess. Even Þornbjörg Eireksdóttir, the most formidably soldierlike of the maiden kings, flees before her future husband Hrólfr Gautreksson's army as soon as her battlements have been breached (earning the damning estimation that she is *hjartaragr*, 'fag-hearted'), then succumbs after a short combat in which she receives a whack to the crotch.[8] Like Þornbjörg, other weapon-wielding women in the sagas last just long enough, at best, for an up-and-coming hero to thump and tame them, earning his laurels.[9] Really the only full exception is the killer

---

[6] See *Gísla saga* capp. 31–32 (ÍF 6: 97–101; a purse is also used as a makeshift weapon in *Laxdœla saga* cap. 15, ÍF 5: 33–36). Auðr later strikes the bounty hunter a debilitating blow with a cudgel while fighting at Gísli's side, but her valor, far from earning her Gísli's respect, is undermined by his backhanded praise: "Þat vissa ek fyrir lǫngu, at ek var vel kvæntr, en þó vissa ek eigi, at ek væra svá vel kvæntr sem ek em. En minna lið veittir þú mér nú en þú mundir vilja eða þú ætlaðir, þó at tilræðit væri gott" [I've known for long that I was well-wived, but still I didn't know that I was so well-wived as I am. Yet you've assisted me less than you might have wished or intended, even though (your) blow was good,] because, given the opportunity, Gísli himself would have struck the man dead (*Gísla saga* cap. 34, ÍF 6: 112); cf. Hallgerðr's notorious refusal to help her husband in his last stand, and Gunnarr's soft-spoken response (*Brennu-Njáls saga* cap. 77, ÍF 12: 189).

[7] See *Laxdœla saga* cap. 35 (ÍF 5: 97–98). For an exceptionally subtle reading of this episode, see Miller (1990: 354–55n35). Miller also notes that Norse women "were not allowed to march out to fight, even though they could gain honor by defending" (2000: 241; cf. 252). Þórðr *kakali*'s sister Steinvör, who means "at . . . taka vápnin ok vita, ef nǫkkurir menn vill fylgja [henni]" [to take up arms and see if some men will follow (her)], acknowledges such action "minnr er at sköpuðu" [accords little with (her) nature] (*Þórðar saga kakala* cap. 2, in *Sturlunga saga* 1946: 2.6; quoted above, chapter IV, n14).

[8] See *Hrólfs saga Gautrekssonar* cap. 13 (FSN 4: 93–96). On maiden kings, see Wahlgren (1938), Kalinke (1990), and Layher (2007). Kalinke notes that "Þornbjǫrg is unique in that she not only rules her country in her capacity as king but also herself leads the country's army. She is maiden king and shield maiden rolled into one" (1986: 65). *Hjartaragr* derives from *ragr*, a loaded term for branding someone a coward, but with strong overtones of sexually deviant effeminacy; see Meulengracht Sørensen (1983: 18–20) and Ármann Jakobsson (2008: 55–63).

[9] E.g., (superhuman females) *Grettis saga* cap. 65 (ÍF 7: 212–13); *Bárðar saga* cap. 8 (ÍF 13: 124); *Gríms saga loðinkinna* cap. 1 (FSN 2: 188–90); *Sturlaugs saga starfsama* cap. 18 (FSN 3: 143); *Illuga saga Gríðarfóstra* capp. 4–6 (FSN 3: 417–24); or (human warrior maidens) Saxo, *Gesta* 3.xxviia [Sela], 5.xlvb [Alvilda], 7.lxviiia [Alvilda], 8.lxxixb [Rusla], 9.xca [Lathgertha] (1886: 87, 149, 229–30 [cited above, chapter V, n15], 267, 301); *Sögubrot af fornkonungum* cap. 9 (FSN 1: 359–60); *Bósa saga ok Herrauðs* cap. 2 (FSN 3: 284). Cf. Jesch (1991: 176–80).

Freydís of *Grænlendinga* saga, capable of executing her violent design with cold-blooded efficiency. Again like Þornbjörg, some women at arms do temporarily assume a defeminized appearance, but none permanently rids herself of her sex attributes, or even threatens to. On the contrary, the potential for resuming femininity is one of these women's most important narrative attributes.[10] Finally, no other Norse woman is rash enough to fight in the nude; men's clothes or, as in the case of Þornbjörg, actual armor are preferred.[11]

In the absence of a substantial Norse tradition of women successfully projecting lethal force against others,[12] a different frame of reference Kirsten Wolf has urged for the Freydís episode may gain credence. Seizing on the seventeenth-century variant in which Freydís actually amputates her breast and throws it at the Natives (above, pp. 26–27), Wolf sees self-inflicted violence as key to the episode. For her, so literal an embodiment of Greek etymology places Freydís closer to Classical myth than to Brynhildr.[13] Wolf suggests that the saga author (and, presumably, audience) would have glossed the "masculine and martial picture of Freydís" by reference to "the terrifying and fascinating image of Amazons," who

---

[10] Cf. Meulengracht Sørensen (1983: 22–23): "The woman in a male role is a moti[f] which carries approval in Old Icelandic literature. It by no means evokes contempt, but on the contrary is often an element in the character of a heroine. On the other hand, it is a feature to be overcome. . . . Even for valkyries, marriage is the proper outcome."

[11] E.g., *Laxdœla saga* cap. 35 (ÍF 5: 97); Saxo, *Gesta* 7.lxixa [Hagbarth in drag], 8.lxxvib [Wisna and Hetha], 9.xca [Norwegian women] (1886: 233, 258, 301); Snorri, *Edda: Skáldskaparmál* 1.2 [Skaði]; cf. *Ljósvetninga saga* cap. 11 [21] (ÍF 10: 59) [the seeress Þórhildr dons britches, a helmet and an axe in order to perform a prophesying ritual]; but cf. Saxo, *Gesta* 2.xiib [Frotho impersonating a female warrior by exchanging clothes with his maidservant] (1886: 41). On cross-dressing women in the sagas, see Wolf (1997c).

[12] Nor is such a tradition common elsewhere in medieval Europe, though Hay (2004) points out that historians have underplayed women's participation in martial affairs; cf. McLaughlin (1990) and Nicholson (1997). As Schulman comments, "the epic literature of the Middle Ages suggests that male members of the audience would have viewed such actions as women killing men with their own hands as horrible and monstrous" (2007: 233n46).

[13] Wolf argues for accepting this late variant as more authoritative than the standard reading of *S* or *H* (1996: 483–85). Cf. Isidore, *Etymologies* 9.2.64: "Amazones dictæ sunt . . . quod adustis dexterioribus mammis essent, ne sagittarum iactus inpediretur, quasi [*aneu mazon*]. Nudabant enim quam adusserant mammam. Has Titianus Vnimammas dicit. Nam hoc est Amazon, quasi [*aneu mazou*], id est sine mamma" [(They) are called Amazons . . . as in (*aneu mazon*), because they have their right breasts seared (off), so as not to impede (them in) hurling missiles; for they bared the breast they seared. Titianus calls them 'one-breasted,' for that is (the meaning of) 'Amazon,' as in (*aneu mazou*), that is 'without a breast'] (1911.1: unpaginated).

were "well known to medieval writers," though she stops short of demonstrating a direct textual link with *Eiríks saga rauða*.[14]

Wolf's attractive hypothesis hangs, however, by the slenderest of evidentiary threads. More importantly, it hardly resolves Freydís's enigma. A medieval audience, if they thought of Freydís as an Amazon, would not likely have perceived in her an antitype of Sigourney Weaver's heroic Lieutenant Ripley. In both Classical and medieval traditions, Amazons—like valkyries, troll-wives, maiden kings, and other exotic ladies—figure primarily as trouncing-fodder for male champions rather than as archetypes of virtuous female derring-do.[15]

Pivotal to Wolf's interpretation is the fact that the violence evoked in Freydís's encounter with the *skrælingar*, whether fully unleashed (as in the late variant) or only hinted at (as in all other manuscripts), specifically targets the breast. Mammary mutilation is indeed typical of Amazons; but they are not the only female figures to endure such sex-specific harm. The richest medieval harvest of ripped bodices and mutilated bodies is a vast corpus of female martyrologies, as well represented in Scandinavia as elsewhere.[16] A typical example is the passion

---

[14] Wolf (1996: 480, 483–84). Establishing such a link, tentatively at least, is not difficult. Isidore's *Etymologies* were known in medieval Iceland, indirectly at least (see Ólafur Halldórsson in ÍF 4: 362–63; cf. chapter V, n12 above for the embellishment of an Old Norse *vita* of St. Nicholas with details from Isidore). The *H* manuscript of *Eiríks saga rauða* also contains a version of *Trójumanna saga* (an Old Norse rendition of *De Excidio Troiae historia*, supplemented from other sources; see Eldevik 1993), where Amazons are mentioned; see, e.g., cap. 29: "I þan tima kom kona sv til moz við Priamo er Pentisilena het með miklv liði. hon va[r] sem karlar. mart var kvena með henni ok varv kallaðar Amazone" [At that time the woman whose name was Pentisilcna came to meet Priam with a great force. She was like men. There were a lot of women with her and they were called Amazons] (in *Hauksbók* 1892–96: 218).

[15] The Amazons known to the Norse, like their sisters elsewhere, come to a bloody end (e.g., *Trójumanna saga* capp. 32–33, in *Hauksbók* 1892–96: 222). On Amazons in Classical antiquity, see Warner (1985: 279–80). Von Bothmer (1957) offers an extensive assemblage of visual evidence. On their medieval descendents, see Kleinbaum (1983: 39–70); Fraser (1988: 23–26); Geary (2006: 26–42); and Bryan (2006). A full book-length study by Suzanne Hagedorn is reportedly underway. Hagedorn suggests (2008) that the first precursor of the modern valorization of Amazons as feminist role models occurs in Christine de Pizan's *Livre de la Cité de Dames*.

[16] For convenient overviews of the genre, see, e.g., Cazelles (1991: 3–86); Winstead (1997); and Crachiolo (2004). Some saints' *vitæ* (most, according to Unger 1877: 2.i-viii) were known to the Norse by the twelfth century, though the oldest manuscript fragments are from the thirteenth; cf. Edgren (1993: 54–56). Cormack (1994: esp. 13–68) reviews the early, maddeningly fragmentary evidence for saints' veneration in Iceland. A taste of the elusiveness of the evidence may be obtained, e.g., from Ari Þorgilsson's mention (ca. 1120–30) of an obscure source: "Ívarr Ragnarssonr loðbrókar lét drepa Eadmund enn helga Englakonung . . . af því es ritit es í sǫgu hans" [Ívarr, son of Ragnarr *loðbrókr*, had St. Edmund, king of the English, killed . . . according to what is written in his tale (*saga*)]

of St. Fides, suffering alongside her sisters Spes and Caritas. She is first stripped and scourged, but refuses to renounce Christ. Flustered, the emperor

> had both breasts cut off her with iron hooks. But all who were nearby and saw these torments and cruelties wept sorely and spoke piteously: "What atrocity have these maidens committed, that they should deserve to have such torment? Your judgment is terribly evil, O king, and these commands of yours are unjust." But from her wounds ran milk and no blood. Then the saintly Fides spoke: "How do these terrors of yours seem to you, O king? For 12 centurions beat me, and they are all exhausted, but have done me no harm. Then you had the breasts cut off me, but milk came out of my wounds and no blood. Yet you foolishly thought that you might be able to separate me from my God by these torments—but that you shall never achieve."

The enraged caesar then orders Fides grilled on a rotisserie, to no avail; nor is she harmed when boiled in pitch. Only the executioner's sword finally dispatches her, "but God's angels bore her soul to heaven, and thus she delivered to Christ the victory of her martyrdom." Like the seventeenth-century variant's Freydís, Fides (and countless other virgin martyrs) loses a breast but wins the battle. Her mastectomy is notable precisely for being so unremarkable, a passing detail in an epic litany of torment—unlike, for instance, the dramatic centrality of this cruelty in the passion of St. Agatha, often emblematized in the later Middle Ages by a dish with her severed breasts. Fides, in contrast, exemplifies just how commonplace the hewing of breasts was in the corpus of female saints' lives, allowing for its wide dissemination in the cultural discourse.[17]

(*Íslendingabók* cap. 1, ÍF 1: 4). The reference, meagre as it is, is generally taken to indicate Ari's familiarity with a *vita* of St. Edmund (Jakob Benediktsson enumerates the candidates in ÍF 1: xxii–xxiii)—yet, as far as I can tell, it could equally refer to a lost **Ívars saga Ragnarssonar*; contrast Jones (1986: 143) and Clunies Ross (2010: 16).

[17] *Fides, Spes, Caritas* cap. 3: "liet . . . slita af henni bædi briostin med iarnkrokum. En allir, þeir er hia voru ok sa þessar pislir ok grimð, gretu sarliga ok mælto med harmi: 'Hvat gerðu þessar meyiar þess endima, at þer skylldu verdar vera at hafa slika pinsl; hardla illr er dómr þinn, konungr, ok raung eru þessi boðorð þin.' En or sárum hennar rann miolk en eigi blod. Þa mælti heilog Fides: 'Hvilikar litaz þer, konungr, ognir þinar þessar, þviat .xii. hundradshofdingiar baurdu mik, ok urdu þeir allir modir, en mik sakadi ecki. Þa leztu briost af mer slita, ok kom miolk ur sárum minum en eigi blod. En þu hugsadir heimsliga, at þu mundir mik mega skilia fra gudi minum i pislum þessum, en þat fær þu alldregi gert.'. . . [e]n aund hennar baru einglar guds til himna, ok færdi hon svo Kristi sigr sins pislarvættiss" (Unger 1877: 1.372–73). Cf. the underlying Latin (Mombritius 1910: 2.380, l. 36—381, l. 46). On the pointed deployment in conversion narratives of the motif of pagan stupidity, see Grønlie (2006: 305, 316n72). For basic orientation in the legend of St. Agatha, see, e.g., Cheney (1996: esp. 5 for the rarity of

Virgin martyrs, however, are in some respects still less like Freydís than Amazons. Even setting aside the pious dimension so absent from *Eiríks saga rauða*, a typical martyr suffers harm that others inflict on her: it is not of her own doing (though she often applauds it as speeding her towards eternal bliss).[18] One category of female martyrs do specialize in self-mutilation, but it is their faces—noses, lips, eyes, ears—that are the targets of preference, not the body parts customarily kept hidden.[19] This is a sensible choice, since their self-violation

---

representations before the twelfth century; I am indebted to Hannah Byland for this reference). For pushing me to ponder the significance of Fides vis-à-vis Agatha, I thank the press's anonymous Reader 1.

[18] Like Fides, other virgin martyrs typically embrace their torments; see, e.g., *Passio Sanctarum Perpetuae et Felicitatis* 21: "tanta femina aliter non potuisset occidi . . . nisi ipsa uoluisset" [such a woman could not be slain unless she herself willed it] (Musurillo 1972: 130). The sole exception I have come across concerns a dedicated virgin so sorely tested—first stabbed in her privates by a lecherous husband, then afflicted in her breast with ergotism—that she wavers momentarily, thinking Mary has abandoned her (King Alfonso X's *Cantiga* 105, 1986: 2.22–24). See Wolf (1997b; revised in 2000: 115–30) for a mainly descriptive survey of the topos of virgin martyrs' mastectomy in Old Norse. Examples of martyred women are too numerous to cite extensively. For some female martyrs whose bosoms are singled out for torture, see *Legenda aurea*, Jacobus (1850: 171): "Quintianus jussit [Agathae] mamillam torqueri et tortam diutissime jussit abscidi" [Quintianus ordered (Agatha's) breast be wrenched and, after (it was) wrenched at great length, ordered (it) cut off] (cf. Unger 1877: 1.3–4, 9; Broby-Johansen 1947: 126); Jacobus (1850: 421): "Julianus mammillas [Christinae] praecidi mandavit" [Julianus commanded (Christina's) breasts be severed] (cf. Broby-Johansen 1947: 154–55); Jacobus (1850: 794): "Rex . . . jussit [reginam] extractis prius mamillis decollari" [the king . . . ordered (the queen) be beheaded, (her) breasts having first been torn (off)] (cf. Unger 1877: 1.417); Jacobus (1850: 900): "jussit impius praeses gladio abscidi mamillas [Barbarae]" [the irreverent governor ordered (Barbara's) breasts be cut off with a sword] (cf. Unger 1877: 1.156; Wolf 2000: 150); Jacobus (1850: 911): "ad mamillas [Dorotheae] faculae ardentes applicatae sunt" [burning brands were applied to (Dorothea's) breasts] (cf. Unger 1877: 1.325; Wolf 1997a: 95). Cf. also the third-century Coptic *Apocalypse of Elijah* 2:35 (in Frankfurter 1993: 309), which predicts that an Antichrist-like king "will command that all the nursing women be seized and be brought to him bound to suckle serpents, that their blood be sucked from their breasts to be given as poison for arrows"; I am indebted to Elizabeth S. Bolman for this reference.

[19] See Schulenburg (1986, rev. as 1998: 127–75; esp. 145–55, 175). Oddly, genital mutilation of men, conspicuously absent from legends of male martyrs tortured by others (Wolf 2000: 119), does appear as a self-inflicted injury in the immensely popular story of a pilgrim to Compostela, tricked by the Devil into castrating and killing himself; for the eleventh-century origins of this tale, see Gripkey (1938: 30). Unlike women's self-mutilation, his act is regarded as a grievous sin; he is miraculously forgiven, but recovers only his life, not his severed member (see, e.g., *Codex Calixtinus* 2.17.150ᵛ-52ᵛ [Herbers and Santos Noia 1998: 172–75]; one of many vernacular adaptations, illustrating the migration of the miracle from the repertoire of St. James to that of the Virgin [cf. p. 76 above],

is committed to preempt a violence deemed worse — a breach of their chastity by rapist or husband — and so must be visibly, revoltingly advertised.[20] At the fall of Acre (1291), for instance, a Franciscan abbess is said to have convened her nuns and urged them, "for our spouse, the Lord Jesus Christ," to follow her example: "Therefore you all do what you see me do!"

> Then the manly woman, gripping a dagger, lopped off her own nose and clotted her entire face with streaming blood. The sisters were all moved to similar love of faith and chastity; and variously wounding their faces and painting [them] with virginal gore, displayed a horrible visage to onlookers. What else [is there to say]? The Saracens entered the monastery with drawn swords, thirsting for Christian blood. The holy virgins met them fearlessly, offering those haggard dogs a horrid rather than decorous sight. Seeing whom they first marveled, then, aghast, cruelly put them all to the sword.[21]

Such virile virgins help throw bare-sarked warriors' play of sex and gender into relief. All violence presupposes a masculine perpetrator; but any specific instance

---

is in King Alfonso X's *Cantiga* 26, 1986: 1.123–26; cf. Crane 1925: 11, Dexter 1927: 23). Between the 1170s and 1221, at least three English victims of judicial castration were more fortunate, regenerating their genitals through saintly intervention; see the stories of Ailward of Westoning and Roger of Durham in William of Canterbury, *Miracula S. Thomæ cantuariensis* 2.3, 6.10–11, and Benedict of Peterborough, *Miracula Sancti Thomæ cantuariensis*, Prologus, 4.2 (1875–85: 1.156–58, 419–23, 2.26, 173–82), an anonymous of Bedford (= Ailward?) in *Thómas saga erkibyskups* cap. 92 (1875–83: 2.102–6, 283–84; cf. Beneit, *Vie de Thomas Becket* stt. 323–25, 1941: 153), and Thomas of Eldersfield in *Miracles of St. Wulfstan* 2.16 (Darlington 1928: 168–75; cf. Hyams 1986). The hagiographers note that both Ailward and Roger, though restored to virility, were less generously endowed than they had been to begin with, however.

[20] By the same logic, men's and women's noses might be targeted by others who sought to inflict cripplingly humiliating injury; see Groebner (1995; rev. as 2004: 67–86) and, for some Norse examples, *Hrólfs saga kraka* cap. 49 (FSN 1: 96) and *DD* 4: 95; cf. Greenberg (1990: esp. 58, 68, 73–74).

[21] [Arnaldus de Serranno?], *Chronica XXIV Generalium*: "'sponso nostro Domino Iesu Christo . . . Quod me igitur facere videritis, hoc omnes faciatis.' Tunc virilis mulier, arrepto gladiolo, nasum proprium mutilavit et fluente sanguine totam faciem cruentavit. Animantur sorores omnes ad simile fidei et castitatis amore et facies suas diversimode vulnerantes et cruore virgineo tingentes aspectum horribilem intuentibus praebuerunt. Quid plura? Intrant Saraceni monasterium evaginatis gladiis christianum sanguinem sitientes. Occurrunt eis sacrae virgines intrepide non vultus decorem, sed horrorem canibus illis famelicis offerentes. Qui videntes eas primo stupent, deinde horrentes omnes gladiis crudeliter occiderunt" (1897: 421). The anonymous *Chronica* was compiled no later than 1374, when the presumed author died (1897: viii-ix). I am indebted to Paul Crawford for this reference.

of violence also fixes the gender of the body it targets. Figures like Freydís or Marguerite d'Artois exhibit a schizophrenic duality, at once both (behaviorally) masculine, as perpetrators of violence, and (physically) feminine, as its victims. Like shield-maidens, however, virgin martyrs, especially those whose martyrdom includes self-mutilation, serve to remind us that victimhood (and its attendant feminine branding) is not only biologically sexed but also behaviorally gendered. Gash-nosed nuns are unusual in seizing the initiative to inflict (part of) their physical torment with their own hands, but ultimately they, too, succumb to the lethal assault of hostile Others. Even women who aspire to masculinity through their violent agency are branded female as soon as their telltale sexual bodies come under attack: one of the most famous of the early female martyrs, St. Perpetua, is a man when she triumphs—in her dreams—but a woman when she dies in the arena.[22] In the case of a detruncating nun or a Vínland vikingess, violence and victimhood are conflated not only spatially but also temporally: rather than await an adversary's blow to re-feminize them (as happens to Þornbjörg, for instance), such women's agent bodies are instantaneously proclaimed feminine by the harm that they direct at themselves. Like other self-violating women whose bosoms happen to remain covered—Théroigne, the *Vœux du héron* queen—virgin martyrs who lop off their own noses should therefore also be classified as bare-sarked warriors (see further Sidebar 8). In this sense (and without in any way subscribing to Freudian interpretation), their mutilated faces may be read as euphemized sex attributes: they ground these women physically in their sex, as Freydís's breasts do her.[23]

Just as the corporeality of violence unleashed on female martyrs serves to anchor them in their sex, so also a litany of imagined assaults on the bodies of personified vices affix them in their gender. There is nothing euphemistic about the vicious targeting of vices' bosoms.[24] The prominence given to these

---

[22] See *Passio Sanctarum Perpetuae et Felicitatis* 10, 18–21 (Musurillo 1972: 116–18, 124–30; cf. Williams 2012). Bynum notes how medieval ideas of female sexuality made "an early demise advisable" for virtuous women: "women's lives can be complete only when death has assured perpetual virginity" (1989: 202–4).

[23] Cf. Groebner (1995: 4; 2004: 71). As Fisher notes (2001: 158), "the modern notion of sexual difference in which physiological features are hierarchized (classed as either primary or secondary characteristics)" need not have obtained in the Middle Ages.

[24] See, e.g., serpents chewing on *Luxuria*'s breasts at Moissac and Auxerre (relief carvings from the second quarter of the twelfth century and ca. 1260, respectively; Hammer-Tugendhat 1987: figs. 6, 9; cf. a similar fourteenth-century Danish image, Broby-Johansen, 1947: 215 and Mills 2004 [M-K 04–046]), or *Luxuria*'s bosom pierced by a spear and gnawed on by snakes at Tavant (early twelfth-century fresco, Yalom 1997: fig. 13; this may be what Weir and Jerman describe as "a woman committing suicide on account of remorse," 1986: 71). A mid-tenth-century Coptic mural of Hell (at Tebtunis in the Fayyum; now apparently destroyed) showed the bosom of a "woman who has given her breasts for [money]" (i.e., a prostitute?) attacked or sucked by demonic serpents (Walters 1989: 202, pl. XXVIII; I am indebted to Elizabeth S. Bolman for this reference). For

8. Interpretation: Noseless maidens

The Poor Clares at Acre are not alone in their martyrdom: beleaguered nuns who cut off their noses seem to migrate among female houses across Europe. Their stories belong to a constellation of uplifting tales about women who spite their faces in desperation, to thwart unwelcome advances and amputate temptation. As St. Elizabeth vows, "if perhaps my uncle were to wish to join me to someone . . . I would slice off my own nose, so that anyone who saw me so defaced would shudder."[1]

How common were such horrific heroics in reality? Jane Tibbetts Schulenburg, the foremost authority on accounts in which nuns first mutilate themselves, then go willingly to their deaths, seems rather too ready to accept such narratives as records of historical events.[2] She cites five instances alleged to have occurred between the eighth and the twelfth century:

(1) Three hundred Hispanic nuns are said to have been martyred when "the Moors who destroyed Spain arrived." The source, however, is a chronicle written ca. 1600.[3]

(2) At Coldingham Abbey on the eve of a viking attack in 870 AD, Ebba, "the abbess, gripping a razor, sliced off her own nose and upper lip, to the very teeth." The other nuns followed suit, and the vikings, "gawking at the abbess and the sisters, each so viciously mutilated and drenched in her own blood from the sole of her foot to the crown of her head . . . set fire to the monastery, burned [it] down with all its outhouses and the recluses themselves." No record of this massacre antedates Matthew Paris's mid-thirteenth-century *Chronica majora*.[4]

---

[1] Jacobus, *Legenda aurea*: "si forte avunculus meus voluerit me alicui copulare . . . nasum mihi proprium detruncarem, ut me sic deformem quilibet exhorreret" (1850: 759). See further exempla cited by Tubach (1969: 271–72, 359, some of whose references, however, are untraceable): §3487 (Nose cut off on wedding day), §3490 (Noses of nuns cut off), §4744b (Temptation resisted by mutilation). Such tales correspond to folk motif T327.1, tale type 706B (Maid sends to her lecherous lover her eyes which he has admired; see Williamson 1932, Thompson 1955–58, and Aarne 1964); in one variant, Arnobius' early fourth-century *Adversus nationes* 5.7, 5.13 (1953: 256, 266), breasts are substituted for eyes.

[2] See Schulenburg (1986: 46 and 1998: 145).

[3] Yepes: "hasta vinieron los moros que destruyeron a España" (1959–60: 1.138).

[4] Matthew Paris: "abbatissa . . . arrepta novacula nasum proprium cum labro superiori ad dentes usque præcide[t]. . . . [T]yranni nequissimi . . . conspicientes abbatissam illam et sorores singulas tam enormiter mutilatas, et in suo sanguine a planta pedis usque ad verticem tabefactas . . . injecto igne monasterium cum omnibus officinis et ipsis sanctimonialibus concremarent" (1872–83: 1.391–92).

(3) At a date no later than the tenth century, a saintly Eusebia and her nuns are said to have suffered a similar fate at Marseilles: "a legend perhaps ancient," comments Henri Leclercq, "but of which there is no mention prior to the seventeenth century."[5]

(4) A similar massacre is located in Barcelona in 986, but, as Schulenburg herself remarks, only attested in modern accounts; thus the nineteenth-century antiquarian Domingo Reventós, for instance, archly refers to "a moth-eaten vellum" as his source for the tale.[6]

(5) At an unspecified date (1187, according to Felix Faber's fifteenth-century retelling), some nuns near Jerusalem "detruncated themselves when the region was conquered by pagans." The reference is inserted into a single (as far as I can tell), thirteenth-century manuscript of Peter the Cantor's twelfth-century *Verbum Abbreviatum*.[7]

When considered by the date of the witness rather than the date ascribed to the event, it seems that Matthew Paris's account of the heroic Ebba may well be the earliest attestation of this particular tale type. Matthew calls the tale an "exemplum" of chastity (as does the *Chronica XXIV Generalium*) — suggesting recognition of its status as edifying fable, not necessarily historical — and projects it onto the Viking Age. The other sources likewise place the events they describe in a dim, distant, and tragically heroic past. The absence of any pre-thirteenth-century witness to any of the alleged atrocities, together with the soaring popularity of this story type in later centuries (attested by its wide distribution in Latin and vernacular preachers' dossiers), points away from any actual event and suggests, instead, a literary topos that became widely disseminated from the thirteenth century onwards.[8]

---

[5] Leclercq: "[une] légende peut-être ancienne, mais dont on ne relève aucune mention [avant la 17e siècle]" (1932: 2272–73); cf. de Rey (1885: 227–30, 237–38).

[6] Reventós: "un arnat pergamí" (1869: 258); cf. Schulenburg (1998: 460n85).

[7] Baldwin: "cum subiugata esset illa regio a paganis exnaseverunt se" (1970: 2.183n29; cf. *Verbum Abbreviatum* 121, *PL* 205: 313a, and other variants cited by Baldwin). Baldwin accepts the attribution to Peter (d. 1197); on the dating of Paris BN Lat. 12011, see Delisle (1868: 33). See also Faber (1843–49: 2.132–33).

[8] See Matthew Paris (1872–83: 1.392) and *Chronica XXIV Generalium* (1897: 420n8). For use of such tales as *exempla* in later preaching, see, e.g., John of Bromyard's ca. 1348 *Summa prædicantium* C.3.6 (1585–86: 1.109^{r-v}) and Johannes Pauli's 1522 *Schimpf und Ernst* 12 (1924: 1.14–15; cf. 2.259 and Vollert 1912: 57–58).

sex attributes serves the dual purpose of associating sin with carnality in general and of feminizing the object of condemnation in particular.[25] Emphatic sexing of the vices mirrors the gendering of martyrs: the breasts and womb which signify socially laudable, essential femininity in the latter[26] function as loci of lust and temptation in the former. The bodily sites of martyrdom for the righteous become sites of torment for the damned.[27]

The impact of such religiously mutilated female bosoms on notions of violence perfectly complements the gendering of violence achieved by institutionalized *hvǫt*. On either side of the dichotomy — the martyr's good breast, wrongly tortured, or vice's bad breast, justly excoriated — such a scenario works to legitimize male violence towards female bodies. The scourging of female sex attributes is what men ought to practice (against evil women), what women should patiently

textual analogues, see, e.g., a Greek *Apocalypse of Mary* §16 (paraphrased in Pernot 1900: 236; the text is at present undatable, Mimouni 1993: 124), or a fifteenth-century Middle English exemplum from the *Gesta Romanorum* (Shepherd 1995: 375–76). The *femme aux serpents* motif is extensively discussed by Weir and Jerman (1986: 58–75) and Hammer-Tugendhat (1987: 20–22). Cf. a fifth- or sixth-century Gotland picture stone which has been interpreted as depicting a 'snake-witch' (Price 2002: 222, fig. 3.106): an apparently female nude (in outline only, with no visible breasts) clutches two snakes poised to strike at her.

[25] This point is subtly borne out in Codex Vindobonensis 2597, "the earliest and most complete" (as well as the only illuminated) extant manuscript of *Le Livre du cuers d'amours espris*, from ca. 1477 (René of Anjou 2001: xxi). The illumination on fol. 25ᵛ shows the personfication of Sloth (*Paresce*) as a woman in a disheveled red dress, unlaced to expose a breast. The corresponding text (57.1) speaks more vaguely of "sa robe descousue en plus de vingt lieux" [her dress, unstitched in more than twenty places] (2001: 54). I am indebted to Thomas D. Hill for this reference.

[26] See, e.g., St. Agatha's words, *Agathu saga meyiar* cap. 3: "Þu enn grimmazti guds ovinr, hvi skammazt þu eigi at skera briost af konu, þar sem þu hefir sialfr sogit briost modur þinnar? En ek hefi heillt briost innan i ǫnd minni, ok fædi ek þadan ǫll vit likama mins, þau sem ek helgada gudi allt fra æsko minni" [you most grievous enemy of God, are you not ashamed to chop off a woman's breast, the same as your mother's breast which you yourself sucked? Still I have an uninjured breast within my soul, from which I feed all of the sense of my body, which I hallowed to God ever since my youth] (Unger, 1877: 1.3–4); cf. the underlying Latin (Mombritius 1910: 1.38, ll. 54–58).

[27] Cf. Gregory the Great's classical formulation: after death, sinners will "cum ipsis quoque membris quibus desideria uoluptatis expleuerunt aeterni iudicii tormenta tolerare, ut tunc eos undique dolor absorbeat, qui nunc suis delectationibus subdeti, undique contra iustitiam iuste iudicantis pugnant" [endure the torments of eternal judgment in those same members with which (they) sated the desires of (their) lust, so that suffering will then wholly swallow up those who now, subject to (their) pleasures, are wholly warring against the justice of the just Judge] (*Moralia in Iob* 9.65.97, 1979–85: 1.526). See also Bynum (1989: 234) and contrast Schreiner (1994: 183). Similarly, late Roman corporal punishments are characterized by "drastic appropriateness" (MacMullen 1986: 159).

endure (from evil men).[28] Moreover, by raising the issues of how victimhood is both physically and behaviorally female and of how men relate to women's violated bodies, virgin martyrs and manifest vices clarify how genital (and *ersatz* genital) mutilation is first gendered, then sexed and, finally, eroticized.[29] That women become targets of exclusionary violence is no arbitrary choice; women are not only marginal Others, they are also objects of desire. The severing of breasts, slitting of wombs, or slicing of noses — affirming women's womanhood and men's violence — becomes a gruesome form of erotic interaction between the sexes.[30]

This pattern of sex-role socialization is striking in its crudely pornographic cocktail of bare bodies, threatened femininity, and physical abuse. Pornography is not supposed to have existed during the medieval millennium.[31] Yet the cultural artifacts discussed here clearly script a behavior gendered by subordinating female sexuality to a male license for wielding physical force:[32] martyrs, mortal sins, and Amazons (frequently depicted in Hellenic and Roman art with an

---

[28] Cf. Cole's (1995) insightful discussion of how violence is socialized into sex roles in contemporary society.

[29] Having already reserved the semantic fields of 'gender' to female and male social conduct and of 'sex' to male and female biology, I am forced to use 'eroticism' (and related terms) to signify the other everyday sense of 'sex,' viz. genital activity. My usage implies no moral or aesthetic approval; e.g., rape is 'erotic,' inasmuch as it involves genital interaction, though of course violent and unwelcome to one party.

[30] Duerr (1993: 286–95) cites numerous, disturbing analogues, from the Middle Ages to the twentieth century; for a Norse example, see *Yngvars saga víðförla* cap. 7 (FSN 2: 445). For convenience, I assume a male heterosexual norm of eroticism. This undoubtedly holds true for Norse culture as idealized in the sagas, and for the discourses of the vast majority of other societies touched on in this study (but cf. Easton 2008: 3–4, 21–24). For some Norse counter-currents, see Phelpstead (2003: esp. 11–14) and Falk (2005).

[31] Histories of pornography, like most pan-chronological sweeps, tend to leapfrog over the Middle Ages with no compunction; see, e.g., Hunt (1993: 10): "the main lines of modern pornographic tradition . . . can be traced back to sixteenth-century Italy and seventeenth- and eighteenth-century France and England (albeit with important antecedents in ancient Greece and Rome)." Cf. Wolf (1997a: 16–17n27 and 2000: 119–24), Easton (2008), and Falk (2013). The catch, of course, is in part in defining pornography, a worried issue into which I do not intend to enter.

[32] Cf. McNair (1996: 94): "Pornography 'consists principally of the exaggeration of culturally standardized sexual cues'" (misquoting Peckham 1969: 170); Cole (1995: 9): "pornography is . . . a practice of sexual subordination in which women's inferior status is eroticized and thus maintained" (cf. further MacKinnon 1989: 221: "sexual harassment . . . eroticizes women's subordination"). For my present purposes, it does not matter whether any of these attempts to define pornography correctly labels the category as a whole; the important point is that some practices of social subordination, at least, do function by exaggerating culturally standardized sexual cues. In other words, the violence underwriting (at least some) gendered power relations is eroticized.

exposed, perfect breast)[33] all breed a snuff-film sensibility, satisfying a desire to undergird men's advantage by subjecting women to eroticism and to violence.[34] Acting out social power relations on distinctively feminine bodies renders the hierarchy of gender relations sexy.

Such socialization is both widespread and effective. It is frequent in romance and ballad, but also farther afield.[35] The Middle Irish prologue to the *Cáin Adamnáin* embodies the same ideology in its clearly critical depiction of a fantastic prehistory, when women went into battle ahead of their husbands. In this barbaric period (which Adamnán is fated to reform, prefiguring the Peace of God councils), "it was the head of a woman, or her two breasts, which were taken as trophies." The aftermath of battle is imagined as littered with infants clinging to their dead mothers' nipples, streaked with milk and blood. Aptly, Adamnán's old mother urges him to resurrect a slain woman, and to "free" women in general, by exclaiming that she would offer the orphan her own breast, were it not dry.[36] The

---

[33] Yalom's interpretation of this motif is that the seared breast is covered (1997: 22–23); Warner suggests instead that the Amazons, in accordance with earliest traditions, do not mutilate themselves (1985: 367n57). In any case, the striking fact is that the (masculine) gaze of those who depicted Amazons chose to focus on an unblemished sexual attribute. Contrast Isidore, *Etymologies* 9.2.64 (cited above, n13 in this chapter): "Nudabant enim quam adusserant mammam."

[34] Cf. Fiske (1993: 134–35) and de Lauretis (1985a: 37). See also Greenshields, who tellingly observes that rape "can be functional without being approved" (1994: 106): the severity with which many patriarchal societies repress and punish individual rapists is in no way inconsistent with their institutional endorsement of the practice.

[35] An arresting example is the tale of a knight beset by a serpent, who can be rescued only by a maiden willing to sacrifice her breast to free him (though she is later magically healed or provided with a prosthesis). A late reflex occurs in Child ballad 301, "The Queen of Scotland": "'How shall I get rid o this foul beast? / It's by it I must dee.'. . . But by there came a weelfaird may, / as Troy Muir did tauk, / The serpent's furious rage to lay, / Cut aff her fair white pap. / As soon as she the same had done, / And in ane hour the wound was heald. / That nae mair pain had she" (stt. 13–15, and cf. st. 18, in Child 1882–98: 5.177). Cf. *First Continuation of Perceval* Carados 3.11–15 (Roach 1949–83: 1.170–231, 2.296–369, 3:1.164–93); Clerk of Troyes, *Renart le contrefait* (Tarbé 1847–64: 13.79–82; Raynaud and Lemaitre 1914: 1.46–47); Wisse and Colin (1888: 115–63); *Chronicon Briocense* capp. 181–82 (Le Duc ante-1987: 29r-31r [BN 6003 60^{r-v} / BN 8899 62^{v}-63^{r}]; I am deeply indebted to André-Yves Bourgès, Michael Jones, Bertrand Yeurc'h, and Isabelle Berthou for making available to me Gwenaël Le Duc's transcription, left unpublished at his death in 2006; see also the French translation in Barthélemy 1866: 241–42, repr. in Le Menn 1985: 21–22); "Santes Henori" (Luzel 1868–90: 1.161–68; cf. Le Menn 1985: 9–20, 59–77); and Campbell (1860–62: 1.xcv-xcvi; see also Le Menn 1985: 36–37, 97–101). See further Harper (1898); Paris (1899); Heller (1940); Fraser (1962); Laurent (1987); and Constantine (1996: 70–72).

[36] *Cáin Adamnáin* 3–8, quoting from Meyer's translation (1905: 2–7); cf. Ní Dhonnchadha's paraphrase (translating snippets; 2001: 26–27) and Márkus's translation

contrast she sets up is stark: a free woman's proper function is to suckle babies, while a woman who risks her life in battle is enslaved. The text's nightmare vision predicates women's indenture in archaic society on their participation in warfare, the violence of which is pictured as unleashed on their bodies. That these bodies are sexed as unfit for war makes them, at the same time, the women's crime and their punishment. Women's liberation takes the form of their exclusion from the sphere of public violence, confining them to domestic nurturing. Brute force is sequestered as a prerogative of men alone.[37]

The seepage of this pornographic acculturation from the religious rhythms of hagiography to secular mythic history, already evident in Adamnán's legend, may be further illustrated with a striking Icelandic example. The mutilation of sex attributes—a fulcrum motif in the martyrdom narratives of virgin saints, demoted to etiologic explanation in the Irish legal tract—is little more than an *obiter dictum* in *Íslendinga saga*'s minute catalogue of outrages committed during a 1228 nighttime raid on a protagonist's farmstead: here, a priest is stabbed over a layman's protests that he should enjoy privilege of clergy; there, a servant is struck down as he steps groggily out of doors; elsewhere, bloody sabres

---

(1997: 8–11). Ní Dhonnchadha, who tentatively seeks an historical basis for this tale (2001: 19–20), assigns the prologue to the late tenth or early eleventh century (2001: 16). I am indebted to Máire Ní Mhaonaigh for bringing this study (updating Ní Dhonnchadha 1982) and Márkus (1997) to my attention. A truncated version of the tale, preserved in the scholia of a martyrology attributed to the ninth-century Oengus Céle Dé, may represent an earlier tradition; in Stokes's translation (1905: 211): "It came to pass that Adamnán was once travelling in Mag Breg with his mother on his back, and they saw two battalions smiting each other. It happened, moreover, that Rónait [Adamnán's mother] saw a woman, with an iron sickle in her hand, dragging another woman out of the opposing battalion, and the sickle was in her pap. For at that time women as well as men used to be delivering battle. Then Rónait said: 'Thou shalt not carry me out of this place, until women are freed for ever from things of yon kind,' i.e., from fighting and hosting. Then Adamnán promised that thing. There chanced to be a great convention in Ireland. So Adamnán with the pick of Ireland's clerics went (thither) and freed the women." On the scholia, see Stokes (1905: xlvii–xlviii), and on the dating of this account, Hull (1940: 336).

[37] Contrast the Egyptian *A(l)-Sha'ab*'s editorial of 1 February 2002, commemorating Wafa Idris, the first Palestinian female suicide bomber, who blew herself up in Jerusalem on 27 January 2002: "It is a woman who teaches you today a lesson in heroism, who teaches you the meaning of Jihad, and the way to die a martyr's death. . . . It is a woman who today teaches you, oh Muslim women, the meaning of true liberation, with which the women's rights activists have tempted you. . . . It is a woman who has now proven that the meaning of [women's] liberation is the liberation of the body from the trials and tribulations of this world . . . and the acceptance of death with a powerful, courageous embrace" (translated, with editorial ellipses, in MEMRI 2002; quoted, without full attribution, in Bloom 2007: 98; see also chapter VIII, n12 below).

are rattled to terrorize the mistress of the household, just risen from childbed.[38] Only towards the end of the anecdote does someone mention in passing that among the injured is a "woman whose two breasts have been hewn off." The victim is not even named, though her identity may be adduced from a later mention of Þorbjörg *ysja* [the Gossip], probably an elderly domestic,[39] who dies of wounds sustained during the raid.

Ysja is no Amazon. The saga's indifference towards the circumstances of her injury and the torments she endures, only fleetingly hinted at, as she slowly expires for two long days are consistent with her low standing in the saga author's eyes.[40] In military and social terms, she is a non-entity; her mutilation appears as

---

[38] *Íslendinga saga* capp. 71–72: "Sveinn prestr Þorvaldsson [tók] hægindi ok bar af sér, er þeir lögðu ok hjuggu til hans [ok] varðist röskliga. Snorri saurr hét sá, er lá næstr honum útar frá. Hann tók til orða: 'Sækið at oss ólærðum mönnum, en látið vera prestrinn í friði.' Var þá sótt at Snorra, ok var hann særðr til ólifis. . . . en Sveinn prestr [var] litt sár" [The priest Sveinn Þorvaldsson (took) a pillow and parried as they stabbed and chopped at him, (and) fended for himself valorously. The man lying farther out next to him was called Snorri *saurr*. He spoke up: 'Attack us *illitterati* but leave the priest in peace.' Snorri was then attacked, and he was mortally injured. . . . but the priest Sveinn (was) slightly wounded] (1946: 1.326–27, 329); "þegar er [Þormóðr] kemr fram í stéttrinar, er höggvit í fang honum, ok var hann særðr til ólifis. . . . Þormóðr valskr hafði mikit sár á bringu" [as soon as (Þormóðr) steps out onto the pavement, he is struck in the breast, and he was mortally injured. . . . Þormóðr *valskr* had a great wound in his chest] (1946: 1.327, 329); "Solveig húsfreyja hafði fætt barn skömmu áðr, ok var hon þá risin af hvílunni ok lá í stofu. . . . Þeir gengu at hvílu Solveigar með brugðnum ok blóðgum vápnum ok hristu at henni ok [hótuðu henni]. En af öllu saman, skapraun hennar ok sjúkleika, þá brá henni nökkut við slík orð" [Mistress Solveig had borne a child shortly before, and she had then risen from bed and lay in the sitting room. . . . They went up to Solveig's bed, brandishing bloodied weapons, and waved (these) at her and (threatened her). But what with everything, her agitation and sickness, she was somewhat shaken by such words] (1946: 1.326–27). This episode is thoroughly treated in Grove (2008).

[39] *Íslendinga saga* cap. 71: "kon[a sú], er brjóstin bæði váru af höggvin" (in *Sturlunga saga* 1946: 1.328). The saga author never explains who Ysja is, nor whether she is indeed the nameless mastectomy victim (an identification which is nevertheless generally accepted). She is described in a verse as a "g[ö]m[ul] . . . kerlin[g]" [old hag] (*Íslendinga saga* v. 37; in *Sturlunga saga* 1946: 1.331); the noun, especially, suggests not only her age but also low social status (cf. Overing 1999: 218). On the other hand, she does merit a name and seems not to be included in an impersonal roll call of injured help staff ("Þá váru enn sárir karlar þrír ok konur tvær" [three (serving) men and two women were also then wounded], 1946: 1.329), and so may be thought to have been an intimate of the master's family; the numbers of casualties, as the editors note (1946: 1.565n72²), do not tally properly anyhow, and so cannot be used to argue her into or out of any grouping. It seems likeliest she should be thought of as a representative of the literary type 'the old nurse.'

[40] See *Íslendinga saga* capp. 71–72: "[Kristrún] sagði þó hlut sárra manna yfrit þungan, þótt hon næði um at binda ok smyrslum á at ríða. Hon sagði ok konu þá, er brjóstin

collateral damage, inflicted unintentionally in the heat of indiscriminate brutalities. She is harmed not as an active subject who pays the dues for having accepted the risks of engaging in violence, but as a mute item of scenery, shattered by a blow gone wide of the mark. Yet precisely because of her insignificance, her killing has propaganda value.[41] As the raid comes to be commemorated in verse, Ysja waxes increasingly visible, irony playing on the tension between the raiders' heroic pretensions of reciprocal, male-on-male violence, and the painfully feminine outcome of their onslaught:

Mikil vas ös, þás Ysju	[What] a great host it was, when fellows
aldrtjón buðu ljónar,	tendered life's termination to Ysja!
sárs ruðu seggir dreyra	Heroes reddened with gore the 'icicle of the
svell, áðr Þorbjörg felli	wound' [=sword], before Þorbjörg might fall [dead].[42]

Fully four of eleven biting verses composed in the wake of the raid mention Ysja's killing; she is singled out by name more often than any other individual involved in the affray. Clearly, the gains to be made from her unhappy end exceed advertisement of the attackers' clumsy incompetence. Ysja—not a wounded cleric or a swooning landlady or other non-combatant victims caught up in political violence in which they may not have a hand—is picked as a shorthand emblem of innocent suffering, bringing calumny on the attackers. It is difficult to avoid the conclusion that what makes her so iconic is not just her sex and age but also the manner in which she died.

Yet nowhere are political dividends cashed by explicitly intercutting her horrific passion with that of virgin martyrs, emblems *par excellence* of victimized innocence. The easiest explanation for such rhetorical oversight is that the saga author (or, taking the saga at historical face value: the verses he cites) reproduces the motif of pectoral mutilation but is not consciously aware of its intertextual depths. In his mind (if Ysja is considered a literary figure), his character's breasts simply must be hacked off to allow her to pose as purity murdered; alternatively

---

bæði váru af höggvin, yfrit þungt at tekna, þótt þau næði smyrslum þeim, er til væri. . . . Þrír önduðust ór sárum. Lifði Þorbjörg ysja tvær nætr" [(Kristrún) said the lot of the injured would be terribly harsh even if she managed to bandage and rub ointments in (their wounds). She also said that the woman, whose two breasts had been hewn off, would have it terribly harsh, even if she got the ointments that were there. . . . Three died of their wounds. Þorbjörg *ysja* lived for two nights] (in *Sturlunga saga* 1946: 1.328–29).

[41] Cf. *Eyrbyggja saga* cap. 18 (ÍF 4: 36–37), where Þórarinn *svarti* is denigrated for having chopped off a woman's hand during a heated mêlée, and *Færeyinga saga* cap. 38 (ÍF 25: 82–83), where Þúríðr's valiant orchestration of the defence of her farmstead is undercut by her taunting of the attackers as setting upon leaderless men ("hǫfuðlaus[ir] menn").

[42] *Íslendinga saga* v. 36 (in *Sturlunga saga*, 1946: 1.330–31); cf. Miller (1990: 208) and Grove (2008: esp. 104).

(if Ysja and the verses composed about her are considered historical), the fact that she alone happened to suffer mastectomy makes her the ideal candidate for the skalds to raise from bare battle statistic to human-interest story. Either way, what grants her tragedy the pathos necessary for corroding her attackers' respectability is its effortless assimilation to hagiographic pornography.[43] Female breasts and male violence make for titillating outrage. In a similar way, we may suspect, Freydís's evocation of mastectomy may aim to shock her audience—not by transgressing against their moral standards and expectations but by confirming them.

There are additional, subtler indications of eroticism in Freydís's presentation. Her unique name, if not as glamorous as Marilyn, certainly befits a pin-up: besides *dís*, 'female spirit,' a common element in feminine personal names, it includes the infrequent theophoric *Frey-*, alluding to the priapic fertility god Freyr or to his licentious female hypostasis, Freyja.[44] The reminiscence, if only faint, of the Virgin's bared bosom may even have washed Freydís in some of Mary's divine sexy glow; the Virgin, simultaneously elevated and humanized into an ideal of impossible femininity—"[e]nough to make any woman suffer, any man dream," in Julia Kristeva's pithy formulation—took over some of the attributes of pre-Christian fertility deities and became the ultimate pin-up herself.[45] Freydís's fortuitous pregnancy further sexualizes her, endowing her with

---

[43] On the question of *Sturlunga saga*'s historicity, see Clover (1985: 255) and Úlfar Bragason (1986 and 2010). A comparable, secular reflex of the hagiographers' mammary fixation occurs in *Raoul de Cambrai* 72, where Bernier's lament for his mother zooms in on "Celes mameles dont ele me norri / [qe] vi je ardoir" [those breasts with which she nourished me, (which) I saw burn] (1992: 96).

[44] Cf. chapter II, n25 above. 'Frey-' is quite a rare theophoric: only Freygerðr (five attestations) and Freysteinn (eleven) have any notable currency (Lind 1905–31: 1.282–85, 2.280–81); I am indebted to Orri Vésteinsson for drawing my attention to this issue. For a famous ithyphallic figurine, interpreted as Freyr, see, e.g., Price (2002: 220, fig. 3.104). For Freyja's promiscuity, see, e.g., "Lokasenna," 30, 32 (in Neckel 1962–68: 1.102–3). Freyja is usually called Freyr's sister, following Snorri Sturluson's thirteenth-century rationalization of the Old Norse pantheon; from both their names ('Lady' and 'Lord,' respectively) and functional attributes, however, it seems likelier that Freyja and Freyr originated in a single divine entity with two (gendered) hypostases. See also Björn Þorsteinsson: "in the *Eiríks saga* [Freydís is] endowed with the appearance of a fertility goddess" (1962–65: 185).

[45] Kristeva (1986: 171). Warner contends that "[t]he Virgin can never . . . be said to be the tutelary goddess of sex" (1976: 278), but amply disproves her own claim (1976: 274–84); Camille (1989: 220–41, esp. 237–41) discusses Mary's appropriation of narrative themes and iconographic motifs associated with Venus. Cf. Drews (1928: 171); Graef (1963–65: 1.226–28, 248–50, 260, 317); Matter (1990: 151–77); Besserman (2006); and Miles (2008: 14–15; cf. 71–74). Likewise, cf. Jacobus's telling need to proclaim that, "cum Maria pulcherrima fuerit, a nullo tamen unquam potuit concupisci . . . quia virtus suae castitatis cunctos adspicientes penetrabat" [although Mary was most beautiful, she could

Figure 8: *Très Riches heures du Duc de Berry*, ca. 1415, 25ᵛ: Adam and Eve

From Longnon and Cazelles (1969: fig. 20; cf. the prominent abdomens of the ladies in some of the better-known calendrical images in this manuscript, e.g., May [5ᵛ]; June [6ᵛ]; August [8ᵛ]; September [9ᵛ])

Figure 9: Piero della Francesca, *Madonna del parto*, fresco, ca. 1460, Museo della Madonna del Parto, Monterchi, Italy
The Virgin's posture is sexually suggestive, even aggressive, with one arm akimbo and gaze directed straight at the viewer; her other hand moves to part her dress, a gesture echoed by the angels' parting of the curtains from which she emerges; her undergarment is already revealed through a slit resembling the vaginal opening.
From Field (2005: fig. 5.31)

an *ad hoc* prominent belly—whose erotic potential blossomed in late medieval iconography, rivalling that of an exposed back in Roman art, or cleavage to a modern eye (see Figs. 8 and 9).[46] Finally, the female bosom, though not fetishized in the same way or to the same extent as in modern discourse, still could enhance Freydís's desirability in medieval eyes, too.[47] This accumulation of signals ensures that, in Freydís, the object of violence is also an object of desire.

Nudity and other, less blatant cues anchor the bare-sarked warrior in femininity, but the weapon in her hand only masculinizes her to the extent that it transforms her into an auto-pornograph. Eroticism and violence, pornographically juxtaposed, pulsate in Irish legal prehistory, in legends of virgin martyrs, even in Ysja's eulogies. Freydís, like the *Vœux du héron* queen, funnels this volatile concoction into a powerful encitement of her male compatriots. The eroticism of some other bare-sarked warriors is still more pronounced, but—since most medieval and modern cultures regard such ribaldry with moral indignation—often only if they are depicted from a hostile viewpoint. Thus, the French printer refers to the "Villette" of the women accompanying Théroigne: these women are fashioned as not merely female but effeminate, not merely bare-bottomed but available for explicitly non-reproductive penetration.[48] Like the female

---

be lusted after by none . . . because the virtue of her chastity pierced all onlookers] (1850: 164 ; likewise, Thomas of Cantimpré, *Bonum universale* 2.28, ca. 1480: [62ʳ] = 2.29.5, 1605: 276). Protestant attacks on the bare-breasted Virgin in iconography (see Marti and Mondini 1994: 84, citing Luther and Zwingli; note esp. the latter's juxtaposition of Mary with "ein Magdalena so huerisch gemaalet"; Heal 2007: 56), as well as Counter-Reformation censorship (see Marti and Mondini 1994: fig. 54; Miles 2008: 10, 25; Heal 2007: 229), confirm an uneasy awareness of Marian eroticism in the sixteenth century. Attempts to differentiate 'truly' erotic images, i.e., ones designed to arouse, from sexually suggestive ones serving other purposes (see, e.g., Johns 1982: 143; Weir and Jerman 1986), strike me as overly precious: cultic imagery capable of sexually arousing worshipers surely must bode well for fertility; cf. Easton (2008: 3–4) and chapter VI, n18 above. See also Clark-Flory (2011).

[46] See Hollander: "In the erotic imagination of [Renaissance] Europe, it was apparently impossible until the late seventeenth century for a woman to have too big a belly" (1978: 98); cf. Easton (2008: 6–7); Miles (1989: figs. 4, 12); as well as the trophy bride in Jan van Eyck's famous Arnolfini double portrait (Hall 1994: pl. 1). Patristic polemics against indulging the belly suggest that laypeople found fleshy bodies alluring in earlier centuries, too; see, e.g., Tertullian, *De Ieiunio* 17.6–7 (1954: 2.1276), and cf. Sandnes (2002: 223–36). For Roman erotic sensibilities, see Montserrat (1996: 214).

[47] Cf., e.g., *Vie de Sainte Marie l'égyptienne* [*T*] 177–80 (Dembowski 1977: 36–37; contrast 641–44, 1977: 47; cf. *Vida de Santa María egipciaca* 221–24, 736–39, Alvar 1970–72: 2.56, 77–78); Marie de France, "Lanval," 100–6 (1944: 60); *Sir Gawain and the Green Knight*, 1740–41 (1967: 48); Chaucer, *Troilus and Criseyde* 3.1250 (1987b: 530); and William Paris, *Life of St. Christina* 441–42 (2003: 239).

[48] See chapter III, n3 above. Cf. Parsons (1995 and 2004) on the angst surrounding awareness of queens' sexuality.

exhibitionism commonplace nowadays in encouragement (or protest) of manly displays of prowess—almost invariably articulated in ways that affirm rather than transgress dominant ideological hierarchies of erotic subordination—the bare-sarked warrior's implied sexual suffering correlates with her viewers' gendered violent pleasure.[49]

---

[49] Cheerleaders offer an obvious gratification of male machismo through (bowdlerized) female exposure, but flashing also erupts frequently at the margins of sports arenas (as evinced, e.g., by a preemptive ban on nudity at the festivities marking the New Orleans Saints' 2010 Super Bowl victory; see TMZ 2010). Larissa Riquelme, a Paraguayan soccer fan who became a staple image of the 2010 World Cup, practically parodied the point: news stories, invariably illustrated with photos celebrating her titanic cleavage, followed Riquelme's reported vow to run naked through the streets of Asunción if her team should win the games—and, after Paraguay dropped out, her renewed vow to do so anyhow, as "a present to all of the players, and for all the people in Paraguay to enjoy" (Huffington Post 2010c; cf. iidem 2010a and 2010b). Bared breasts may occasionally even be observed in encitement to armed combat; see, e.g., Duerr (1993: fig. 6), Liebrecht (2009), Mak (2014). For subversive appropriation of the ritual juxtaposition of eroticism and violence, aimed at discouraging violence, see, e.g., Johnston (2008), Khaleeli (2011) and Pilkington (2011).

VIII. Rehabilitating a Vínland Vet

Freydis yelled — no one heard her — "Cowards!" . . .
　　　　　She stood hard-winded against a tree,
Her eyes in a blaze of fury fit to consume countrymen,
　Norwegians, and foe — all or any alive . . . .
　　　　　As the Skraelings rushed,
　Freydis moved out like a tranced woman,
Gray in the face — hair mad — the bodice torn full off
　her great breasts.
She seized the huge sword. Turning she screamed
　at the Skraelings,
And wildly advancing, she struck the blade flat to her
　naked flesh. They stopped — slings slack,
And in that moment an arch of arrows curved from the woods
　and shattered upon them.
　　　　　　　　　　Scott, *The Dark Sister* (1958: 93–94)[1]

Freydís's story fits snugly into a cultural matrix which may fairly be described, in a terminology distinctly no longer fashionable, as patriarchal.[2] This subliminal patriarchy helps explain the ease with which *Eiríks saga rauða* elides the encounter with ethnic aliens into an intra-societal confrontation, in which the Other is female rather than American. Scrutinizing Freydís solely as a passive object of violence (and of desire), however, risks downplaying her role as an agent subject. Even where she is said to lose a breast, it is at her own hands: if her injury (like those of Fides and Ysja) is inflicted in the course of male-on-female violence, then it is a sequence in which she gets to play both the female and the male roles. And, like ill-used virgin martyrs and the hapless woman whom Adamnán resurrected, Freydís gets to see her passion play lead to triumph. A happy ending,

---

[1] Cf. Hewlett (1918: 250–51), Boyer (1976: 214–19), and Clark (1994: 260–61).

[2] Phelpstead finds a similar ideology of patriarchy in *Hrólfs saga kraka*, a text he (like others) believes to be based on traditions going as far back as the fifth century but which he sensibly reads in its extant form as a fourteenth- or early fifteenth-century saga (2003: 1–2, 4–5, 17). The ideological consonance between *Hrólfs saga kraka* and *Eiríks saga rauða* may lend further, indirect support to a late dating of the latter (cf. chapter V, n43 above).

then, for Freydís? Is she, as Aileen Ajootian characterizes Classical hermaphrodites, an ultimate "happy couple"?[3]

What ensures the bare-sarked warrior's effectiveness is a literary need to balance her topless-heavy womanhood with some hardcore manliness. She is simultaneously the victim on the receiving end of eroticizing violence and the virile perpetrator who unleashes it. A whetting (or supplicant) stance, exhibitionism, and victimhood all help overdetermine the bare-sarked warrior's femininity. At the same time, the special cross-gendering political license of *hvǫt* (or flyting), an aggressive breach of modesty, and her willingness to wield a weapon in anger all grant her access to effective (though temporary) masculinity. A *femina femininissima* in so many respects, she is accorded honorary hyper-masculinity to even the odds. Lesser men must fight if they are to conquer: a Freydís or a Théroigne just needs to stand there, bearing the insignia of her *topos*, for all to tremble.[4] In a sense, then, the reading of Freydís's performance as battlefield magic has something to commend it—means and end are indeed causally discontinuous—but bare-sarked magic has more to do with the literary pursuit of ideological purposes than with any practices real-life Norsewomen may have engaged in. I do not trivialize the probability that the Norse had various superstitions concerned with manipulating cosmic powers through human agency, perhaps even ritual techniques similar to those which the saga depicts. But the question of actual magical practices is largely irrelevant to Freydís's efficacy against the *skrælingar*. As a structural feature of the *topos*, a bare-sarked warrior's magic has to do with more mundane sleight of hand: an author's skill in redirecting attention from the clash between ingroup and outgroup men to the symbolism of internal gender turmoil.[5]

In a patriarchal hierarchy where genders are stratified, the bare-sarked warrior's excess virility elevates her above most men, just as her superfluity of feminine indices degrades her below most women.[6] There are no half measures with her. As victim, she does not lag behind the most piteous martyr; as warrior, she puts to flight enemies against whom male heroes would have had to risk life and limb. Unlike everyday whetters or supplicants, the bare-sarked warrior emerges where society faces a catastrophic threat from categorical Others. Against these she is able to wage total war; but her secret weapon is not so much to overcome the alien risk as to divert attention away from it and onto domestic concerns,

---

   [3] Ajootian (1997).

   [4] Marguerite d'Artois and Philippa in the *Vœux du héron* attain impressive victories, too, though more difficult to gauge because they are not directly waged against an enemy. The nuns at Acre go to their deaths; but for *sponsae Christi*, this too is an ultimate triumph.

   [5] Cf. Poole's perceptive comments on the similarity of metaphor and magic (1991: 131).

   [6] As Hanawalt (1998) notes, marginalization should not be equated with degradation: social elevation or horizontal differentiation may spell exclusion just as well as relegation to an inferior status.

transubstantiating historical reality into literary convention. To be able to reorder risk priorities, she must herself breach category boundaries; thanks to her excessive gender characteristics, she is able to overcome Others too perilous for anyone else to deal with. As Jacques Moreau writes, "'shameless women' . . . apply the most desperate remedy to a terrible danger: normally, their act would lead to disastrous consequences, but . . . [i]n a dire situation, the monstrous, the dreadful may effect salvation." Capitalizing on "the reversability of pure and impure," the bare-sarked warrior short-circuits cosmic power lines, to explosive effect.[7]

At the same time, however, the very transgression that arms her for conflict with the threatening interlopers turns her into a conceptual abomination, herself a source of danger for her society. The recurring resort to a bare-sarked warrior proves that this intra-social risk is more acceptable than the external one: although dangerous ("polluting," in Mary Douglas's terminology, or "abject," in Kristeva's), this categorical abomination is at least a familiar chimera. Her known ambivalence disambiguates a situation where society faces an unknown, supplying a framework in which the routine of engrained ritual can take over from the laborious desperation of conscious decision making.[8] By calling attention to the symbolic peril they themselves embody, Freydís, Théroigne, the *Vœux du héron* queen—even the persistent Ethiopic Virgin—obviate the urgency of facing up to the real and indomitable perils of *skrælingar*, conscripted regulars, the flower of French knighthood, or human sinfulness. They hijack the podium for themselves, muzzling the fearsome foreign foes whom they muscle aside. This silencing of riotous Others at last allows the bare-sarked warrior's male allies to find their own voice, too, rallying their sense of their own agency.

None of this diversionary skirmishing, of course, may take place on actual battlefields; it is strictly the prerogative of retrospective retellings. Yet, because such retellings (or, in Théroigne's case, foretelling) allow themselves to be read as historiography, they mold societies' concrete sense of their own histories. The tag

---

[7] Moreau: "Il faut, je crois, tenir compte avant tout du caractère ambigu du sacré, de la réversibilité du pur et de l'impur. . . . [L]es 'femme impudiques' . . . appliquent-elles à un danger terrible le remède le plus désespéré: en temps normal, leur acte entraînerait des conséquences désastreuses, mais . . . [d]ans une situation critique, le monstrueux, le redoutable peuvent apporter le salut" (1951: 300). Cf. also Bloom: "women defying tradition to sacrifice their lives for the Palestinian cause ha[ve] drawn more attention to the despair of the Palestinian people" (2007: 100).

[8] See Douglas (1966: 68–72; cf. 1966: 155–56 and Rayner 1992: 91) and Kristeva (1982). The very existence, let alone the definition and understanding, of 'ritual' is hotly contested in the scholarship; for the present purposes, all that matters is that the behaviors some scholars identify as ritual are "repetitive, standardized," and as such can be performed more-or-less automatically, with little cognitive effort (Muir 2005: 6); cf. Falk (forthcoming), cap. 5.

"exemplum," attached to the nuns at Acre, tends to drop from view; the banner of the real flies over Fides, Philippa, and Freydís. For this reason, to insist, as I have done throughout this book, that the bare-sarked warrior is a literary topos rather than a class of actual persons does not in the least diminish her historical significance or impact. "Cultural acts," Clifford Geertz observes, in his inimitable style, "the construction, apprehension, and utilization of symbolic forms, are social events like any other; they are as public as marriage and as observable as agriculture." The bare-sarked warrior is an ideological fantasy, a prism through which a society purposefully (mis)perceives its own historical reality and strives to project its priorities onto a still nascent future. She is, in Daniel Kahneman's words, a "[n]arrative fallacy" (albeit one with very tangible consequences) "aris[ing] inevitably from our continuous attempt to make sense of the world," and she fosters the "pernicious illusion . . . that the world is more knowable than it is[: that] we understand the past, which implies that the future should also be knowable."[9] By rendering past events foreseeable in retrospect, playing the cultural searchlight of ideational reality on the insufferable opacity of lived experience, the bare-sarked warrior confirms a society's capacity for making sense of its past and controlling its circumstances into the present and future.

Violently or otherwise, Freydís fails to engage the Natives directly because (as the *Grœnlendinga saga* author succinctly puts it) "neither understood the other's speech."[10] With no reciprocity between the two peoples, the saga author—like Freydís and, in all likelihood, the historical Norse explorers of Vínland—has no language for figuring First Contact in a terminology of intra-societal exchange. The *skrælingar* are too unfathomable to be the primary audience of Freydís's display in any believable sense. On the far side of the glade, the Norse men find Freydís almost as uncanny. Her Otherness is qualitatively quite different, however: whereas the Natives are exempt from Norse structures of signification, Freydís's alienation from her compatriots stems from her inability to be incorporated into male-on-male sociability, not from novelty.[11] Her generic enough

---

[9] Geertz (1966: 91); Kahneman (2011: 199, 201). Anticipating Kahneman, Geertz goes on to say: "Man depends upon symbols and symbol systems with a dependence so great as to be decisive for his creatural viability and, as a result, his sensitivity to even the remotest indication that they may prove unable to cope with one or another aspect of experience raises within him the gravest sort of anxiety: '[Man] can adapt himself somehow to anything his imagination can cope with; but he cannot deal with Chaos. Because his characteristic function and highest asset is conception, his greatest fright is to meet what he cannot construe—the "uncanny," as it is popularly called'" (1966: 99, quoting Langer 1957: 287).

[10] *Grœnlendinga saga* cap. 6: "Hvárigir skilðu annars mál" (ÍF 4: 262).

[11] Again, it is neither necessary nor desirable to subscribe to a Freudian interpretation of the uncanny in order to recognize the aptness of his description of the phenomenon as a "species of the frightening that goes back to what was once well known and had long been familiar," especially liable to occur when "beliefs that have been *surmounted*

evocations of the heroic and pornographic commonplaces of male-on-female violence, or of female-on-male manipulation, embroil Freydís in patriarchal gender politics but do not gain her entry into normative masculinity. For all her efforts, the bare-sarked warrior never wins full acceptance into men's ingroup definition of Mankind; she is oil on water, defining the margins of this membership by floating just outside them. Freydís thus serves the saga author as a vehicle for intruding perennial worries over women's Otherness into the unique story of the historic meeting between two ethnic groups who are as much each other's Other as Earth's narrow confines will allow.

For the Théroigne printer, an armed woman in raised skirts emblematizes a world fractured and disarrayed, much like the fictional prehistory imagined in the prologue to *Cáin Adamnáin*. A similar imaginary world-disorder governs Freydís's medieval Canadian extravaganza. In the Icelandic author's social ethos, too, *hvatr* conduct is gendered masculine, *blauðr* feminine; women are excluded from the political public sphere, except through narrowly circumscribed channels (like whetting), and from the martial sphere, except as victims; and women's sexuality is taboo, except as an eroticized object of masculine violence. Only in the specific set scenario prescribed by the bare-sarked topos (i.e., under an external threat so severe that the men, society's regular defensive arm, waver) do certain women acquire special dispensation to transgress against each of these exclusions. Such women teeter perilously close to the line demarcating the genders, embodying a challenge to the men in their vicinity: that they should come to their rescue by reinstating order—or rather, that they should rescue order by reinstating their womanhood.[12] The Son of God Himself is not immune to such manipulation.

---

appear to be once again confirmed"; predictably, Freud also pauses to note that, for many men, "there is something uncanny about the female genitals" (2003: 124, 155, 151, emphasis original). The bare-sarked warrior toys with men's perception of femininity, representing it in a fashion that at once confirms and supersedes male stereotypes. As I have argued above (and cf. pp. 121–22 below), however, her uncanny effect is culturally and historically constructed, rather than deriving inevitably from any innate psychology.

[12] Much the same analysis may be applied to the English court in the *Vœux du héron*, to the convent of Poor Clares in Acre, etc. Cf. King (1986: 65, 67–68), and Geary on the valence of Amazon tales in Classical sources (2006: 29–30). Cf. *A(l)-Sha'ab*'s eulogy for suicide bomber Wafa Idris: "It is a woman who teaches you today a lesson in heroism, who teaches you the meaning of Jihad, and the way to die a martyr's death. It is a woman who has inscribed, in letters of fire, the battle of martyrdom that horrified the heart of the enemy's entity. It is a woman who has shocked the enemy, with her thin, meager, and weak body. . . . It is a woman who blew herself up, and with her exploded all the myths about women's weakness, submissiveness, and enslavement. . . . It is a woman, a woman, a woman who is a source of pride for the women of this nation and a source of honor that shames the submissive men with a shame that cannot be washed away except by blood" (in MEMRI's translation, 2002; see also chapter VII, n37 above).

The Freydís episode—couched (within the text) in the Norse idiom of whetting, aimed (beyond the text) to entertain and educate an audience steeped in the
values of European patriarchy—stresses interaction between the sexes within
civilized society, at the expense of representing confrontation across the inter-
continental cultural divide. The homely familiarity of Freydís's gendered Otherness and the imponderable vastness of the gulf between societies are wholly
codependent; both are complementary effects generated by the text, assimilating
Freydís firmly to culturally resonant stereotypes so as to distract from the genuinely problematic, unintelligible, unrepresentable alienness of the *skrælingar*. The
saga author strips Freydís for the same reason that he impregnates her: to mark
her with the utmost biological stigmata of femininity. He needs to anchor her in
a sissy physique as a foil to attributing to her a butch course of action. The blade
he puts into her hand is thus reserved for beating her own breast: her usurped
masculine aggressiveness is aimed not at an external enemy but at Karlsefni and
his men.

Yet the *skrælingar* also play an indispensable role in the author's edifying
drama. As abominable to the Norsemen as a *sans-culotte* mob to ancien-régime
aristocrats, they incarnate the farthest reaches of unthinkable barbarity and port
it into tangible, terrifying proximity.[13] Like the count of Flanders in the fifteenth century and the Austrian army in the eighteenth, Karlsefni is exposed to
potentially devastating criticism. If, on the whole, he enjoys the author's accla-
mation for resourcefulness and valor, in this instance he is denied the opportunity to wage cathartic warfare and cannot quite recover from the humiliation
Freydís subjects him to. In some retellings (such as the epigraph at the head of
this chapter, where the Natives' flaccid slings give the measure of their *débandement* even before the Norsemen's erectile arrows pierce them), modern authors
have sought to remedy this defect, shifting the act that secures victory back from
Freydís's hands to Karlsefni's: she is allowed the role of catalyst, but actual triumph is effected by those of the correct sex. "Then bare-breasted she whirled the
great sword over her head and began to lay about her like a man," narrates Maurice Hewlett; "[t]he savages fell back before her, and at the entry were caught by
Karlsefne, returning from chasing a horde of them, and all killed." The Norsemen's ignominious flight has been emended to heroic pursuit, and Freydís, for all
that she is allowed to "lay about her like a man," has been demoted to shooing
errant *skrælingar* into the jaws of a patriarchal killing machine.[14] In the medieval
saga, too, Karlsefni's sullen, half-hearted praise of the woman who beat back
the *skrælingar*—emphasizing luck, not pluck—as well as his haste to murder a

---

[13] Morse points out that "a culture [uses] what it considers most unthinkable (paradoxical as that is) horrors as characteristic . . . of its enemies. . . . These atrocities are [a]
mark of the wickedness of [the Other]—a dramatization of their *ethos*" (1991: 118).

[14] Hewlett (1918: 251). Cf. also Chapin's invention of the male character Gest to
supplement Freydis (1934: 101, epigraph to chapter IV above).

handful of Natives encountered by chance a short time later, are readily under-standable. For all its *hvatr* pretensions, Norse society is exposed by Freydís as eminently unorganized for real war.[15]

Finally, however, it is Freydís who pays the highest personal price for step-ping out of her womanly place. When she tried to run, the saga says she "wished to follow [Karlsefni's men]" (*Freydís vildi fylgja þeim*). But though the terrain they traverse may be physically identical, conceptually they navigate utterly distinct spaces. The men had fled along a riverbank (*halda* [*þeir*] *undan upp með ánni*); in contrast, Freydís hobbles into a forest (*gekk hon . . . í skóginn*). Consciously or not, then, the saga author has picked his words in such a way as to send the men scur-rying through one type of landscape, while directing Freydís deep into another: *skóggangr*, "going [into the] forest," is the Icelandic legal term for outlawry. Tech-nically, then, Freydís becomes an outlaw, if only for the brief duration of her unforeseen tour of duty. The Icelandic legal system knew no harsher sentence; not to be harbored, the outlaw was to be treated as a wolf, a price set on his head. *Skóggangr* thus spelled immediate expulsion, a social death sentence, with physi-cal annihilation following inevitably on its heels (though sometimes deferred). Freydís appears to be unique in cheating death.[16]

---

[15] See *Eiríks saga rauða* cap. 11: "fundu fimm Skrælinga í skinnhjúpum, sofnaða, nær sjó. . . . Þóttusk þeir Karlsefni þat skilja, at þessir menn myndi hafa gǫrvir brott af landinu; þeir drápu þá" [(they) found five *skrælingar* in skin-jackets, sleeping by the sea. . . . As best Karlsefni and his men could make out, these men had likely been driven away from the land. They slew them] (ÍF 4, 1985: [*H*] 230; cf. [*S*] 430). Cf. Falk (forthcom-ing), cap. 4.

[16] On *skóggangr*, see Byock (2001: 231–32), and cf. Hastrup (1985: 144, 256n5). Freydís is also unique inasmuch as no female outlaws are recorded (but cf. *Hervarar saga ok Heiðreks* cap. 4: "[Hervör tamdist] meir við skot ok skjöld ok sverð en við sauma eða borða. . . . [H]ljóp hún á skóga ok drap menn til fjár sér" [(Hervör trained) more with shot and shield and sword than with sewing and needlework. . . . She ran off into the woods and killed people for their money], FSN 2: 11). Although this glossing of Freydís's forest stroll is not made explicit in *Eiríks saga rauða*, I believe it is inevitably latent in the text: "for the writer, [it is overdetermined] by the (historically specified) universe of dis-courses available, which Eco calls at different times 'the world of the encyclopedia' and 'the format of the semantic space'; for the reader, it is overdetermined as much by [his or her] knowledge of codes and frames as by the text's own project" (de Lauretis 1985b: 60, drawing on Umberto Eco and Louis Althusser). Contrast Gunnar Karlsson's skepticism towards symbolic interpretation: "when the early Icelanders built a wall, *garðr*, around their hay-making *tún* or *taða*, they certainly did it for practical purposes, to keep the sheep and cattle out while the grass was growing. . . . I find it difficult to accept that this entirely practical distinction between what was *útangarðs* and *innangarðs* could symbolize a general distinction between the world of human and the world of non-human beings, as Kirsten Hastrup maintains. . . . And if no one ever thought this thought, where did the system of thought exist until the anthropologist discovered it?" (1993: 22).

Like other veterans of harsh campaigns, however, the bare-sarked warrior is bound to discover that reintegration into respectable society is the toughest phase in her martial career—assuming she had been a part of such society to begin with. The textual silence enveloping Freydís strongly suggests that she never was. In both *Grœnlendinga saga* and *Eiríks saga rauða*, she materializes only when narratively called for, without so much as a nod to introducing her into the plot ahead of time or locating her among the other characters,[17] and she vanishes from the text just as abruptly. In the case of Théroigne de Méricourt, the same conclusion may be reached from opposite considerations—a wealth, in her case, of evidence, much of it satirical and all of it implacably hostile; nor was her exclusion limited to the textual world of the pamphlets. "As a Patriot," writes Helga Grubitzsch, "Théroigne attracted the political hatred of the Royalists; as a woman, she experienced it in the form of slanders of her sex; as a fighter for the rights of women, she was treated even by her own comrades with distrust." In May 1793, a little over a year after the publication of the *Grand débandement* print, the real Théroigne fell victim to a brutal and humiliating physical assault: associated with the Girondins, she was publicly stripped and whipped by women who supported Marat's Montagne. It was Marat himself who rescued her from their hands. Théroigne, however, lost all social footing and toppled headlong into insanity. She was confined in 1794 and spent the long years up to her death in 1817 in asylums, consumed by a lonely passion for ideals which the rush of events had rendered obsolete. Théroigne's madness merely gave a label to the social and political fact which, in 1793, the Royalist printer could already take for granted: that she was a monster, a freak, an outcast by her own hand—an abomination.[18] By comparison, the martyrs at Acre have it easiest, perhaps: hurried on to their final destination by the beastly Saracens, they are spared the difficulties of homecoming. Not so Freydís. Her sojourn beyond gender places her not only beneath society (as supreme woman) or above it (as superman) but outside it altogether.[19]

---

[17] Early introduction of characters who play no role until later on is the norm in the sagas; see, e.g., *Egils saga*'s handling of Berg-Ǫnundr (first mentioned in cap. 37, ÍF 2: 94, but only active from cap. 56, ÍF 2: 148), or even of Egill's *ad hoc* son Gunnarr (introduced in cap. 66, ÍF 2: 211, summarily killed in cap. 78, ÍF 2: 245, 254).

[18] Grubitzsch: "Als Patriotin zog Théroigne den politischen Haß der Royalisten auf sich, als Frau erfuhr sie ihn in Form von Schmähungen ihres Geschlechts, als Kämpferin für die Rechte der Frauen begegneten ihr auch die eigenen Genossen mit Mißtrauen" (1992: 99). For Théroigne's ordeal, see Goldsmith (1935: 63–64); Roudinesco (1991: 137–39); and Grubitzsch and Bockholt (1991: 387–96). On her unravelling, see Schama (1989: 873–75), esp. his telling verdict: "Sympathy seems out of place here, for in a sense the madness of Théroigne de Méricourt was a logical destination for the compulsions of revolutionary Idealism. . . . [She] now lived entirely inside the Revolution and the Revolution inside her" (1989: 875).

[19] Modern studies of Post-Traumatic Stress Disorder victims suggest that an inability to set aside extreme (and hypermasculine) battlefield personae, which combatants

Conceptualizing the bare-sarked warrior as a distinct, coherent topos thus helps solve the puzzle that has long dogged *Eiríks saga rauða* cap. 11: why does Freydís bare her breast and beat it with the sword, and why do her actions so terrorize the *skrælingar*? More broadly, identifying this topos allows us to see clearly the double bind in which Freydís and her sisters at arms are often caught, pincered in the crossfire of contradictory cultural conventions. For them, sex and gender, Otherness and familiarity, violence and eroticism all constitute a repertoire of constraining enablements. Hemmed in on all sides, the bare-sarked warrior is repeatedly damned if she does obey her culture's directives, and all the more damned if she doesn't. Members in this sisterhood, strewn across the histories of many societies, times, and places, face a grimly familiar repertoire of oppression, denial, and exclusion. Familiar, yet also diverse and elastic enough to bend with the cultural currents flowing through individual contexts and with the political agendas of individual authors: all bare-sarked warriors, Tolstoy might have reflected, endure the same universal fate, but each suffers it in her own, historically specific way.

The question of the universality and historicity of the topos might be pressed just a tad farther. As a narrative structure, the bare-sarked warrior is, in theory, timeless, and may manifest herself in any literary context where she might serve as both emblem of gender anxieties and mitigator of the angst aroused by menacing aliens. The bare-sarked warriors surveyed in the preceding pages, however, all belong to a definite temporal range—unlike the more ubiquitous bare-bosomed supplicants, tart-tongued whetters, or the participants in acerbic flyting. They first appear in (perhaps) the thirteenth century, facing down *skrælingar* or Saracens, and continue to flourish throughout the later Middle Ages and beyond, translating the global concussions of the Hundred Years' War and the Revolution into their own intimate idiom of danger. This timeline coincides with Europe's development into what R.I. Moore has influentially labeled a "persecuting society," one in which portable "patterns, procedures and rhetoric of persecution [acquired] the power of infinite and indefinite self-generation and self-renewal." The victimization of diverse groups branded as outsiders became a mainstay of the technology of power.[20] Moore, his disciples, and his critics have concerned themselves with the question of relations between the dominant groups who did (or sometimes did not) have recourse to the arsenal of persecu-

---

must be able to assume temporarily, may be responsible for their later dysfunction in civilian life; see, e.g., Karner (1998); cf. also Grossman (1995).

[20] Moore (2007: 155). See also such other explicit statements of the thesis as "the identity of the victim[s] was socially constructed, and persecution justified, or rationalised, largely in terms of the constructed persona"; and "[i]n the history of power[,] persecution was part of the process of intensification. Its function (irrespective of the ideology and conscious personal motives of those involved) was to carry wherever and whenever might be desired the new political and cultural regime" (2007: 153, 169).

tion and those whom they targeted (sometimes conjuring their group identity into being through the very process of extirpating them). Native Americans were too negligible a category of the medieval European imagination to warrant these scholars' attention,[21] and so Freydís, too, has escaped their notice. In the context of the long arc described by these scholars, an arc of growing trepidation over the integrity of the ingroup and urgency in excluding outgroups, Freydís and her topos sisters may be seen to have emerged as canaries in the cultural coalmine, providing a hyper-sensitive gauge of the proximity of peril to society's boundaries. It is not that, where a bare-sarked warrior appears, persecution of *skrælingar* or Saracens, French or Englishmen, Flemings or *sans-culottes* will follow. Rather, her appearance signals the brink at which the powers operating through persecution teeter, unable either to back down from the logic of their relentless discourse or extend their reach outwards effectively to suppress the threat they have externalized. Where the bare-sarked warrior appears, historical persecuting society has come up short against an Other it could only tame through displacement into the constraining structure of the literary topos.

Freydís's only recourse for countering the otherworldly malevolence of the *skrælingar* is to step literally beyond the margins of her civilization, to run outlaw into the forest. Her penalty for this transgression in *Eiríks saga rauða* is as merciless as her fate in *Grænlendinga saga* had been: although heroic, she receives praise only for her good fortune; although victorious, she disappears from the tale; and although heavy with child, she bears no prosperous descendants.[22] *Skóggangr* and silence are her only deserts. Freydís plunges headfirst out of history and into myth, her identity entirely obliterated by the façade the saga author has plastered over her to meet his narrative needs. Even in modern reworkings of her tale, rehabilitation can only barely be imagined, and then only as an unlikely subjunctive clause:

---

[21] Moore rightly insists, however, on the longevity of the persecuting social machinery debuted in the High Middle Ages, and the early modern history of the subjugation of the Americas certainly bears out the extension of this type of society forward in time and outwards in space. See, e.g., Pagden (1982), Todorov (1984), and Stannard (1992).

[22] Cf. Leifr's prediction about Freydís's progeny in *Grænlendinga saga*, mentioned above (pp. 10–11). See also Morison (1971–74: 1.57), Barnes (2001: 32–33), Perkins (2004: 48), and Brown (2007: 275n); and, imaginatively, Hewlett (1918: 253, where Freydis gives birth to a girl she loves "more than life itself," a rehabilitation of sorts), Boyer (1976: 246–47, 297, where Freydís's child is stillborn, a misfortune blamed on the mother's martial exertions), Vollmann (1990: 303n, 330, where Freydís, impregnated by a demon, gives birth to a lump of ice), and esp. Désy's bizarre narrative (1990: 97–98, where Freydis Karlsevni dies in childbirth but is reincarnated as her own daughter). In analysing the character of the outlaw-hero Grettir, Hastrup persuasively argues for the necessity of transgressing against the boundaries of society in order to combat threats from beyond them (1998: 91).

Nils and Halfdan together with Perek and their Indian friends waited in vain for the return of their comrades, but the Vikings never returned. Whether the dragon ship was sunk on the long voyage home or blown off its course by the violent winds of the northern seas, or if Freydis and her men, desperate for their freedom, recaptured the vessel and turned pirate, no one knows.[23]

A multicultural utopia reigns on the shores of Vínland in this closing vignette of William Resnick's romantic adaptation. Yet even in this happy land, Freydís may find no rest. Having bought her society's welfare with her sacrifice, the bare-sarked warrior remains a cypher—feared, unloved, misunderstood, all too hastily sunk below the horizon into uneasy oblivion.

---

[23] Resnick (1942: 213). Cf. the doleful tone even of accounts sympathetic to Freydís, e.g., Hewlett (1918: 252–56), Boyer (1976: 301–3), and Vollmann (1990: 330).

WORKS CITED

Manuscripts, facsimiles, transcriptions, and incunabula

AM 770 4to. Stofnun Árna Magnússonar, Reykjavík, Iceland. [photographs]

Herbers, Klaus, and Manuel Santos Noia (ed.), 1998. *Liber Sancti Jacobi: Codex Calixtinus*. Santiago de Compostela: Xunta de Galicia. [references by book, chapter and folio number]

John of Bromyard, 1585–86. *Svmma prædicantivm omni ervditione refertissima . . .*, 2 vols. Venice: Dominicus Nicolinus. [references by index letter, chapter, and article number]

Le Duc, Gwenaël, [ante 1987]. *Chronicon Briocense de Rebus gestis Brittonum*. Based on BN 6003, comparing BN 9888 [i.e., 8899]. Vol. 2, notebook 1. CIRDoMoC (Centre International de Recherche et de Documentation sur le Monachisme Celtique) Library, Landévennec, Brittany. [uncatalogued transcription]

Longnon, Jean, and Raymond Cazelles, 1969. *The Très Riches Heures of Jean, Duke of Berry: Musée Condé, Chantilly*, tr. Victoria Benedict, Preface Millard Meiss. New York: George Braziller.

Mettler, Ruth, Nigel Morgan and Michelle Brown (ed.), 1990. *Die Lambeth Apokalypse: Faksimile-Ausgabe von MS 209 der Lambeth Palace Library London*, tr. Ruth Mettler. Stuttgart: Verlag Müller & Schindler.

Neumüller, Willibrord (ed.), 1997. *Speculum humanae salvationis: Codex Cremifanensis 243 des Benediktinerstiftes Kremsmünster*. Glanzlichter und Buchkunst, 7. Graz: Akademische Druck- u. Verlagsanstalt. [reduced facsimile]

Pseudo-Bartolo (Innocent III?), [post-1500]. *Processus Sathane procuratoris infernalis contra genus humanum Coram deo nostro Iesu christo. Eius quidem generis ipsa intemerata virgo Maria aduocata existit*. In *Ordo iudicii*. [Cologne: Cornelis de Zierikzee,] ff. B.vii^v-C.vii^v.

Thomas of Cantimpré, [ca. 1480]. *Bonum vniuersale de proprietatibus apum*. [Cologne: Johann Koelhoff.] [references by book and chapter number]

Wichner, Jacob, 1888. *Catalog of Manuscripts in Stift Admont, Austria*. Authorized facsimile of a handwritten catalogue. Ann Arbor and London: University Microfilms International.

Edited and translated primary sources

Aeschylus, 1893. *The 'Choephori'*, ed. and tr. A.W. Verrall. London and New York: Macmillan and Co.

Albert the Great, 1916. *Alberts des Großen Homilie zu Luc. 11, 27*, ed. Paulus Maria von Loë, OP. Bonn: Peter Hanstein. [references by section number]

Alfonso X, el sabio, 1986. *Cantigas de Santa María*, ed. Walter Mettmann, 3 vols. Colección Clásicos Castalia, ed. Alonso Zamora Vicente. Madrid: Castalia.

Alvar, Manuel (ed.), 1970–72. *Vida de Santa María egipciaca: Estudios, vocabulario, edición de los textos*, 2 vols. Clásicos hispánicos, ser. 2, 18–19, ed. Rafael de Balbín Lucas. Madrid: Consejo superior de investigaciones científicas. [references by line number]

Ambroise, 1897. *L'Estoire de la guerre sainte: Histoire en vers de la troisième croisade (1190–1192)*, ed. Gaston Paris. Collection de documents inédits sur l'histoire de France. Paris: Imprimerie Nationale. [reference by column number]

Ambrose of Milan, [1948]. *De Virginibus libri tres*, ed. Egnatius Cazzaniga. Corpus Scriptorum Latinorum Paravianum. Turin et al.: G.B. Paravia.

Anselm of Canterbury, *Oratio lii: Ad Sanctam Virginem Mariam. PL* 158: 952c–59b.

Aristophanes, 1990. *Lysistrata*, ed. and tr. Alan H. Sommerstein. The Comedies of Aristophanes, 7. Warminster: Aris & Phillips. [references by line number]

[Arnaldus de Serranno?], 1897. *Chronica XXIV Generalium ordinis Minorum*, ed. anon. Fathers of Collegium S. Bonaventurae. Analecta Franciscana, 3. Florence: Quaracchi.

Arnobius of Sicca, 1953. *Adversus nationes*, ed. C. Marchesi, 2nd ed. Turin: G.B. Paravia. [references by book and chapter number]

el-Baghdadi, Iyad (ed. and tr.), 2011. "Meet Asmaa Mahfouz and the vlog that Helped Spark the Revolution." *YouTube*. Available at <http://www.youtube.com/watch?v=SgjIgMdsEuk> [references by time marker]

Bárðar saga Snæfellsáss, in *ÍF* 13, 99–172.

Bede, *Homilia ii: In vigilia Paschæ. PL* 94: 139c–44c.

———, *Hymnus xi: In Natali sanctæ Dei Genitricis. PL* 94: 631b–32b.

Benedict of Peterborough, *Miracula Sancti Thomæ Cantuariensis*, in Robertson (1875–85), 2.21–281. [references by book and chapter number]

Beneit, 1941. *La Vie de Thomas Becket: Poème anglo-normand du XIIᵉ siècle*, ed. Börje Schlyter. Études romanes de Lund, 4, ed. Alf Lombard. Lund and Copenhagen: CWK Gleerup and Ejnar Munksgaard.

Benson, Larry D. (ed.), 1987. *The Riverside Chaucer*, 3rd ed. Boston et al.: Houghton Mifflin.

Bernard of Clairvaux, *Epistola cccxxii. PL* 182: 527a–28b.

Bernardino of Siena, 1950–65. *S. Bernardini Senensis, Ordinis Fratrum Minorum, opera omnia*, ed. Pacificus M. Perantoni and Augustinus Sépinski, 9 vols. Florence: Quaracchi. [references by sermon, article and chapter number]

Biblia Sacra iuxta Vulgatam Versionem, ed. Robertus Weber, 1983. 2 vols. 3rd ed., rev. Bonifatius Fischer et al. Stuttgart: Deutsche Bibelgesellschaft. [references by abbreviated book title, chapter and verse number]

Bósa saga ok Herrauðs, in FSN 3, 281–322.

Branigan, Tania, and John Vidal, 2002. "Hands Up or We Strip!" *The Guardian*. Available at <http://www.guardian.co.uk/world/2002/jul/22/gender.uk1> (originally posted 22 July 2002).

Brennu-Njáls saga, in ÍF 12.

Brown, Carleton (ed.), 1932. *English Lyrics of the XIIIth Century*. Oxford: Clarendon Press.

——— (ed.), 1952. *Religious Lyrics of the XIVth Century*, 2nd ed., rev. G.V. Smithers. Oxford: Clarendon Press.

Budge, E.A. Wallis, 1933. *One Hundred and Ten Miracles of Our Lady Mary Translated from Ethiopic Manuscripts . . . .* London: Oxford University Press.

Caesar, 1917 [repr. 1963]. *The Gallic War*, ed. and tr. H.J. Edwards. Loeb Classical Library. London and Cambridge, MA: William Heinemann and Harvard University Press. [references by book and chapter number]

Caesarius of Heisterbach, 1851. *Caesarii Heisterbacensis monachi, ordini Cisterciensis, Dialogus Miraculorum*, ed. Josephus Strange, 2 vols. Cologne, Bonn and Brussels: J.M. Heberle. [references by distinction and chapter number]

Campbell, J.F. (ed. and tr.), 1860–62. *Popular Tales of the West Highlands*, 4 vols. Edinburgh: Edmonston and Douglas.

[Cassius] Dio, 1961–69. *Dio's Roman History*, tr. Herbert Baldwin Foster and Earnest Cary, 9 vols. Loeb Classical Library. London and New York: William Heinemann and Harvard University Press. [references by book, chapter and section number]

Chariton, 1995. *Callirhoe*, ed. and tr. G.P. Goold. Loeb Classical Library, 481. Cambridge, MA and London: Harvard University Press. [references by book, chapter and section number]

Chaucer, Geoffrey, 1987a. "The Miller's Tale," in *The Canterbury Tales*. In Benson (1987), 68–77. [references by line number]

———, 1987b. *Troilus and Criseyde*. In Benson (1987), 471–585. [references by book and line number]

Child, Francis James (ed.), 1882–98 [repr. 1965]. *The English and Scottish Popular Ballads*, 5 vols. Boston and New York: Houghton, Mifflin and Company [repr. New York: Dover].

Christine de Pizan, 1997 [repr. 1998]. *La Città delle Dame*, ed. Earl Jeffrey Richards, tr. Patrizia Caraffi. Milan: Luni Editrice. [references by book and chapter number]

[Clerk of Troyes,] *Le roman de Renart le contrefait*, in Tarbé (1847–64: 13.49–160) and Raynaud and Lemaitre (1914).

Collier, J. Payne, 1868 [repr. 1968]. *Broadside Black-letter Ballads, Printed in the Sixteenth and Seventeenth Centuries.* Burt Franklin Bibliography & Reference Series, 107. New York: Burt Franklin.

Crane, T[homas] F[rederick] (ed.), 1911. "Miracles of the Virgin." *The Romanic Review* 2:3: 235–79. [references by chapter number]

———— (ed.), 1925. *Liber de Miraculis Sanctae Dei Genitricis Mariae, Published at Vienna, in 1731, by Bernard Pez, O.S.B.* Cornell University Studies in Romance Languages and Literature, 1. Ithaca and London: Cornell University Press, Humphrey Milford, and Oxford University Press.

Darlington, Reginald R. (ed.), 1928. *The Vita Wulfstani of William of Malmesbury; to which are added the extant Abridgments of this work and the Miracles and Translation of St. Wulfstan.* Camden Society, 3rd ser., 40. London: Royal Historical Society. [references by work, book and chapter number]

Davis, Judith M., and F.R.P. Akehurst (trs.), Gérard Gros (ed.), 2011. *Our Lady's Lawsuits in L'Advocacie Nostre Dame (Our Lady's Advocacy) and La Chapelerie Nostre Dame de Baiex (The Benefice of Our Lady's Chapel in Bayeux).* Medieval and Renaissance Texts and Studies, 393. Tempe: ACMRS. [references by line number]

DD = Diplomatarium danicum, 1st ser., ed. Niels Skyum-Nielsen et al., 1957–90, 7 vols. Copenhagen: C.A. Reitzels Boghandel.

Dembowski, Peter F. (ed.), 1977. *La Vie de Sainte Marie l'égyptienne: Versions en ancien et en moyen français.* Publications romanes et françaises, 144, ed. Alexandre Micha. Geneva: Librairie Droz. [references by version siglum and line number]

Dexter, Elise F. (ed.), 1927. *Miraculae Sanctae Virginis Mariae.* University of Wisconsin Studies in the Social Sciences and History, 12. Madison: University of Wisconsin Press.

Diodorus of Sicily, 1933–67. *Library of History*, ed. and tr. C.H. Oldfather and Francis R. Walton, 12 vols. Loeb Classical Library. Cambridge, MA and London: Harvard University Press and William Heinemann. [references by book, chapter and section number]

Dirr, Adolf (tr.), 1920. *Kaukasische Märchen.* Die Märchen der Weltliteratur, ed. Friedrich von der Leyen and Paul Zaunert. Jena: Eugen Diederich.

Dracontius, Blossius Æmilius, 1905. *Orestis Tragoedia.* In *Monumenta Germaniae historica, auctorum antiquissimorum* 14: *Merobaudes, Dracontius, Eugenius Toletanus*, ed. Fridericus Vollmer, 197–226. Berlin: Weidmann.

Dreves, Guido Maria, Clemens Blume and Henry Marriott Bannister (eds.), 1886–1922. *Analecta hymnica medii aevi*, 55 vols. Leipzig: O.R. Reisland [et al.].

Eadmer of Canterbury, *Liber de excellentia Virginis Mariæ. PL* 159: 557c–579c.

Egils saga Skallagrímssonar, in ÍF 2.

Eiríks saga rauða, in ÍF 4, 193–237 [*H = Hauksbók*], 401–34 [*S = Skálholtsbók*].

Ekkehard of Aura, *Chronicon universale, id est abbreviatio Epythome Eusebii de sequenti opere. PL* 154: 497–1060a.

Ekrem, Inger, and Lars Boje Mortensen (eds.), 2003. *Historia Norwegie*, tr. Peter Fisher. Copenhagen: Museum Tusculanum Press, University of Copenhagen. [references by chapter number]

Ernaud of Bonneval, *Libellus de laudibus B. Mariæ Virginis. PL* 189: 1725–34.

Euripides, 1987. *Orestes*, ed. and tr. M.L. West. Warminster: Aris and Phillips. [references by line number]

———, 1988. *Phoenician Women*, ed. and tr. Elizabeth Craik. Warminster: Aris and Phillips. [references by line number]

———, 1995. *Children of Heracles, Hippolytus, Andromache, Hecuba*, ed. and tr. David Kovacs. Loeb Classical Library, 484. Cambridge, MA and London: Harvard University Press. [references by line number]

———, 1998. *Supplicant Women, Electra, Heracles*, tr. David Kovacs. Loeb Classical Library, 9. Cambridge, MA and London: Harvard University Press. [references by line number]

Eyrbyggja saga, in ÍF 4, 1–186.

Faber, Felix, 1843–49. *Fratris Felicis Fabri Evagatorium in Terræ Sanctæ, Arabiæ et Egypti Peregrinationem*, ed. Conrad Dietrich Haßler, 3 vols. Bibliothek des Literarischen Vereins in Stuttgart, 2–4. Stuttgart: Societas literaria stuttgardiensis.

Færeyinga saga, in ÍF 25, 1–121.

First Continuation of Perceval, in Roach (1949–83), vol. 1–3. [references by section name and number, and by episode number]

Flóamanna saga, in ÍF 13, 229–327.

Frechulf of Lisieux, *Chronicon. PL* 106: 915d–1258b. [references by book, chapter and section number]

Froissart, Jehan, 1869–1975. *Chroniques*, ed. Siméon Luce et al., 15 vols. Paris: Jules Renouard. [references by book, chapter and section number]

FSN = *Fornaldar sögur Norðurlanda*, ed. Guðni Jónsson, 1954, 4 vols. [Reykjavík:] Íslendingasagnaútgáfan.

Geoffrey of Monmouth, 2007. *The History of the Kings of Britain: De gestis Britonum [Historia Regum Britanniae]*, ed. Michael D. Reeve, tr. Neil Wright. Arthurian Studies, 69, ed. Norris J. Lacy. Woodbridge: Boydell Press.

Getatchew Haile (ed. and tr.), 1992. *The Mariology of Emperor Zär'a Ya'əqob of Ethiopia*. Orientalia Christiana Analecta, 242, ed. Robert F. Taft, SJ. Rome: Pontificium Institutum Studiorum Orientalium.

——— (ed. and tr.), 2006. *The Gə'əz Acts of Abba Ǝsṭifanos of Gʷəndagʷənde*, 2 vols. Corpus Scriptorum Christianorum Orientalium, 619–620, Scriptores Aethiopici, 110–111. Louvain: Peeters.

Gísla saga Súrssonar, in ÍF 6, 1–118.

Gregory the Great, 1979–85. *S. Gregorii Magni Moralia in Iob*, ed. Marcus Adriaen, 3 vols. Corpus Christianorum Series Latina, 143. Turnhout: Brepols. [references by book, chapter and section number]

Grettis saga Ásmundarsonar, in ÍF 7, 1–290.

Gríms saga loðinkinna, in FSN 2, 183–98.

Grænlendinga saga, in ÍF 4, 239–69.

Guibert of Nogent, *Liber de laude Sanctæ Mariæ*. PL 156: 537b–578d.

Hallfreðar saga, in ÍF 8, 133–200.

"Hárbarð[s]l[j]óð." In Neckel and Kuhn (1962–68), 1.78–87. [references by strophe number]

Harðar saga, in ÍF 13, 1–97.

Hardy, Thomas Dufus, and Charles Price Martin (eds.), 1888. *Gesta Herwardi incliti exulis et militis*. In *Lestorie des Engles solum la translacion maistre Geffrei Gaimar*. 2 vols., 1: 339–404. Rolls Series, 91. London: Eyre and Spottiswoode.

Harvey, P.D.A., 1996. *Mappa Mundi: The Hereford World Map*. Toronto and Buffalo: University of Toronto Press.

Hauksbók, [ed. Finnur Jónsson,] 1892–96. Copenhagen: Thieles Bogtrykkeri.

Henry of Huntingdon, 1996. *Historia Anglorum: The History of the English People*, ed. and tr. Diana Greenway. Oxford Medieval Texts. Oxford: Clarendon Press. [references by book and chapter number]

Hervarar saga ok Heiðreks, in FSN 2, 1–71.

Hænsa-Þóris saga, in ÍF 3, 1–47.

Homer, 1999. *The Iliad*, 2nd ed., ed. and tr. A.T. Murray, rev. William F. Wyatt, 2 vols. Loeb Classical Library. London and Cambridge, MA: Harvard University Press. [references by book and line number]

Honorius Augustodunensis, *Sigillum Beatæ Mariæ*. PL 172: 495a–518d.

Horstmann, Carl (ed.), 1875. "Kindheit Jesu." In *Altenglische Legenden*, ed. idem, 3–61. Paderborn: Ferdinand Schöningh.

Hrólfs saga Gautrekssonar, in FSN 4, 51–176.

Hrólfs saga kraka og kappa hans, in FSN 1, 1–105.

Huffington Post, 2010a. "Larissa Riquelme, Lingerie Model, Will Run Naked If Paraguay Wins World Cup." Accessible at <http://www.huffingtonpost.com/2010/06/29/larissa-riquelme-lingerie_n_629975.html#s109666> (originally posted 29 June 2010).

———, 2010b. "Larissa Riquelme Naked Pledge Ends In Heartbreak." Accessible at <http://www.huffingtonpost.com/2010/07/03/larissa-riquelme-naked-pl_n_634886.html#s110117> (originally posted 3 July 2010).

———, 2010c. "Larissa Riquelme Will Run Nude As 'Present' To Players." Accessible at <www.huffingtonpost.com/2010/07/06/larissa-riquelme-nude-pho_n_637063.html/> (originally posted 6 July 2010).

ÍF = *Íslenzk Fornrit*, 1933–. Reykjavík: Hið íslenzka fornritfélag.
    1: Jakob Benediktsson (ed.), 1986. *Íslendingabók, Landnámabók*.

2: Sigurður Nordal (ed.), 1933. *Egils saga Skalla-Grímssonar.*
3: Sigurður Nordal and Guðni Jónsson (ed.), 1938. *Borgfirðinga sǫgur.*
4: Einar Ól. Sveinsson and Matthías Þórðarson (eds.), Óláfur Halldórsson (rev.), 1985. *Eyrbyggja saga* et al.
5: Einar Ól. Sveinsson (ed.), 1934. *Laxdœla saga* et al.
6: Björn K. Þórólfsson and Guðni Jónsson (eds.), 1943. *Vestfirðinga sǫgur.*
7: Guðni Jónsson (ed.), 1936. *Grettis saga Ásmundarsonar* et al.
8: Einar Ól. Sveinsson (ed.), 1939. *Vatnsdœla saga* et al.
10: Björn Sigfússon (ed.), 1940. *Ljósvetninga saga* et al.
11: Jón Jóhannesson (ed.), 1950. *Austfirðinga sǫgur.*
12: Einar Ól. Sveinsson (ed.), 1954. *Brennu-Njáls saga.*
13: Þórhallur Vilmundarson and Bjarni Vilhjálmsson (eds.), 1991. *Harðar saga* et al.
14: Jóhannes Halldórsson (ed.), 1959. *Kjalnesinga saga* et al.
25: Ólafur Halldórsson (ed.), 2006. *Færeyinga saga*; Oddr munkr Snorrason, *Óláfs saga Tryggvasonar.*
26–28: Snorri Sturluson, 1941–51. *Heimskringla*, ed. Bjarni Aðalbjarnarson.
Isidore of Seville, 1911. *Isidori Hispalensis episcopi etymologiarum sive originum libri XX*, ed. W.M. Lindsay, 2 vols. Scriptorum classicorum bibliotheca Oxoniensis. Oxford: Clarendon Press. [references by book, chapter and section number; unnumbered pages]
———, *Mysticorum Expositiones Sacramentorum, seu Quæstiones in Vetus Testamentum: in Genesin. PL* 83: 207b–88a. [references by chapter and section number]
Íslendinga saga, in *Sturlunga saga*, vol. 1, 229–534.
Íslendingabók, in ÍF 1, 1–28.
Jacobus a Voragine, 1850. *Legenda aurea*, ed. Th. Graesse, 2nd ed. Leipzig: Libraria Arnoldiana.
Jacoby, Felix (ed.), [1925? (repr. 1961)]. *Die Fragmente der grieschichen Historiker (F Gr Hist)*, part 2, vol. A: *Zeitgeschichte: Universalgeschichte und Hellenika.* Leiden: E.J. Brill.
[J]acopone da Todi, 1977. *Laude*, ed. Franco Mancini. Rome and Bari: Laterza & Figli.
———, 1982. *The Lauds*, tr. Serge and Elizabeth Hughes. The Classics of Western Spirituality. New York, Ramsey, Toronto: Paulist Press.
Jerome, *Epistola xiv: Ad Heliodorum monachum. PL* 22: 347–55. [references by section number]
———, *Epistola lxxvii: Ad Oceanum de morte Fabiolæ. PL* 22: 691–98. [references by section number]
John of Salisbury, 1909 [repr. 1965]. *Policraticus, sive De nugis curialium et vestigiis philosophorum*, ed. Clemens C.I. Webb, 2 vols. London and Oxford: Clarendon Press [repr. Frankfurt a.M.: Minerva]. [references by book and chapter number]

Johnston, Jacqueline, 2008. "Code Pink Demonstrators Bare Breasts to Protest War." *The Daily Californian Online*. Accessible at <http://www.dailycal.org/printable.php?id=10910/> (originally posted 16 June 2008).

Jón Árnason (ed.), 1862–64. *Íslenzkar þjóðsögur og æfintýri*, 2 vols. Leipzig: J.H. Hinrichs.

Josephus, 1926–65. [*Works*], ed. and tr. H.St.J. Thackeray et al., 10 vols. Loeb Classical Library. London, New York, and Cambridge, MA: William Heinemann, G.P. Putnam's Sons and Harvard University Press. [references by book, chapter and section number]

Justin, 1972. *M. Iuniani Iustini epitoma historiarum Philippicarum Pompei Trogi, accedunt prologii in Pompeium Trogum*, ed. Otto Seel. Stuttgart: B.G. Teubner. [references by book, chapter and section number]

Kervyn de Lettenhove (ed.), 1879–80. *Istore et croniques de Flandres, d'après les textes de divers manuscrits*, 2 vols. Brussels: F. Hayez.

Króka-Refs saga, in ÍF 14, 117–60.

Kunstmann, Pierre (ed.), 1981. *Treize miracles de Notre-Dame: Tirés du Ms. B.N. fr. 2094*. Publications médiévales de l'Université d'Ottawa, 6. Ottawa: Université d'Ottawa.

Lactantius, Lucius Cæcilius Firmianus, 1748 [repr. 1783]. *Opera omnia*, 2 vols, ed. Joannes Bapt. le Brun and Nicolaus Lenglet du Fresnoi. Würzburg: Libraria Staheliana. [references by book and chapter number]

La Fontaine, [Jehan], 1762. *Contes et nouvelles en vers*, 2 vols. Amsterdam.

———, 1961 [repr. 1966]. *Contes et Nouvelles en vers*, ed. Georges Couton. Classiques Garnier. [Paris:] Garnier Frères.

Laȝamon, 1963–78. *Brut*, 2 vols, ed. G.L. Brook and R.F. Leslie. Early English Text Society, 250, 270. London, New York, Toronto: Oxford University Press. [references by line number]

Landnámabók, in ÍF 1, 29–397. [references to *Skálholtsbók* (*S*) and *Hauksbók* (*H*)]

Laxdœla saga, in ÍF 5, 1–248.

Le Bel, Jean, 1904–5. *Chronique*, ed. Jules Viard and Eugène Déprez, 2 vols. Paris: Librairie Renouard. [references by chapter number]

Liebrecht, Richard, 2009. "Women Bare Breasts to Boost Edmonton's Finest." *Edmonton Sun*. Accessible at <http://www.edmontonsun.com/news/edmonton/2009/06/28/9960196-sun.html/> (originally posted 28 June 2009).

Ljósvetninga saga, in ÍF 10, 1–106.

"Lo[k]asenna." In Neckel and Kuhn (1962–68), 1: 96–110. [references by strophe number]

Lupus of Olmedo, *Regula monachorum, ex scriptis Hieronymi collecta*. PL 30: 319a–92b. [references by chapter number]

Luzel, F.M. (ed. and tr.), 1868–90 [repr. 1971]. *Chants et chansons populaires de la Basse-Bretagne*, rev. Donatien Laurent, 4 vols. [to date]. Paris: G.P. Maisonneuve & Larose.

Machiavelli, Niccolò, 1971–99. *Opere*, ed. Rinaldo Rinaldi et al., 4 vols. Classici Italiani, ed. Giorgio Bárberi Squarotti. Turin: Unione Tipografico-Editrice Torinese. [references by volume, part (where appropriate), and page number]

————, *Discorsi sopra la prima Deca di Tito Livio*, in Machiavelli (1971–99), 1:1: 411–943 and 1:2: 945–1200. [references by book and chapter number]

————, *Istorie fiorentine*, in Machiavelli (1971–99), 2: 273–751. [references by book and chapter number]

Marie de France, 1944 [repr. 1965]. "Lanval." In *Lais*, ed. Alfred Ewert, 58–74. Blackwell's French Texts, ed. Alfred Ewert. Oxford: Basil Blackwell. [references by line number]

Márkus, Gilbert OP (tr.), 1997. *Adomnán's "Law of the Innocents"; Cáin Adomnáin: A Seventh-Century Law for the Protection of Non-Combatants*. Glasgow: Blackfriars Books.

Matthew Paris, 1872–83. *Chronica majora*, ed. Henry Richards Luard, 7 vols. Rolls Series, 57. London et al.: Longman et al.

Mayer, Hans Eberhard (ed.), 1962. *Das Itinerarium peregrinorum: Eine zeitgenössische englische Chronik zum dritten Kreuzzug in ursprünglicher Gestalt*. Schriften der Monumenta Germaniae historica, 18. Stuttgart: Anton Hiersemann.

McKenna, L[ambert] SJ (ed. and tr.), [1922]. *Dán Dé: The Poems of Donnchadh Mor O Dálaigh, and the Religious Poems in the Duanaire of the Yellow Book of Lecan*. Dublin: The Educational Company of Ireland.

———— (ed. and tr.), 1935–38. *Aithdioġluim Dána: A Miscellany of Irish Bardic Poetry, Historical and Religious, including the Historical Poems of the Duanaire in the Yellow Book of Lecan*, 2 vols. Irish Text Society, 27, 40. Dublin: Irish Text Society (1939–40 for 1935–38).

MEMRI (The Middle East Media Research Institute), 2002. "Wafa Idris: The Celebration of the First Female Palestinian Suicide Bomber—Part II." Accessible at <http://www.memri.org/report/en/0/0/0/0/0/0/610.htm> (originally posted 13 February 2002).

Meyer, Kuno (ed. and tr.), 1905. *Cáin Adamnáin: An Old-Irish Treatise on the Law of Adamnan*. Anecdota Oxoniensia, 12. Oxford: Clarendon Press. [references by section number]

Mills, James, 2004. "The Mills-Kronborg Collection of Danish Church Wall Paintings." Available at <http://ica.princeton.edu/mills/index.php>.

Molinier, Émile (ed.), 1882. *Chronique normande du XIVᵉ siècle*. Paris: Librairie Renouard.

Mombritius, Boninus (ed.), 1910 [repr. 1978]. *Sanctuarium seu Vitae Sanctorum*, 2 vols. Paris: Albert Fontemoing [repr. Hildesheim and New York: Georg Olms Verlag].

Mone, F.J. (ed.), 1854. *Lateinische Hymnen des Mittelalters*, 2 vols. Freiburg im Breisgau: Herder'sche Verlagshandlung.

Montgomery, James E., 2000. "Ibn Faḍlān and the Rūsiyyah." *Journal of Arabic and Islamic Studies* 3: 1–25.

Musurillo, Herbert (ed. and tr.), 1972. *Acts of the Christian Martyrs*. Oxford: Clarendon Press.

Neckel, Gustav (ed.), 1962–68. *Edda: Die Lieder des Codex Regius nebst verwandten Denkmälern*. 2 vols. 4th ed., rev. Hans Kuhn. Heidelberg: Carl Winter Universitätsverlag.

Neumann, Hans, and Gisela Vollmann-Profe (ed.), 1990–93. *Mechthild von Magdeburg 'Das fließende Licht der Gottheit': Nach der Einsiedler Handschrift in kritischem Vergleich mit der gesamten Überlieferung*. 2 vols. Münchener Texte und Untersuchungen zur deutschen Literatur des Mittelalters, 100–101. Munich and Zurich: Artemis [and Max Niemeyer].

Nève, Joseph (ed.), 1924. *Sermons choisis de Michel Menot (1508–1518)*. Bibliothèque du XVe siècle, 29. Paris : Édouard Champion.

Niesner, Manuela, 1995. *Das Speculum humanae salvationis der Stiftsbibliothek Kremsmünster: Edition der mittelhochdeutschen Versübersetzung und Studien zum Verhältnis von Bild und Text*. Pictura et Poësis: Interdisziplinäre Studien zum Verhaltnis von Literatur und Kunst, 8, ed. Ulrich Ernst, Joachim Gaus and Christel Meier. Cologne, Weimar, and Vienna: Böhlau Verlag.

O'Rahilly, Cecile (ed. and tr.), 1976. *Táin Bó Cúailnge: Recension I*. Dublin: Dublin Institute for Advanced Studies. [references by line number]

Orosius, Paulus, 1882 [repr. 1967]. *Historiarum adversum paganos libri vii*, ed. [Karl] Zangemeister. Corpus scriptorum ecclesiasticorum latinorum, 5. Vienna: C. Gerold [repr. Hildesheim: Georg Olms Verlagsbuchhandlung]. [references by book, chapter and section number]

Othlo of St. Emmeram, *Vita Sancti Wolfkangi episcopi Ratisbonensis*. PL 146: 389b–428a. [references by section number]

Ovid[ius], Publius Naso, 1916 [repr. 1922]. *Metamorphoses*, ed. and tr. Frank Justus Miller, 2 vols. Loeb Classical Library. London and New York: William Heinemann and G.P. Putnam's Sons. [references by book and line number]

Page, D.L. (ed.), 1962. *Poetae Melici Graeci*. Oxford: Clarendon Press.

Paris, Gaston, and Ulysse Robert (eds.), 1876–93. *Miracles de Nostre Dame par personnages*, 8 vols. Paris: Librairie de Firmin Didot.

Paul the Deacon, 1908. "Miraculum S Marie De Theophilo penitente." In Petsch (1908), 1–10. [references by section number]

Pauli, Johannes, 1924. *Schimpf und Ernst*, ed. Johannes Bolte, 2 vols. Alte Erzähler, 1–2, ed. Johannes Bolte. Berlin: Herbert Stubenrauch. [references by chapter number]

Pernot, Hubert (ed.), 1900. "Descente de la Vierge aux Enfers d'après les manuscrits grecs de Paris." *Revue des Études Grecques* 13: 232–57.

Peter of Blois, *Sermo lxv: Ad populum*. PL 207: 750d–776b.

Peter the Cantor, *Verbum Abbreviatum*. PL 205: 21a–554d.

Petsch, Robert (ed.), 1908. *Theophilus: Mittelniederdeutsches Drama in drei Fassungen herausgegeben*. Germanische Bibliothek, 2nd ser., 2, ed. W. Streitberg. Heidelberg: Carl Winter's Universitätsbuchhandlung.

PL = Patrologia cursus completus, series latina, ed. J.-P. Migne, 1844–65, 221 vols. Paris: Fratres Garnier. [references by volume and column number]

Plutarch, 1927–69. *Moralia*, tr. Frank Cole Babbitt et al., 15 vols. Loeb Classical Library. London, New York, and Cambridge, MA: William Heinemann, G.P. Putnam's Sons and Harvard University Press. [references by section, chapter (if applicable), and page number and letter in the Stephanus (1572) edition]

Polyaenus, 1994. *Stratagems of War*, ed. and tr. Peter Krentz and Everett L. Wheeler, 2 vols. Chicago: Ares Publishers.

Polybius, 1922–27. *The Histories*, tr. W.R. Paton, 6 vols. Loeb Classical Library. London and New York: William Heinemann and G.P. Putnam. [references by book, chapter, and section number]

Procopius, 1914–41. *[Works]*, tr. H.B. Dewing and Glanville Downey, 7 vols. Loeb Classical Library. London, New York, and Cambridge, MA: William Heinemann, Macmillan, Harvard University Press. [references by work, book, chapter, and section number]

Pseudo-Jerome, *Homilia ad monachos*. *PL* 30: 311b-18d.

Pseudo-Seneca, *Hercules Oetaeus*. In Seneca (1917), 2: 183–341.

Rabelais, François, 1994. *Œuvres complètes*, ed. Mireille Huchon and François Moreau. Bibliothèque de la Pléiade, 15. [Liège:] Gallimard. [references by book name and chapter number]

Rafn, C.C. (ed.), 1837. *Antiquitates americanæ*. Copenhagen: Officina Schultziana.

Raoul de Cambrai, ed. and tr. Sarah Kay, 1992. Oxford: Clarendon Press. [references by fitt number]

Raynaud, Gaston, and Henri Lemaitre (eds.), 1914. *Le roman de Renart le contrefait*, 2 vols. Paris: Librairie Ancienne Honoré Champion.

Reames, Sherri L. (ed.), 2003. *Middle English Legends of Women Saints*. Middle English Texts, ed. Russell A. Peck. Kalamazoo: TEAMS and Western Michigan University.

René of Anjou, 2001. *The Book of the Love-Smitten Heart (Le Livre du cuers d'amours espris)*, ed. and tr. Stephanie Viereck Gibbs and Kathryn Karczewska. New York and London: Routledge. [references by section and verse number]

Richard of St. Laurent, *De Laudibus B. Mariæ Virginis libri xii*, 1890–99. Vol. 36 in *B. Alberti Magni, Ratisbonensis episcopi, Ordinis Prædicatorum, opera omnia*, ed. Auguste and Émile Borgnet, 38 vols. [references by book, chapter, and section number]

Roach, William (ed.), 1949–83. *The Continuations of the Old French Perceval*, 5 vols. Philadelphia: University of Pennsylvania Press.

Robertson, James Craigie [and J. Brigstocke Sheppard] (eds.), 1875–85. 7 vols. *Materials for the History of Thomas Becket, Archbishop of Canterbury (Canonized by Pope Alexander III, A.D. 1173)*. Rolls Series, 67. London: Longman.

Rutherfurd, Andrew (tr.), 1897. "The Apocalypse of the Virgin." In *The Ante-Nicene Fathers: Additional Volume*, ed. Allan Menzies, 167–74. 2nd ed. New York: The Christian Literature Company.

Saxo Grammaticus, 1886. *Gesta Danorum*, ed. Alfred Holder. Strassburg: Karl J. Trübner. [references by book and folio number]

Scragg, D.G. (ed.), 1992. *The Vercelli Homilies and Related Texts*. Early English Text Society, o.s. 300. Oxford et al.: Oxford University Press.

Seneca, Lucius Annaeus, 1917 [repr. 1927–29]. *Tragedies*, ed. and tr. Frank Justus Miller, 2 vols. Loeb Classical Library. London and New York: William Heinemann and G.P. Putnam's Sons. [references by line number]

———, 1987. *Seneca's Phaedra*, ed. and tr. A.J. Boyle. Latin and Greek Texts, 5, ed. F. Cairns and I.S. Moxon. Liverpool and Wolfeboro: Francis Cairns. [references by act and line number]

Shepherd, Stephen H.A. (ed.), 1995. *Middle English Romances: Authoritative Texts, Sources, and Background Criticism*. A Norton Critical Edition. New York and London: W.W. Norton.

Sinclair, K.V. (ed.), 1971. *Tristan de Nanteuil: Chanson de geste inédite*. Assen: Van Gorcum & Comp. [references by line number]

Sir Gawain and the Green Knight, ed. J.R.R. Tolkien and E.V. Gordon, rev. Norman Davis, 1967 [repr. 1985]. Oxford: Clarendon Press. [references by line number]

Skjd = *Den norsk-islandske skjaldedigtning*, ed. Finnur Jónsson, 1910–15. A: Tekst efter håndskrifterne, 2 vols.; B: Rettet Tekst, 2 vols. Copenhagen and Christiania: Gyldendalske Boghandel and Nordisk Forlag. [references by volume letter & number and page number]

Snorri Sturluson, *Edda*, ed. Anthony Faulkes, 1982–98. 3 vols. 1: *Prologue and Gylfaginning* (1982); 2: *Skáldskaparmál*, 2 parts (1998); 3: *Háttatal* (1991). Oxford [and London]: Clarendon and Viking Society for Northern Research with University College London. [references by volume title, part (for vol. 2) and page number]

———, *Heimskringla*, in ÍF 26–28.

———, *Ynglinga saga*, in ÍF 26, 9–83.

Sögubrot af fornkonungum, in FSN 1, 337–63.

Song of Dermot = *The Song of Dermot and Earl Richard Fitzgilbert: Le Chansun de Dermot e li Quens Richard Fiz Gilbert*, ed. Denis J. Conlon, 1992. Studien und Dokumente zur Geschichte der Romanischen Literaturen, 24, ed. Hans-Joachim Lope. Frankfurt a.M. et al.: Peter Lang.

SPSMA = *Skaldic Poetry of the Scandinavian Middle Ages*, ed. Margaret Clunies Ross et al., 2007–. Turnhout: Brepols. [references by volume and part number]

Statius, Publius Papinius, 1928 [repr. 1961]. *Silvae, Thebaid, Achilleid*, tr. J.H. Mozley, 2 vols. Loeb Classical Library. Cambridge, MA and London: Harvard University Press and William Heinemann.

Stokes, Whitley (ed. and tr.), 1905. *Félire Óengusso Céli Dé: The Martyrology of Oengus the Culdee*. Henry Bradshaw Society, 29. London: Harrison and Sons.

Sturlaugs saga starfsama, in FSN 3, 105–60.

Sturlu saga, in *Sturlunga saga*, vol. 1, 63–114.

Sturlunga saga, ed. Jón Jóhannesson, Magnús Finnbogason and Kristján Eldjárn, 1946. 2 vols. Reykjavík: Sturlunguútgáfan.

Suetonius, Caius Tranquillus, 1997. *Lives of the Caesars and Lives of Illustrious Men*, tr. J.C. Rolfe, rev. K.R. Bradley, 2 vols. Loeb Classical Library. Cambridge, MA and London: Harvard University Press. [references by Emperor, chapter and section number]

Tacitus, Publius Cornelius, 1925–37. *The Histories and the Annals*, tr. Clifford H. Moore and John Jackson, 4 vols. Loeb Classical Library. London and Cambridge, MA: William Heinemann, Harvard University Press. [references by book and chapter number]

———, 1938. *De origine et situ Germanorum*, ed. and tr. J.G.C. Anderson. Oxford: Clarendon Press. [references by chapter and section number]

Tarbé, P. (ed.), 1847–64. *Poètes de Champagne Antérieurs au XVIᵉ siècle*, 24 vols. Reims.

Tertullian, Quintus Septimus Florens, 1954. *Opera*, 2 vols. Corpus Christianorum Series Latina, 1–2. Turnhout: Brepols. [references by volume and page number]

———, *De ieiunio adversus Psychicos*, ed. A. Reifferschied and G. Wissowa, in Tertullian (1954), 2: 1255–77 [references by chapter and section number]

Theodulf of Orleans, *Carmina libri vii. PL* 105: 283a–380d. [references by book and song number]

Thomas of Cantimpré, 1605. *MIRACVLORVM, ET EXEMPLORVM memorabilium sui temporis LIBRI DVO. In quibus præterea, ex mirifica APVM Repub. universa vitæ bene & Christiane instituendæ ratio (quò vetus, BONI VNIVERSALIS, alludit inscriptio) traditur, & artificiosé pertractatur*, ed. George Colveneere. Douai: Baltazar Bellerus. [references by book, chapter, and section number]

Thómas saga erkibyskups, ed. and tr. Eiríkr Magnússon, 1875–83. 2 vols. Rolls Series, 65. London: Longman.

Þórðar saga kakala, in *Sturlunga saga*, vol. 2, 1–86.

Þorskfirðinga saga eða Gull-Þóris saga, in ÍF 13, 173–227.

Þorsteins þáttr stangarhǫggs, in ÍF 11, 67–79.

"Þryms[k]viða." In Neckel and Kuhn (1962–68), 1: 111–15. [references by strophe number]

TMZ, 2010. "Boob Crackdown Ordered for Saints Parade." Accessible at <http://www.tmz.com/2010/02/09/new-orleans-saints-parade-super-bowl-boobs-flashing/> (originally posted 9 February 2010).

Trounce, A.McI. (ed.), 1951. *Athelston: A Middle English Romance*, rev. ed. Early English Text Society, 224. London: Oxford University Press.

Unger, C.R. (ed.), 1871. *Mariu saga: Legender om Jomfru Maria og hendes Jertegn efter gamle Haandskrifter*, 4 vols. Christiania: Brögger & Christie. [references by miracle number]

—— (ed.), 1877. *Heilagra Manna Søgur: Fortællinger og Legender om hellige Mænd og Kvinder*, 2 vols. Christiania: B.M. Bentzen.

Valerius Maximus, 2000. *Memorable Doings and Sayings*, ed. and tr. D.R. Shackleton Bailey, 2 vols. Loeb Classical Library. Cambridge, MA and London: Harvard University Press. [references by book, chapter and exemplum number]

Valo, Peter, 1990. *August '68 na Slovensku: Pocta fotoreportérovi Ladislavovi Beilikovi a všetkým ostatným, ktorí dokumentovali demonštráciu sily / August 1968 in Slovakia: In Honour of the Photographer Ladislav Bielik and of All the Others who Documented the Display of Force*, tr. Peter Tkáč. OKO Editorial Series Slovakia in Photography, 1, ed. Pavel Meluš and Juraj Králik. Bratislava: OKO.

Vápnfirðinga saga, in ÍF 11, 21–65.

Vatnsdœla saga, in ÍF 8, 1–131.

Les Vœux du héron = The Vows of the Heron (Les Voeux du héron): A Middle French Vowing Poem, ed. John L. Grigsby and Norris J. Lacy, tr. N.J. Lacy, 1992. Garland Library of Medieal Literature, ser. A, 86. New York and London: Garland. [references by line number]

Wace, 1999. *Roman de Brut: A History of the British*, ed. and tr. Judith Weiss. Exeter Medieval English Texts and Studies. Exeter: University of Exeter.

Wenzel, Siegfried, 1971. "A Latin Miracle with Middle English Verses." *Neuphilologische Mitteilungen* 72: 77–85.

—— (ed.), 1989. *Fasciculus Morum: A Fourteenth-Century Preacher's Handbook*. University Park and London: Pennsylvania State University Press.

William of Canterbury, *Miracula S Thomæ Cantuariensis*, in Robertson (1875–85), 1: 137–546. [references by book and chapter number]

William Paris, *Life of St. Christina*, in Reames (2003), 227–48. [references by line number]

Wisse, Claus, and Philipp Colin, 1888. *Parzifal*, ed. Karl Schorbach. Elsässische Litteraturdenkmäler aus dem XIV–XVII. Jahrhundert, 5, ed. Ernst Martin and Erich Schmidt. Strassburg: Karl J. Trübner. [references by column number]

Wolf, Kirsten (ed.), 1997a. *The Icelandic Legend of Saint Dorothy*. Studies and Texts, 130. Toronto: Pontifical Institute of Mediaeval Studies.

—— (ed.), 2000. *The Old Norse–Icelandic Legend of Saint Barbara*. Studies and Texts, 134. Toronto: Pontifical Institute of Mediaeval Studies.

Wolfram von Eschenbach, 1952 [tr. 1977, repr. 1996]. *Parzival: Mittelhochdeutsch / Neuhochdeutsch*, ed. Karl Lachmann, 2 vols. 7th ed., tr. Wolfgang Spiewok. Stuttgart: Philipp Reclam.

de Yepes, Antonio, 1959–60. *Cronica general de la Orden de San Benito*, ed. Justo Perez de Urbel, 3 vols. Biblioteca de autores españoles (continuación), 123–25. Madrid: Real Academia Española.

Yngvars saga víðförla, in FSN 2, 423–59.

Fiction and creative nonfiction adaptations

Ballantyne, R.M., 1872. *The Norsemen in the West, or, America before Columbus: A Tale*. London: James Nisbet & Co.

Berry, Francis, 1977. *I Tell of Greenland: An Edited Translation of the Sauðarkrokur Manuscripts*. London, Henley and Boston: Routledge & Kegan Paul.

Boyer, Elizabeth, 1976. *Freydis and Gudrid*. Novelty, OH: Veritie.

Brown, Nancy Marie, 2007. *The Far Traveler: Voyages of a Viking Woman*. Orlando: Harcourt.

Busch, Fritz-Otto, 1966. *Wikingersegel vor Amerika: Die Saga von Gudrid und Freydis*. Hameln-Hannover: Adolf Sponholtz Verlag.

Chapin, Henry, 1934. *Leifsaga: A Narrative Poem of the Norse Discoveries of America*. [New York:] Farrar & Rinehart.

Clark, Joan, 1994. *Eiriksdottir: A Tale of Dreams and Luck*. Toronto: Macmillan Canada.

Désy, Jean, 1990. *La saga de Freydis Karlsevni: roman*. Montreal: L'Hexagon.

Elphinstone, Margaret, 2000. *The Sea Road*. Toronto: McArthur & Company.

Hewlett, Maurice, 1918. *Gudrid the Fair: A Tale of the Discovery of America*. New York: Dodd, Mean and Company.

Irwin, Constance, 1974. *Gudrid's Saga: The Norse Settlement in America: A Documentary Novel*. New York: St. Martin's Press.

Jensen, Malcolm C., 1979. *Leif Erikson the Lucky*. A Visual Biography. New York and London: Franklin Watts.

Jónas Kristjánsson, 1998. *Veröld víð: Skáldsaga um ævi og örlög Guðríðar Þorbjarnardóttur—víðförlustu konu miðalda*. Reykjavík: Vaka-Helgafell.

Kamban, Gudmundur, 1936. *Jeg ser et stort skønt Land*. Copenhagen: Gyldendal.

Pedersen, Sigfred, 1952. *Vinland det gode*. Copenhagen: Branner og Kroch.

Resnick, William S., 1942. *The Dragon Ship: A Story of the Vikings in America*. New York: Coward-McCann.

Scott, Winfield Townley, 1958. *The Dark Sister*. New York: New York University Press.

Vollmann, William T., 1990 [repr. 1993]. *The Ice-Shirt: A Novel*. Seven Dreams: A Book of North American Landscapes, 1. New York et al.: Penguin.

Secondary literature

Aarne, Antti, 1964. *The Types of the Folktale*, tr. and enl. Stith Thompson. Helsinki: Suomalianen tiedeakatemia.

Abels, Richard, 2006. "'Cowardice' and Duty in Anglo-Saxon England." *The Journal of Medieval Military History* 4: 29–49.

Ajootian, Aileen, 1997. "The Only Happy Couple: Hermaphrodites and Gender." In *Naked Truths: Women, Sexuality, and Gender in Classical Art and Archaeology*, ed. Olga Koloski-Ostrow and Claire L. Lyons, 220–42. London: Routledge.

Almqvist, Bo, 2001. "'My Name is Guðríðr': An Enigmatic Episode in *Grœnlendinga saga*." In Wawn and Þórunn Sigurðardóttir (2001), 15–30.

Andersen, Jørgen, 1977. *The Witch on the Wall: Medieval Erotic Sculpture in the British Isles*. Copenhagen: Rosenkilde and Bagger.

Anderson, Joel, 2013. "Disseminating and Dispensing Canon Law in Medieval Iceland." *Arkiv för nordisk filologi* 128: 78-95.

Ármann Jakobsson, 2008. "The Trollish Acts of Þorgrímr the Witch: The Meanings of *troll* and *ergi* in Medieval Iceland." *Saga-Book* 32: 39–68.

Arnold, Martin, 2006. *The Vikings: Culture and Conquest*. London: Hambledon Continuum.

———, 2007. *The Vikings: Wolves of War*. Critical Issues in History. Lanham et al.: Rowman & Littlefield.

Astell, Ann W., 1990. *The Song of Songs in the Middle Ages*. Ithaca and London: Cornell University Press.

Baitsholts, Kenneth, 2003. "Humour, Irony, and Insight: The First European Accounts of Native North Americans." In Lewis-Simpson (2003), 365–75.

Baldwin, John W., 1970. *Masters, Princes and Merchants: The Social Views of Peter the Chanter & his Circle*, 2 vols. Princeton: Princeton University Press.

Banning, Knud (ed.), 1976–82. *A Catalogue of Wall-Paintings in the Churches of Medieval Denmark 1100–1600*. 4 vols. Copenhagen: Akademisk Forlag.

de Barante, 1838. *Histoire des ducs de Bourgogne de la maison de Valois, 1364–1477*, rev. M. Gachard, 2 vols. Brussels: Société typographique belge.

Baraz, Daniel, 1994. "Bartolomeo da Trento's Book of Marian Miracles: A New Insight into the Arabic Collections of Marian Legends." *Orientalia Christiana Periodica* 60: 69–85.

Bardsley, Sandy, 2006. *Venomous Tongues: Speech and Gender in Late Medieval England*. The Middle Ages Series, ed. Ruth Mazo Karras. Philadelphia: University of Pennsylvania Press.

Barnes, Geraldine, 2001. *Viking America: The First Millennium*. Cambridge: D.S. Brewer.

Bart, Pauline B., and Patricia H. O'Brien, 1985. *Stopping Rape: Successful Survival Strategies*. The Athene Series: An International Collection of Feminist Books, ed. Gloria Bowles and Renate Duelli-Klein. Pergamon International

Library of Science, Technology, Engineering and Social Studies. New York et al.: Pergamon.

de Barthélemy, A., 1866. "La légende de Saint Budoc et de Sainte Azénor." *Bulletins et mémoires de la Société d'Émulation des Côtes-du-Nord* 4 (1867 for 1866): 235–51.

Bartlett, Robert, 2004. *The Hanged Man: A Story of Miracle, Memory, and Colonialism in the Middle Ages.* Princeton and Oxford: Princeton University Press.

Baumgartner, Walter, 1993. "Freydís in Vinland oder die Vertreibung aus dem Paradies." *Skandinavistik* 23: 16–35.

Bausi, Francesco, 1991. "Machiavelli e Caterina Sforza." *Archivio storico italiano* 149:550: 887–92.

Bellon-Méguelle, Hélène, 2008. *Du temple de Mars à la chambre de Venus: Le beau jeu courtois dans les Vœux du paon.* Essais sur le Moyen Âge, 38, ed. Jean DuFournet. Paris: Honoré Champion.

Belmont, Nicole, 1995. "L'enfant cuit.'" *Ethnologie française* 25.2: 180–86.

Berlin, Gail, 2007. "Regard the Breast: A Gesture and Its History." Paper presented at the 42nd International Congress on Medieval Studies, Kalamazoo, MI.

Besserman, Lawrence, 2006. "*Imitatio Christi* in the Later Middle Ages and in Contemporary Film: Three Paradigms." *Florilegium* 23.1 (2008 for 2006): 223–49.

Bétérous, Paule-V., 1975. "A propos d'une des légendes mariales les plus répandues: Le 'lait de la Vierge.'" *Bulletin de l'Association Guillaume Budé: Revue de culture générale*, 4th ser. 3: 403–11.

Björn Þorsteinsson, 1962–65. "Some Observations on the Discoveries and the Cultural History of the Norsemen." *Saga-Book* 16: 173–91.

Blackledge, Catherine, 2003 [repr. 2004]. *The Story of V: A Natural History of Female Sexuality.* New Brunswick, NJ: Rutgers University Press.

Bloom, Mia, 2007. "Female Suicide Bombers: A Global Trend." *Dædalus: Journal of the American Academy of Arts & Sciences* 136.1: 94–102

Bolman, Elizabeth S., 2005. "The Enigmatic Coptic Galaktotrophousa and the Cult of the Virgin Mary in Egypt." In *Images of the Mother of God: Perceptions of the Theotokos in Byzantium*, ed. Maria Vassilaki, 13–22. Aldershot and Burlington: Ashgate.

Bolte, Johannes, and Georg Polívka, 1937. "Das Mädchen ohne Hände." In *Anmerkungen zu den Kinder- und Hausmärchen der Brüder Grimm*, eds. iidem, 1: 295–311, §31. Leipzig: Dieterich'sche Verlagsbuchhandlung.

Bonner, Campbell, 1920. "The Trial of Saint Eugenia." *American Journal of Philology* 41.3: 253–64.

von Bothmer, Dietrich, 1957. *Amazons in Greek Art.* Oxford Monographs on Classical Archaeology, 5, ed. J.D. Beazley and Paul Jacobsthal. Oxford: Clarendon Press.

Brecher, Ruth and Edward, 1958. "The Enigma of Dighton Rock." *American Heritage* 9.4: 62–64, 91–92.

Broby-Johansen, R. (ed.), 1947. *Den danske billedbibel: De middelalderlige kalkmalerier i de danske kirker*. Copenhagen: Gyldendalske Boghandel, Nordisk Forlag.

Brøgger, A.W., 1937. *Vinlandsferdene*. Oslo: Gyldendal norsk forlag.

Brown, Peter, 1973. "A Dark Age Crisis: Aspects of the Iconoclastic Controversy." In idem, *Society and the Holy in Late Antiquity*, 251–301. Berkeley and Los Angeles: University of California Press, 1982.

Bruder, Reinhold, 1974. *Die germanische Frau im Lichte der Runeninschriften und der antiken Historiographie*. Quellen und Forschungen zur Sprach- und Kulturgeschichte der germanischen Völker, 57 (181), ed. Stefan Sonderegger. Berlin and New York: Walter de Gruyter.

Bryan, Elizabeth J., 2006. "Amazons and Ursulines." In Wheeler (2006), 21–30.

Buc, Philippe, 2001. *The Dangers of Ritual: Between Early Medieval Texts and Social Scientific Theory*. Princeton and Oxford: Princeton University Press.

Burne, Alfred H., 1955. *The Crecy War: A Military History of the Hundred Years War from 1337 to the Peace of Bretigny, 1360*. London: Eyre & Spottiswoode.

Burrow, J.A., 2002. *Gestures and Looks in Medieval Narrative*. Cambridge Studies in Medieval Literature, ed. Alastair Minnis. Cambridge et al.: Cambridge University Press.

Bynum, Caroline Walker, 1982. *Jesus as Mother: Studies in the Spirituality of the High Middle Ages*. Publications of the Center for Medieval and Renaissance Studies, UCLA, 16. Berkeley, Los Angeles and London: University of California Press.

———, 1986. "The Body of Christ in the Later Middle Ages: A Reply to Leo Steinberg." Repr. in Bynum (1991), 79–117.

———, 1987. *Holy Feast and Holy Fast: The Religious Significance of Food to Medieval Women*. The New Historicism: Studies in Cultural Poetics, ed. Stephen Greenblatt. Berkeley, Los Angeles and London: University of California Press.

———, 1989. "The Female Body and Religious Practice in the Later Middle Ages." Repr. in Bynum (1991), 181–238.

———, 1991. *Fragmentation and Redemption: Essays on Gender and the Human Body in Medieval Religion*. New York: Zone Books.

Byock, Jesse L., 1982. *Feud in the Icelandic Saga*. Berkeley and Los Angeles: University of California Press.

———, 1988 [repr. 1990]. *Medieval Iceland: Society, Sagas, and Power*. Berkeley, Los Angeles and London: University of California Press.

———, 2001. *Viking Age Iceland*. London: Penguin.

Calmette, Joseph, 1962 [orig. 1949]. *The Golden Age of Burgundy: The Magnificent Dukes and their Courts*, tr. Doreen Weightman. London: Weidenfeld and Nicholson.

Cameron, Vivian, 1991. "Political Exposures: Sexuality and Caricature in the French Revolution." In *Eroticism and the Body Politic*, ed. Lynn A. Hunt, 90–107. Baltimore: Johns Hopkins University Press.

Camille, Michael, 1989. *The Gothic Idol: Ideology and Image-Making in Medieval Art*. Cambridge New Art History and Criticism, ed. Norman Bryson. Cambridge et al.: Cambridge University Press.

Carpenter, Jennifer, and Sally-Beth MacLean (ed.), 1995. *Power of the Weak: Studies on Medieval Women*. Urbana and Chicago: University of Illinois Press.

Carroll, Michael P., 1986. *The Cult of the Virgin Mary: Psychological Origins*. Princeton: Princeton University Press.

———, 1992. *Madonnas that Maim: Popular Catholicism in Italy since the Fifteenth Century*. Baltimore and London: Johns Hopkins University Press.

Cazelles, Brigitte, 1991. *The Lady as Saint: A Collection of French Hagiographical Romances of the Thirteenth Century*. Middle Ages Series, ed. Edward Peters. Philadelphia: University of Pennsylvania Press.

Cerulli, Enrico, 1943. *Il Libro etiopico dei miracoli di Maria, e le sue fonti nelle letterature del medio evo latino*. R. Università di Roma, Studi orientali pubblicati a cura della Scuola Orientale, 1. Rome: Giovanni Bardi.

———, 1966. "Un episodio della storia culturale medievale: Il Libro dei Miracoli di Maria nelle letterature europee e orientali." *Cultura e scuola* 19: 117–23.

———, 1969. "'Il suicidio della peccatrice' nelle versioni araba ed etiopica del Libro dei Miracoli di Maria." *Annali dell'Istituto orientale di Napoli* n.s. 29.2: 147–79.

Cheney, Liana De Girolami, 1996. "The Cult of Saint Agatha." *Women's Art Journal* 17:1: 3–9.

Chojnacki, Stanisław, 1983. *Major Themes in Ethiopian Painting: Indigenous Developments, the Influence of Foreign Models and their Adaptation from the 13th to the 19th Century*. Äthiopistische Forschungen, 10, ed. Ernst Hammerschmidt. Wiesbaden: Franz Steiner.

Christian, William A., Jr., 1981. *Local Religion in Sixteenth-Century Spain*. Princeton: Princeton University Press.

Ciggaar, Krijnie N., 1996. *Western Travellers to Constantinople: The West and Byzantium, 962–1204: Cultural and Political Relations*. The Medieval Mediterranean: Peoples, Economies and Cultures, 400–1453, 10, ed. Michael Whitby, Paul Magdalino, Hugh Kennedy, David Abulafia, Benjamin Arbel, and Mark Meyerson. Leiden, New York, and Cologne: Brill.

Clark-Flory, Tracy, 2011. "When Porn Meets Real Motherhood." *Salon*. Accessible at <http://www.salon.com/life/feature/2011/08/16/madison_young/index.html> (originally posted 16 August 2011).

Clausen, Birthe L. (ed.), 1993. *Viking Voyages to North America*. [Roskilde:] The Viking Ship Museum.

Clayton, Mary, 1986. "Delivering the Damned: A Motif in Old English Homiletic Prose." *Medium Ævum* 55.1: 92–102.

——, 1990. *The Cult of the Virgin Mary in Anglo-Saxon England*. Cambridge Studies in Anglo-Saxon England, 2, ed. Simon Keynes and Michael Lapidge. Cambridge: Cambridge University Press.

Clendinnen, Inga, 1991. "'Fierce and Unnatural Cruelty': Cortés and the Conquest of Mexico." *Representations* 33: 65–100.

Clover, Carol J., 1979. "*Hárbarðsljóð* as Generic Farce." *Scandinavian Studies* 51.2: 124–45.

——, 1980. "The Germanic Context of the Unferþ Episode." *Speculum* 55.3: 444–68.

——, 1985. "Icelandic Family Sagas (*Íslendingasögur*)." In Clover and Lindow (1985), 239–315.

——, 1986a. "Maiden Warriors and Other Sons." *Journal of English and Germanic Philology* 85.1: 35–49.

——, 1986b. "Hildigunnr's Lament." In Lindow, Lönnroth & Weber (1986), 141–83.

——, 1993. "Regardless of Sex: Men, Women, and Power in Early Northern Europe." *Speculum* 68.2: 363–87.

——, and John Lindow (eds.), 1985. *Old Norse-Icelandic Literature: A Critical Guide*. Islandica 45. Ithaca: Cornell University Press.

Clunies Ross, Margaret, 1973. "Hildr's Ring: A Problem in the Ragnarsdrápa, Strophes 8–12." *Mediaeval Scandinavia* 6: 75–92.

——, 1981. "An Interpretation of the Myth of Þórr's Encounter with Geirrøðr and his Daughters." In Dronke et al. (1981), 370–91.

——, 2010. *The Cambridge Introduction to the Old Norse–Icelandic Saga*. Cambridge Introductions to Literature. Cambridge et al.: Cambridge University Press.

Cole, Susan G., 1995. *Power Surge: Sex, Violence & Pornography*. Toronto: Second Story Press.

Constantine, Mary-Ann, 1996. *Breton Ballads*. Aberystwyth: CMCS Publications.

Copet-Rougier, Elisabeth, 1986. "'Le Mal Court': Visible and Invisible Violence in an Acephalous Society—Mkako of Cameroon." In *The Anthropology of Violence*, ed. David Riches, 50–69. Oxford and New York: Basil Blackwell.

Cormier, Raymond J., 1981. "Pagan Shame or Christian Modesty?" *Celtica* 14: 43–46.

Coser, Lewis A., 1956 [repr. 1968]. *The Functions of Social Conflict*. International Library of Sociology and Social Reconstruction, ed. W.J.H. Sprott.

——, 1966. "Some Social Functions of Violence." *Annals of the American Academy of Political and Social Science* 364: 8–18.

De Costa, B.F., 1901. *The Pre-Columbian Discovery of America by the Northmen*, 3rd rev. ed. Albany: Joel Munsell's Sons.

Couch, Julie Nelson, 2006. "Misbehaving God: The Case of the Christ Child in MS Laud Misc. 108 'Infancy of Jesus Christ'." In Wheeler (2006), 31–43.

Crachiolo, Beth, 2004. "Seeing the Gendering of Violence: Female and Male Martyrs in the *South English Legendary*." In Meyerson et al. (2004), 147–63.

Davies, Malcolm (ed.), 1988. *Epicorum Graecorum Fragmenta*. Göttingen: Vandenhoeck & Ruprecht.

Davis, Natalie Zemon, 1973. "The Rites of Violence." In eadem, *Society and Culture in Early Modern France*, 152–87, 315–26. Stanford: Stanford University Press, 1975.

——, 1983. *The Return of Martin Guerre*. Cambridge, MA: Harvard University Press.

DeForest, M., 1993. "Clytemnestra's Breast and the Evil Eye." In *Women's Power, Man's Game: Essays on Classical Antiquity in Honor of Joy K. King*, ed. eadem, 129–48. Wauconda: Bolchazy-Carducci.

Delisle, Léopold, 1868. *Inventaire des manuscrits de Saint-Germain-des-Prés conservés à la Bibliothèque impériale sous les numéros 11504–14231 du fonds latin*. Paris: Auguste Durand et Pedone-Lauriel.

DeMarco, Patricia A., 1997. *Chivalry in Crisis: The Representation of the Subject of Violence in Late Medieval Literature*. Ph.D. Diss., Duke University, Durham, NC.

Deonna, W., 1914. "Le dévoilement prophylactique du corps." *Anzeiger für schweizerische Altertumskunde / Indicateur d'antiquités suisses* n.s. 16 (1915 for 1914): 62–66.

Desan, Suzanne, 2004. *The Family on Trial in Revolutionary France*. Studies on the History of Society and Culture, 51, ed. Victoria E. Bonnell and Lynn Hunt. Berkeley, Los Angeles, and London: University of California Press.

Dogaer, Georges, and Marguerite Debae (eds.), 1967. *La Librairie de Philippe le Bon: Exposition organisée à l'occasion du 500ᵉ anniversaire de la mort du duc*. Brussels: Bibliothèque Albert 1ᵉʳ.

Domínguez Rodríguez, Ana, 1998. "'Compassio' y 'co-redemptio' en las cantigas de Santa María: Crucifixión y Juicio final." *Archivo Español de Arte* 71.281: 17–35.

Douglas, Mary, 1966. *Purity and Danger: An Analysis of the Concepts of Pollution and Taboo*. London: Routledge & Kegan Paul.

——, 1970. *Natural Symbols: Explorations in Cosmology*. New York: Pantheon Books.

Drews, Arthur, 1928. *Die Marienmythe*. Erstes bis drittes Tausend. Jena: Eugen Diederich.

Driscoll, Matthew, 2005. "Late Prose Fiction (*lygisögur*)." In McTurk (2005), 190–204.

Dronke, Ursula, 1984. "*Óminnis hegri.*" In Fidjestøl et al. (1984), 53–60.

——, Guðrún P. Helgadóttir, Gerd Wolfgang Weber, and Hans Bekker-Nielsen (eds.), 1981. *Specvlvm Norroenvm: Norse Studies in Memory of Gabriel Turville-Petre.* Odense: Odense University Press.

Duerr, Hans Peter, 1993. *Der Mythos vom Zivilisationsprozeß,* vol. 3: *Obszönität und Gewalt.* Frankfurt a.M.: Suhrkamp.

Duffy, Eamon, 2005. *The Stripping of the Altars: Traditional Religion in England 1400–1580,* 2nd ed. New Haven and London: Yale University Press.

Dupeux, Cécile, 1991. "La Lactation de Saint Bernard de Clairvaux: Genèse et évolution d'une image." In *L'Image et la production du sacré: Actes du colloque de Strasbourg (20–21 janvier 1988),* ed. Françoise Dunand, Jean-Michel Spieser, and Jean Wirth, 165–93. Paris: Méridiens Klincksieck.

Easton, Martha, 2008. "'Was It Good For You, Too?' Medieval Erotic Art and Its Audiences." *Different Visions: A Journal of New Perspectives on Medieval Art* 1: 1–30.

Ebel, Else, 1994. "Fiktion und Realität in den Vínlandsagas." In *Studien zum Altgermanischen: Festschrift für Heinrich Beck,* ed. Heiko Uecker, 89–100. Ergänzungsbände zum Reallexikon der Germanischen Altertumskunde, 11, ed. Heinrich Beck, Heiko Steuer, and Dieter Timpe. Berlin and New York: Walter de Gruyter.

Edgren, Helena, 1993. *Mercy and Justice: Miracles of the Virgin Mary in Finnish Medieval Wall-Paintings,* tr. Jüri Kokkonen. Finska Fornminnesföreningens Tidskrift 100. Helsinki: Vammala.

Eldevik, Randi, 1993. "Trójumanna saga." In Pulsiano et al. (1993), 658–59.

Ellington, Donna Spivey, 2001. *From Sacred Body to Angelic Soul: Understanding Mary in Late Medieval and Early Modern Europe.* Washington, DC: The Catholic University of America Press.

Ellis Davidson, H.R., 1976. *The Viking Road to Byzantium.* London: George Allen & Unwin.

Enright, Michael J., 1996. *Lady with a Mead Cup: Ritual, Prophecy and Lordship in the European Warband from La Tène to the Viking Age.* Dublin: Four Courts Press.

Falk, Oren, 1998. "Searching for Skrælings: Images of Native Americans in the Vínland Sagas (*Grænlendinga saga* and *Eiríks saga rauða*)." Paper presented at the 33rd International Congress on Medieval Studies, Kalamazoo, MI.

——, 2004. "Review of *Approaches to Vínland,* ed. Andrew Wawn and Þórunn Sigurðardóttir (Reykjavík: Sigurður Nordal Institute, 2001)." *Speculum* 79.2: 581–83.

——, 2005. "Beardless Wonders: 'Gaman vas Sǫxu' (The Sex was Great)." In *Verbal Encounters: Anglo-Saxon and Old Norse Studies for Roberta Frank,* ed. Antonina Harbus and Russell Poole, 223–46. Toronto Old English Series. Toronto: University of Toronto Press.

———, 2011. "Medievalism and Medieval Studies: A Case Study of Freydís Eiríksdóttir." Paper presented at the Sixth Annual Fiske Conference on Medieval Icelandic Studies, Cornell University, Ithaca, NY.

———, 2013. "Bestiality, Inside Out: Two Notes on 'Moriuht,' lines 231–34." *Mittellateinisches Jahrbuch* 48.3: 399–413.

———, forthcoming. *This Spattered Isle: Violence and Risk in Medieval Iceland.* Unpublished manuscript.

Farr, James R., 1988. *Hands of Honor: Artisans and Their World in Dijon, 1550–1650.* Ithaca and London: Cornell University Press.

Faulkes, Anthony, and Richard Perkins (ed.), 1993. *Viking Revaluations: Viking Society Centennary Symposium, 14–15 May 1992.* London: Viking Society for Northern Research.

Feilberg, H.F., 1901. "Der böse Blick in nordischer Überlieferung." *Zeitschrift des Vereins für Volkskunde* 11: 304–30 and 420–30.

Fidjestøl, Bjarne, Eyvind Fjeld Halvorsen, Finn Hødnebø, Alfred Jakobsen, Hallvard Magerøy, and Magnus Rindal (eds.), 1984. *Festskrift til Ludvig Holm-Olsen: på hans 70-årsdag den 9. juni 1984.* [Bergen:] Alvheim & Eide Akademisk Forlag.

Field, J.V., 2005. *Piero della Francesca: A Mathematician's Art.* New Haven and London: Yale University Press.

Fischer, Svante, 1999. "Ännu ett runfynd i Hagia Sofia?" *Nytt om runner* 14: 27.

Fischhoff, Baruch, 1980. "For Those Condemned to Study the Past: Reflections on Historical Judgment." In *Fallible Judgment in Behavioral Research*, ed. Richard A. Shweder, 79–93. New Directions for Methodology of Social and Behavioral Science, 4, ed. Donald W. Fiske. San Francisco: Jossey-Bass.

Fisher, Will, 2001. "The Renaissance Beard: Masculinity in Early Modern England." *Renaissance Quarterly* 54.1: 155–87.

Fiske, John, 1993. *Power Plays, Power Works.* London and New York: Verso.

Fitzhugh, William W., and Elisabeth I. Ward (eds.), 2000. *Vikings: The North Atlantic Saga.* Washington, DC and London: Smithsonian Institute Press and the National Museum of Natural History.

Foote, Peter, 1984. "Things in Early Norse Verse." In Fidjestøl et al. (1984), 74–83.

Frankfurter, David, 1993. *Elijah in Upper Egypt: The Apocalypse of Elijah and Early Egyptian Christianity.* Studies in Antiquity and Christianity. Minneapolis: Fortress Press.

Fraser, Antonia, 1988. *Boadicea's Chariot: The Warrior Queens.* London: Weidenfeld and Nicholson.

Fraser, Sloane, 1962. "The Queen of Scotland." *Folklore* 73.1: 41–54.

Freccero, John, 1993. "Medusa and the Madonna of Forlì: Political Sexuality in Machiavelli." In *Machiavelli and the Discourse of Literature*, ed. Albert Russell Ascoli and Victoria Kahn, 161–78. Ithaca and London: Cornell University Press.

Freud, Sigmund, 2003 [orig. 1919]. "The Uncanny." In *The Uncanny*, tr. David McLintock, 121–62. The New Penguin Freud, ed. Adam Phillips. London et al.: Penguin.

Frey, Dagobert, 1952. "Ikonographische Bemerkungen zur Passionsmystik den späten Mittelalters." In *Neue Beiträge zur Archäologie und Kunstgeschichte Schwabens, Julius Baum zum 70. Geburtstag am 9. April 1952 gewidmet*, ed. [Fritz Kauffmann (?)], 107–23 and pll. 47–54. Stuttgart: W. Kohlhammer.

Frieß, Peter, 1994. "Biblische Automaten in der Münchner Frauenkirche." In *Monachium sacrum: Festschrift zur 500-Jahr-Feier der Metropolitankirche Zu Unserer Lieben Frau in München*, ed. Georg Schwaiger and Hans Ramisch, 2 vols, 2: 533–56. Munich: Deutscher Kunstverlag.

Fulton, Rachel, 2009. "Mary." In *The Cambridge History of Christianity*, vol. 4: *Christianity in Western Europe c. 1100–c. 1500*, ed. Miri Rubin and Walter Simons, 283–96. Cambridge et al.: Cambridge University Press.

Gathorne-Hardy, G.M., 1921. *The Norse Discoverers of America: The Wineland Sagas*. Oxford: Clarendon Press.

Geary, Patrick J., 1979a. "Humiliation of Saints." Repr. in idem (1994), 95–115.

——, 1979b. "Coercion of Saints in Medieval Religious Practice." Repr. in idem (1994), 116–24.

——, 1994. *Living with the Dead in the Middle Ages*. Ithaca and London: Cornell University Press.

——, 2006. *Women at the Beginning: Origin Myths from the Amazons to the Virgin Mary*. Princeton: Princeton University Press.

Gebhart, Émile, [ca. 1906]. *L'Italie mystique: Histoire de la rénaissance réligieuse au Moyen Age*. Bibliothèque de littérature. [Paris:] Hachette.

Geertz, Clifford, 1966. "Religion as a Cultural System." Repr. in idem (1973), 87–125.

——, 1972. "The Politics of Meaning." Repr. in idem (1973), 311–26.

——, 1973. *The Interpretation of Cultures*. New York: Basic Books.

Getatchew Haile, 1983. "The Cause of the Ǝsṭifanosites: A Fundamentalist Sect in the Church of Ethiopia." *Paideuma: Mitteilungen zur Kulturkunde* 29: 93–119.

Geyer, Rudolf, 1909. "Die arabischen Frauen in der Schlacht." *Mitteilungen der anthropologischen Gesellschaft in Wien* 39: 148–55.

Gillingham, John, 1992. "Conquering the Barbarians: War and Chivalry in Twelfth-Century Britain." *Haskins Society Journal* 4: 67–84.

Gísli Sigurðsson, 2004 [orig. 2002]. *The Medieval Icelandic Saga and Oral Tradition: A Discourse on Method*, tr. Nicholas Jones. Publications of the Milman Parry Collection of Oral Literature, 2; Cambridge, MA and London: Harvard University Press.

Glauser, Jürg, 2005. "Romance (Translated *riddarasögur*)." In McTurk (2005), 372–87.

Goldsmith, Margaret, 1935 [repr. 1976]. *Seven Women against the World*. Pioneers of the Women's Movement. London: Methuen & Co.

Gordon, E.V., [1957]. *An Introduction to Old Norse*, 2nd ed., rev. A.R. Taylor. Oxford: Clarendon Press.

Graef, Hilda, 1963–65. *Mary: A History of Doctrine and Devotion*, 2 vols. New York: Sheed and Ward.

Gray, Madeleine, and Salvador Ryan, 2007. "Mother of Mercy: The Virgin Mary and the Last Judgment in Welsh and Irish Tradition." In *Ireland and Wales in the Middle Ages*, ed. Karen Jankulak and Jonathan M. Wooding, 246–61. Dublin: Four Courts Press.

Greenberg, Kenneth S., 1990. "The Nose, the Lie, and the Duel in the Antebellum South." *American Historical Review* 95.1: 57–74.

Greenshields, Malcolm, 1994. *An Economy of Violence in Early Modern France: Crime and Justice in the Haute Auvergne, 1587–1664*. University Park, PA: The Pennsylvania State University Press.

Grigsby, John L., 2000. *The Gab as a Latent Genre in Medieval French Literature: Drinking and Boasting in the Middle Ages*, ed. Joseph J. Duggan. Medieval Academy Books, 103. Cambridge, MA: The Medieval Academy of America.

Gripkey, Mary Vincentine, 1938 [repr. 1969]. *The Blessed Virgin Mary as Mediatrix in the Latin and Old French Legend prior to the Fourteenth Century*. The Catholic University of America Studies in Romance Languages and Literatures, 17. Washington, DC: The Catholic University of America [repr. New York: AMS Press].

Groebner, Valentin, 1995. "Losing Face, Saving Face: Noses and Honour in the Late Medieval Town," tr. Pamela Selwyn. *History Workshop Journal* 40: 1–15.

———, 2004 [orig. 2003]. *Defaced: The Visual Culture of Violence in the Later Middle Ages*, tr. Pamela Selwyn. New York: Zone Books.

Grønlie, Siân, 2006. "'No Longer Male and Female': Redeeming Women in the Icelandic Conversion Narratives." *Medium Ævum* 75.2: 293–318.

Grossman, Dave, 1995. *On Killing: The Psychological Cost of Learning to Kill in War and Society*. Boston et al.: Little, Brown and Company.

Grubitzsch, Helga, 1989. "Théroigne de Méricourt." In *Sklavin oder Bürgerin? Französische Revolution und neue Weiblichkeit 1760–1830*, ed. Viktoria Schmidt-Linsenhoff, 88–102. Kleine Schriften des Historischen Museum Frankfurt, 44. Frankfurt a.M.: Jonas Verlag.

———, [1992]. "Die Autobiographie der Théroigne de Méricourt. Überlegungen zum feministischen Umgang mit autobiographischen Texten." In *Bildersturm im Elfenbeinturm: Ansätze feministischer Literaturwissenschaft*, ed. Karin Fischer, Eveline Kilian, and Jutta Schönberg, 96–115. Attempto Studium Generale. Tübingen: Attempto.

———, and Roswitha Bockholt, 1991. *Théroigne de Méricourt: Die Amazone der Freiheit*. Pfaffenwiler: Centaurus.

Gunnar Harðarson and Stefán Karlsson, 1993. "Hauksbók." In Pulsiano et al. (1993), 271–72.

Gunnar Karlsson, 1993. "A Century of Research on Early Icelandic Society." In Faulkes and Perkins (1993), 15–25.

Haastrup, Ulla, and Robert Egevang, 1985–92. *Danske kalkmalerier*, 8 vols. Copenhagen: Nationalmuseet.

Haberland, Eike, 1976. *Altes Christentum in Süd-Äthiopien: Eine vergessene Missionsepoche.* Frankfurter historische Vorträge, 2. Wiesbaden: Franz Steiner Verlag.

Hagedorn, Suzanne, 2008. "Amazons: Women Warriors & the Medieval Imagination." Quodlibet presentation at Cornell University, Ithaca, NY (6 November).

Hairston, Julia L., 2000. "Skirting the Issue: Machiavelli's Caterina Sforza." *Renaissance Quarterly* 53.3: 687–712.

Hall, Edwin, 1994. *The Arnolfini Betrothal: Medieval Marriage and the Enigma of van Eyck's Double Portrait.* California Studies in the History of Art, Discovery Series, 3. Berkeley and Los Angeles: University of California Press.

Hallberg, Peter, 1987. "Recent Trends in Saga Research." In *Proceedings of the Seventh Biennial Conference of Teachers of Scandinavian Studies in Great Britain and Northern Ireland held at University College London, March 23–25 1987,* ed. R.D.S. Allen and M.P. Barnes, 78–95. [London:] University College London.

Halldór Hermannsson, 1936 [repr. 1966]. *The Problem of Wineland.* Islandica, 25. Ithaca: Cornell University Press [repr. New York: Kraus Reprint Corporation].

Halsall, Guy, 1992. "Playing by whose Rules? A Further Look at Viking Atrocity in the Ninth Century." *Medieval History* 2.2: 2–12.

Hammer-Tugendhat, Daniela, 1987. "Venus und Luxuria: Zum Verhältnis von Kunst und Ideologie im Hochmittelalter." In *Frauen - Bilder - Männer - Mythen: Kunsthistorische Beiträge,* ed. Ilsebill Barta, Zita Breu, Daniela Hammer-Tugendhat, Ulrike Jenni, Irene Nierhaus, and Judith Schöbel, 13–34. Berlin: Dietrich Reimer.

Hammerschmidt, Ernst, 1963. *Stellung und Bedeutung des Sabbats in Äthiopien.* Studia Delitzschiana: Abhandlungen und Texte aus dem Institutum Judaicum Delitzschianum Münster (Westfalen), 7, ed. Karl Heinrich Regenstorf. Stuttgart: W. Kohlhammer.

Hanawalt, Barbara A., 1998. "Rituals of Inclusion and Exclusion: Hierarchy and Marginalization in Medieval London." In eadem, *'Of Good and Ill Repute': Gender and Social Control in Medieval England,* 18–34. New York and Oxford: Oxford University Press.

Harper, Carrie A., 1898. "Carados and the Serpent." *Modern Language Notes* 13.7: 209–16.

Hastrup, Kirsten, 1985. *Culture and History in Medieval Iceland: An Anthropological Analysis of Structure and Change.* Oxford: Clarendon Press.

——, 1998. *A Place Apart: An Anthropological Study of the Icelandic World.* Oxford Studies in Social and Cultural Anthropology. Oxford: Clarendon Press.

Haugen, Einar, 1981. "Was Vínland in Newfoundland?" In *Proceedings of the Eighth Viking Congress, Århus 24–31 August 1977,* ed. Hans Bekker-Nielsen, Peter Foote, and Olaf Olsen, 3–8. Odense: Odense University Press.

Hay, David, 2004. "Attitudes towards Female Military Leaders up to the Time of Gratian: Some Canonical Texts and Their Historical Contexts." In Meyerson et al. (2004), 287–313.

Heal, Bridget, 2007. *The Cult of the Virgin Mary in Early Modern Germany: Protestant and Catholic Piety, 1500–1648.* Past and Present Publications, ed. Lyndal Roper and Chris Wickham. Cambridge et al.: Cambridge University Press.

Heckenbach, Josephus, 1911. *De nuditate sacra sacrisque vinculis.* Religionsgeschichtliche Versuche und Vorarbeiten, 9.3, ed. Richard Wünsch and Ludwig Deubner. Gießen: Alfred Töpelmann.

Heldman, Marilyn E., 1994. *The Marian Icons of the Painter Frē Ṣeyon: A Study in Fifteenth-Century Ethiopian Art, Patronage, and Spirituality.* Orientalia Biblica et Christiana, 6, ed. Eckart Otto and Siegbert Uhlig. Wiesbaden: Harrassowitz.

Helgi Þorláksson, 2001. "The Vínland Sagas in a Contemporary Light." In Wawn and Þórunn Sigurðardóttir (2001), 63–77.

Heller, Kurt Edmund, 1940. "The Story of the Sorcerer's Serpent: A Puzzling Mediaeval Folk Tale." *Speculum* 15.3: 338–47.

Heller, Rolf, 1958. *Die literarische Darstellung der Frau in den Isländersagas.* Saga: Untersuchungen zur nordischen Literatur- und Sprachgeschichte, 2, ed. Walter Baetke. Halle (Saale): Max Niemeyer Verlag.

Hermann Pálsson, 2000. "Vínland Revisited." *Northern Studies: The Journal of the Scottish Society for Northern Studies* 35: 11–38.

Hill, Joyce, 1983. "From Rome to Jerusalem: An Icelandic Itinerary of the Mid-Twelfth Century." *Harvard Theological Review* 76.2: 175–203.

Hill, Thomas D., 1992. "Delivering the Damned in Old English Anonymous Homilies and Jón Arason's *Ljómur.*" *Medium Ævum* 61.1: 75–82.

——, 2010. "'Thomas Rhymer (A)' and the Tradition of Early Modern Feminist Theology." *Harvard Theological Review* 103.4: 471–83.

[Hlynur Páll Pálsson, (2002).] *Saga Museum Program*[, tr. Martin Regal]. [Reykjavík:] E. Backman Advertising Agency.

[Hockman, Lynne (ed.)], 1988. *French Caricature and the French Revolution, 1789–1799.* Los Angeles: Grunwald Center for the Graphic Arts, Wight Art Gallery and University of California Press.

Holand, Hjalmar R., 1940. *Norse Discoveries & Explorations in America, 982–1362: Leif Erikson to the Kensington Stone.* New York: Dover.

Hollander, Anne, 1978. *Seeing through Clothes*. New York: Viking Press.

Holthausen, Ferdinand, 1948. *Vergleichendes und etymologisches Wörterbuch des Altwestnordischen: Altnorwegisch-isländischen*. Göttingen: Vandenhoeck & Ruprecht.

Hovgaard, William, 1914. *The Voyages of the Norsemen to America*. Scandinavian Monographs 1. New York: The American-Scandinavian Foundation.

Howley, James P., 1915. *The Beothucks or Red Indians: The Aboriginal Inhabitants of Newfoundland*. Cambridge: Cambridge University Press.

Høyersten, Jon Geir, 1998. *Personlighet og avvik: En studie i islendingesagaens menneskebilde, med særlig vekt på Njála*. Bergen: Universitetet i Bergen.

Huet, Marie-Hélène, 1993. *Monstrous Imagination*. Cambridge, MA and London: Harvard University Press.

Hufton, Olwen H., 1992. *Women and the Limits of Citizenship in the French Revolution*. The Donald G. Creighton Lectures 1989. Toronto et al.: University of Toronto Press.

Hull, Vernam, 1940. "How St. Adamnan Released the Women of Ireland from Military Service." *Zeitschrift für celtische Philologie* 21: 335–38.

Huneycutt, Lois, 1995. "Intercession and the High-Medieval Queen: The Esther Topos." In Carpenter and MacLean (1995), 126–46.

Hunt, Lucy-Anne, 2007. "Eastern Christian Iconographic and Architectural Traditions: Oriental Orthodox." In *The Blackwell Companion to Eastern Christianity*, ed. Ken Parry, 388–419. Malden, MA and Oxford: Blackwell.

Hunt, Lynn, 1992. *The Family Romance of the French Revolution*. Berkeley and Los Angeles: University of California Press.

———, 1993 [repr. 1996]. "Introduction: Obscenity and the Origins of Modernity, 1500–1800." In *The Invention of Pornography: Obscenity and the Origins of Modernity, 1500–1800*, ed. eadem, 9–45. New York: Zone Books.

HWdA = *Handwörterbuch des deutschen Aberglaubens*, ed. E. Hoffmann-Krayer and Hanns Bächtold-Stäubli, 1927–42. 10 vols. Berlin and Leipzig: W. de Gruyter.

Hyams, Paul R., 1986. "The Strange Case of Thomas of Eldersfield." *History Today* 36.6: 9–15.

Immenkötter, Herbert, 1995. "Glaubensbilder der Renaissance in Deutschland: Ikonographische Folgen der Reformation." In *Das 16. Jahrhundert: Europäische Renaissance*, ed. Hildegard Kuester. Eichstätter Kolloquium 2, ed. Roland Hagenbüchle, 167–79. Regensburg: Verlag Friedrich Pustet.

Ingstad, Helge, 1985. *The Norse Discovery of America*, vol. 2: *The Historical Background and the Evidence of the Norse Settlement Discovered in Newfoundland*. Oslo et al.: Norwegian University Press.

Iverslie, P.P., 1912. *Gustav Storms Studier over Vinlandsreiserne*. Minneapolis: P.P. Iverslie.

Jansson, Sven B.F., 1944. *Sagorna om Vinland*, vol. 1: *Handskrifterna till Erik den rödes saga*. Lund: Håkan Ohlssons Boktryckeri.

————, 1958. "Eiríks saga rauða." In *Kulturhistorisk leksikon for nordisk middelalder, fra vikingetid til reformationstid*, 3: 536–40. Copenhagen: Rosenkilde og Bagger.

Jarring, Gunnar, 1978. "Evliya Çelebi och marmorlejonet från Pireus." *Fornvännen* 73: 1–4.

Jesch, Judith, 1991. *Women in the Viking Age*. Woodbridge: Boydell Press.

Jezler, Peter (ed.), 1994a. *Himmel, Hölle, Fegefeuer: Das Jenseits im Mittelalter*. Katalog [einer] Ausstellung des Schweizerischen Landesmuseums. . . . Munich: Wilhelm Fink.

————, 1994b. "Jenseitsmodelle und Jenseitsvorsorge—eine Einführung." In Jezler (1994a), 13–26.

Jochens, Jenny, 1995. *Women in Old Norse Society*. Ithaca and London: Cornell University Press.

————, 1996. *Old Norse Images of Women*. Philadelphia: University of Pennsylvania Press.

————, 2002. "Vikings Westward to Vínland: The Problem of Women." In *Cold Counsel: Women in Old Norse Literature and Mythology*, ed. Sarah M. Anderson and Karen Swenson, 81–92. New York and London: Routledge.

J[ó]hanna Katr[í]n Fri[ð]riksd[ó]ttir, 2010. *Women, Bodies, Words and Power: Women in Old Norse Literature*. PhD Diss., Oxford University.

————, 2013. *Women in Old Norse Literature: Bodies, Words, and Power*. The New Middle Ages, ed. Bonnie Wheeler. New York: Palgrave Macmillan.

Johns, Catherine, 1982. *Sex or Symbol: Erotic Images of Greece and Rome*. A Colonnade Book. London: British Museum Publications.

Jón Jóhannesson, 1962–65 [orig. 1956]. "The Date of the Composition of the Saga of the Greenlanders," tr. Tryggvi J. Oleson. *Saga-Book* 16: 54–66.

Jónas Kristjánsson, 1988 [orig. 1974]. *Eddas and Sagas: Iceland's Medieval Literature*, tr. Peter Foote. Reykjavík: Hið íslenska bókmenntafélag.

Jones, Gwyn, 1986. *The Norse Atlantic Saga*, 2nd ed. Oxford and New York: Oxford University Press.

Kaeuper, Richard W., 1999. *Chivalry and Violence in Medieval Europe*. Oxford: Oxford University Press.

Kahle, Bernhard, 1903. "Noch einiges von bösen Blick." *Zeitschrift des Vereins für Volkskunde* 13: 213–16.

Kahneman, Daniel, 2011. *Thinking, Fast and Slow*. New York: Farrar, Straus and Giroux.

Kalinke, Marianne E., 1986. "The Misogamous Maiden Kings of Icelandic Romance." *Scripta Islandica: Isländska sällskapets årsbok* 37: 47–71.

————, 1990. *Bridal-Quest Romance in Medieval Iceland*. Islandica, 46. Ithaca: Cornell University Press.

[Kålund, Kristian (ed.)], 1888–94. *Katalog over den arnamagnæanske Håndskriftsamling*. 2 vols. Copenhagen: Gyldendalske Boghandel.

Karner, Tracy Xavia, 1998. "Engendering Violent Men: Oral Histories of Military Masculinity." In *Masculinities and Violence*, ed. Lee H. Bowker, 197–232. Research on Men and Masculinities, 10, ed. Michael S. Kimmel. Thousand Oaks, CA et al.: Sage Publications.

Kauffmann, C.M., 2003. *Biblical Imagery in Medieval England 700–1550*. London and Turnhout: Harvey Miller Publishers.

Kedar, Benjamin Z., and Chr. Westergård-Nielsen, 1978–79. "Icelanders in the Crusader Kingdom of Jerusalem: A Twelfth-Century Account." *Mediaeval Scandinavia* 11 (1982 for 1978–79): 193–211.

Kellogg, Robert, 2001. "The Vínland Sagas: A Romance of Conversion." In Wawn and Þórunn Sigurðardóttir (2001), 31–38.

Kelly, Eamonn P., 1996. *Sheela-na-Gigs: Origins and Functions*. Dublin: Country House and The National Museum of Ireland.

Khaleeli, Homa, 2011. "The Nude Radicals: Feminism Ukrainian Style." *The Guardian*. Accessible at <http://www.guardian.co.uk/lifeandstyle/2011/apr/15/ukrainian-feminists-topless-campaign> (originally posted 15 April 2011).

King, Helen, 1986. "Agnodike and the Profession of Medicine." *Proceedings of the Cambridge Philological Society* 212 (n.s. 32): 53–77.

Klapisch-Zuber, Christiane, 1983. "Parents de sang, parents de lait: La Mise en nourrice à Florence (1300–1530)." *Annales de démographie historique* (Mères et nourrissons): 33–64.

Kleinbaum, Abby Wettan, 1983. *The War against the Amazons*. New York et al.: McGraw-Hill Book Company.

Kline, Naomi Reed, 2001. *Maps of Medieval Thought: The Hereford Paradigm*. Woodbridge: Boydell.

Knipping, John B., 1974 [orig. 1939–42]. *Iconography of the Counter Reformation in the Netherlands*, [tr. H. Jones and Elizabeth Barrow,] 2 vols. Nieuwkoop and Leiden: B. de Graaf and A.W. Sijthoff.

Knirk, James E., 1999. "Runer i Hagia Sophia i Istanbul." *Nytt om runer* 14: 26–27.

Koepplin, D., 1970. "Interzession Mariä und Christi vor Gottvater." In *Lexikon der christlichen Ikonographie*, ed. Engelbert Kirschbaum SJ et al., 8 vols., 2: 346–52. Rome et al.: Herder.

Kolodny, Annette, 2012. *In Search of First Contact: The Vikings of Vinland, the Peoples of the Dawnland, and the Anglo-American Anxiety of Discovery*. Durham, NC: Duke University Press.

Kolsrud, Oluf, 1910. "Kjættarskapen og den norske Kyrkja under Katolisismen." *Syn og Segn* 16: 57–64, 105–19.

Körner, Hans, 1988. "Hans Baldungs 'Muttergottes mit der Weintraube.'" *Pantheon: Internationale Jahreszeitschrift für Kunst* 46: 50–60.

Koziol, Geoffrey, 1992. "Monks, Feuds, and the Making of Peace in Eleventh-Century Flanders." In *The Peace of God: Social Violence and Religious Response in France around the Year 1000*, ed. Thomas Head and Richard Landes, 239–58. Ithaca and London: Cornell University Press.

Kristeva, Julia, 1977 [orig. 1983, repr. 1990]. "Stabat Mater," tr. Léon Roudiez. In *The Kristeva Reader*, ed. Toril Moi, 160–86. Oxford: Basil Blackwell.

———, 1982 [orig. 1980]. *Powers of Horror: An Essay on Abjection*, tr. Leon S. Roudiez. New York: Columbia University Press.

Kuhn, Hans, 1968. "Kämpen und Berserker." *Frümittelalterliche Studien: Jahrbuch des Instituts für Frühmittelalterforschung der Universität Münster* 2: 218–27.

Künstle, Karl, 1926–28. *Ikonographie der christlichen Kunst*, 2 vols. Freiburg: Herder.

Kvilhaug, Maria, 2004. "The Maiden with the Mead: A Goddess of Initiation Rituals in Old Norse Mythology?" MA Thesis, University of Oslo.

Lacour, Léopold, 1900. *Trois femmes de la Révolution: Olympe de Gouges, Théroigne de Méricourt, Rose Lacombe. Les Origines du féminisme contemporain*. Paris: Plon.

Lane, Barbara G., 1973. "The 'Symbolic Crucifixion['] in the Hours of Catherine of Cleves." *Oud-Holland* 87:1: 4–26.

Langer, Susanne K., 1957 [repr. 1971]. *Philosophy in a New Key: A Study in the Symbolism of Reason, Rite, and Art*, 3rd ed. Cambridge, MA: Harvard University Press.

Laurent, Donatien, 1987. "Enori et le roi de Brest." In *Etudes sur la Bretagne et les pays celtiques: Mélanges offerts à Yves Le Gallo*, ed. Chantal Guillou, 207–24. Cahiers de Bretagne Occidentale, 6. Brest: Centre de Recherche Bretonne et Celtique, l'Institut Culturel de Bretagne, and Le Conseil général du Finistère.

de Lauretis, Teresa, 1985a. "The Violence of Rhetoric: Considerations on Representation and Gender." Repr. in de Lauretis (1987), 31–50.

———, 1985b. "Gaudy Rose: Eco and Narcissism." Repr. in de Lauretis (1987), 51–69.

———, 1987. *Technologies of Gender: Essays on Theory, Film, and Fiction*. Bloomington: Indiana University Press.

Layher, William, 2007. "Caught between Worlds: Gendering the Maiden Warrior in Old Norse." In *Women and Medieval Epic: Gender, Genre, and the Limits of Epic Masculinity*, ed. Sara S. Poor and Jana K. Schulman, 183–208. New York and Basingstoke: Palgrave-Macmillan.

Leach, Edmund R., 1964. "Anthropological Aspects of Language: Animal Categories and Verbal Abuse." In *Mythology: Selected Readings*, ed. Pierre Maranda, 39–67. Harmondsworth: Penguin, 1972.

Leclant, Jean, 1960. "Le rôle de l'allaitement dans le cérémonial pharaonique du couronnement." In *Proceedings of the IXth International Congress for the History of Religions, Tokyo and Kyoto, 1958, August 27th—September 9th*, [ed. Teruji Ishizu et al.], 135–45. Tokyo: Maruzen.

Leclercq, Henri, 1932. "Marseille." In *Dictionnaire d'archéologie chrétienne et de liturgie*, ed. Fernand Cabrol and Henri Leclercq, 10: 2204–93. Paris: Letouzet et Ané. [references by column number]

Le Menn, Gwennolé, 1985. *La femme au sein d'or: Des chants populaires bretons . . . aux légendes celtiques*. Revue SKOL, 86–88. Saint-Brieuc: SKOL—DAS-TUM and l'Institut Culturel de Bretagne.

Lévi-Strauss, Claude, 1963–76 [orig. 1958]. *Structural Anthropology*, tr. Claire Jacobson, Brooke Grundfest Schoepf and Monique Layton, 2 vols. New York and London: Basic Books.

Lewis, Shannon, 2000. "*Hvatr ok Blauðr*: Interdisciplinary Approaches to Gender in Hiberno-Norse Society." MA Thesis, University of York.

Lewis-Simpson, Shannon (ed.), 2003. *Vínland Revisited: The Norse World at the Turn of the First Millennium; Selected Papers from the Viking Millennium International Symposium, 15–24 September 2000, Newfoundland and Labrador*. St. John's, NL: Historic Sites Association of Newfoundland and Labrador.

Lind, E.H., 1905–31. *Norsk-isländska dopnamn ock fingerade namn från medeltiden*, 2 vols. Uppsala and Leipzig: A.-B. Lundequistska Bokhandeln and Otto Harrassowicz [vol. 1]; Oslo, Uppsala and Copenhagen: Jacob Dybwads Bokhandel, A.-B. Lundequistska Bokhandeln and G.E.C. Gads Boghandel [supplement].

Linden, Eugene, 2004. "The Vikings: A Memorable Visit to North America." *Smithsonian* 35.9: 92–99.

Lindow, John, 1994. "Bloodfeud and Scandinavian Mythology." *alvíssmál* 4: 51–68.

Linke, Uli, 1996. "The Origin of Poetry: Narratives of Masculinity and Female Disempowerment in Icelandic Mythology." In *Denying Biology: Essays on Gender and Pseudo-Procreation*, ed. Warren Shapiro and Uli Linke, 129–65. Lanham et al.: University Press of America.

Lodewyckx, A., 1955. "Freydís Eiríksdóttir rauda and the Germania of Tacitus." *Arkiv för nordisk filologi* 70: 182–87.

Lundberg, Oskar, 1946. "Holmgång och Holmgångsblot." *Arv* 2: 125–38.

Lundén, Tryggve, 1981. "Jungfru Maria såsom corredemptrix eller medåter-lösarinna framställd i teologisk litteratur och bildkonst från Sveriges medeltid." *Konsthistorisk tidskrift* 50.1: 33–42.

Macdonald, Sharon, 1987. "Boadicea: Warrior, Mother and Myth." In *Images of Women in Peace and War: Cross-Cultural and Historical Perspectives*, ed. Sharon Macdonald, Pat Holden, and Shirley Ardener, 40–61. Women in Society: A Feminist List, ed. Jo Campling. London: Macmillan Education.

MacKinnon, Catharine A., 1979. *Sexual Harassment of Working Women: A Case of Sex Discrimination*. Foreword by Thomas I. Emerson. New Haven and London: Yale University Press.

———, 1989 [repr. 1997]. "Rape: On Coercion and Consent." In *Writing on the Body: Female Embodiment and Feminist Theory*, ed. Katie Conboy, Nadia

Medina, and Sarah Stanbury, 42–58. A Gender and Culture Reader, ed. Carolyn G. Heilbrun and Nancy K. Miller. New York: Columbia University Press.

———, 1994. "Rape, Genocide, and Women's Human Rights." In *Mass Rape: The War against Women in Bosnia-Herzegovina*, ed. Alexandra Stiglmayer, tr. Marion Faber, 183–96. Foreword by Roy Gutman. Lincoln and London: University of Nebraska Press.

MacMullen, Ramsay, 1986. "Judicial Savagery in the Roman Empire." *Chiron: Mitteilungen der Kommission für alte Geschichte und Epigraphik des deutschen archäologischen Instituts* 16: 147–66.

Magnus Magnusson and Hermann Pálsson, 1965. "Introduction." In *The Vinland Sagas: The Norse Discovery of America*, ed. and tr. iidem, 7–43. Harmondsworth: Penguin.

Mak, Tim, 2014. "Sexy Selfies Flood In for Israeli Troops." *The Daily Beast*. Accessible at <http://www.thedailybeast.com/articles/2014/07/25/a-new-facebook-page-dedicated-to-the-idf-is-being-flooded-with-sexy-selfies. html> (originally posted 25 July 2014).

Mancini, J.M., 2002. "Discovering Viking America." *Critical Inquiry* 28.4: 868–907.

[Marchal, J., (ed.)], 1842. *Catalogue des manuscrits de la Bibliothèque royale des ducs de Bourgogne*, 3 vols. Brussels and Leipzig: C. Muquardt.

Marti, Susan, and Daniela Mondini, 1994. "'Ich manen dich der brüsten min, Das du dem sünder wellest milte sin!' Marienbrüste und Marienmilch im Heilsgeschehen." In Jezler (1994a), 79–90.

Marshall, Ingeborg, 1996. *A History and Ethnography of the Beothuk*. Montreal & Kingston et al.: McGill-Queen's University Press.

Mathiez, A., 1898–99. "Étude critique sur les journées des 5 & 6 octobre, 1789." *Revue Historique* 68.1 (1898): 241–81, 68.2 (1898): 258–94, and 69.1 (1899): 41–66.

Matter, E. Ann, 1990. *The Voice of My Beloved: The Song of Songs in Western Medieval Christianity*. Philadelphia: University of Pennsylvania Press.

Matthías Þórðarson, 1930 [orig. 1929]. *The Vinland Voyages*, tr. Thorstina Jackson Walters. American Geographical Society Research Series, 18. New York: American Geographical Society.

McKinnell, John, 2005. *Meeting the Other in Norse Myth and Legend*. Cambridge: D.S. Brewer.

McLaughlin, Megan, 1990. "The Woman Warrior: Gender, Warfare and Society in Medieval Europe." *Women's Studies: An Interdisciplinary Journal* 17.3–4: 193–209.

McNair, Brian, 1996. *Mediated Sex: Pornography and Postmodern Culture*. London et al.: Arnold.

McTurk, Rory (ed.), 2005. *A Companion to Old Norse-Icelandic Literature and Culture*. Blackwell Companions to Literature and Culture, 31. Malden, MA and Oxford: Blackwell.

Meier, Theo, 1959. *Die Gestalt Marias in geistlichen Schauspiel des deutschen Mittelalters*. Philologische Studien und Quellen, ed. Wolfgang Stammler. Berlin: Erich Schmidt.

Meiss, Millard, 1954. "An Early Altarpiece from the Cathedral of Florence." *The Metropolitan Museum of Art Bulletin* n.s. 12.10: 302–17.

Meulengracht Sørensen, Preben, 1983 [orig. 1980]. *The Unmanly Man: Concepts of Sexual Defamation in Early Northern Society*, tr. Joan Turville-Petre. The Viking Collection: Studies in Northern Civilization, 1. Odense: Odense University Press.

———, 1993a [orig. 1977]. *Saga and Society: An Introduction to Old Norse Literature*, tr. John Tucker. Studia Borealia, 1. [Odense:] Odense University Press.

———, 1993b. "Historical Reality and Literary Form." In Faulkes and Perkins (1993), 172–81.

———, 1993c. *Fortælling og ære: Studier i islændingesagaerne*. Århus: Århus universitetsforlag.

Meyerson, Mark D., Daniel Thiery and Oren Falk (ed.), 2004. *'A Great Effusion of Blood'? Interpreting Medieval Violence*. Toronto: University of Toronto Press.

Michelet, Jules, 1847–53 [repr. 1952]. *Histoire de la Révolution française*, ed. Gérard Walter. 2 vols. Bibliothèque de la Pléiade, 55–56. [Paris:] Gallimard.

Miles, Margaret R., 1986. "The Virgin's One Bare Breast: Female Nudity and Religious Meaning in Tuscan Early Renaissance Culture." In *The Female Body in Western Culture: Contemporary Perspectives*, ed. Susan Rubin Suleiman, 193–208. Cambridge, MA and London: Harvard University Press.

———, 1989. *Carnal Knowing: Female Nakedness and Religious Meaning in the Christian West*. Boston: Beacon.

———, 2008. *A Complex Delight: The Secularization of the Breast, 1350–1750*. Berkeley and Los Angeles: University of California Press.

Miller, William Ian, 1990. *Bloodtaking and Peacemaking: Feud, Law, and Society in Saga Iceland*. Chicago and London: University of Chicago Press.

———, 2000. *The Mystery of Courage*. Cambridge, MA and London: Harvard University Press.

Mimouni, Simon Claude, 1993 [repr. 2011]. "Les *Apocalypses de le Vierge*: Etat de la question." In idem, *Les traditions anciennes sur la Dormition et l'Assomption de Marie: Études littéraires, historiques et doctrinales*, 117–28. Supplements to Vigiliae Christianae: Texts and Studies of Early Christian Life and Language, 104, ed. J. den Boeft et al. Leiden and Boston: Brill.

Moeglin, Jean-Marie, 1994. "Edouard III et les six bourgeois de Calais." *Revue historique* 292.2: 229–67.

Montserrat, Dominic, 1996. *Sex and Society in Graeco-Roman Egypt.* London and New York: Kegan Paul International.

Moore, R.I., 2007. *The Formation of a Persecuting Society: Authority and Deviance in Western Europe 950–1250,* 2nd ed. Malden, MA et al.: Blackwell.

Moreau, Jacques, 1951. "Les guerriers et les femmes impudiques." *Annuaire de l'Institut de Philologie et d'Histoire Orientales et Slaves* 11 (*Mélanges Henri Grégoire*): 283–300.

Morgan, Nigel, 1991. "Texts and Images of Marian Devotion in Thirteenth-Century England." In *England in the Thirteenth Century: Proceedings of the 1989 Harlaxton Symposium,* ed. W.M. Ormrod, 69–97 and pll. 5–20. Harlaxton Medieval Studies, 1, Paul Watkins Medieval Studies, 9, ed. Shaun Tyas. Stamford: Paul Watkins.

Morison, Samuel Eliot, 1971–74. *The European Discovery of America,* 2 vols. New York: Oxford University Press.

Morse, Ruth, 1991. *Truth and Convention in the Middle Ages: Rhetoric, Representation and Reality.* Cambridge: Cambridge University Press.

Mowat, Farley, 1965. *Westviking: The Ancient Norse in Greenland and North America.* Boston and Toronto: Little, Brown and Company.

Much, Rudolf, 1909. "Die germanischen Frauen in der Schlacht." *Mitteilungen der anthropologischen Gesellschaft in Wien* 39: 156–62.

Muir, Edward, 2005. *Ritual in Early Modern Europe.* 2nd ed. New Approaches to European History, ed. William Beik and T.C.W. Blanning. Cambridge: Cambridge University Press.

Mundt, Marina, 1993. *Zur Adaption orientalischer Bilder in den Fornaldarsögur Norðrlanda: Materialien zu einer neuen Dimension altnordischer Belletristik.* Frankfurt a.M. et al.: Peter Lang.

Mussafia, A., 1886. "Studien zu den mittelalterlichen Marienlegenden I." *Sitzungsberichte der philosophisch-historische Classe der kaiserlichen Akademie der Wissenschaften* 113: 917–94.

Næshagen, Ferdinand Linthoe, 2000. "Medieval Norwegian Religiosity: Historical Sources and Modern Social Science." *Scandinavian Journal of History* 25.4: 297–316.

Nansen, Fridtjof, 1911. *In Northern Mists: Arctic Exploration in Early Times,* tr. Arthur G. Chater, 2 vols. London: William Heinemann.

Ness, Cindy D., 2007. "The Rise in Female Violence." *Dædalus* 136.1: 84–93.

Ní Dhonnchadha, Máirín, 1982. "The Guarantor List of *Cáin Adomnáin,* 697." *Peritia* 1: 178–215.

———, 2001. "Birr and the Law of the Innocents." In *Adomnán at Birr, AD 697: Essays in Commemoration of the Law of the Innocents,* ed. Thomas O'Loughlin, 13–32. Dublin: Four Courts Press.

Nicholas, David, 1985. *The Domestic Life of a Medieval City: Women, Children, and the Family in Fourteenth-Century Ghent.* Lincoln and London: University of Nebraska Press.

————, 1992. *Medieval Flanders*. London and New York: Longman.

Nicholson, Helen, 1997. "Women on the Third Crusade." *Journal of Medieval History* 23.4: 335–49.

Nip, Renée, 1995. "Godelieve of Gistel and Ida of Boulogne." In *Sanctity and Motherhood: Essays on Holy Mothers in the Middle Ages*, ed. Anneke B. Mulder-Bakker, 191–223. Garland Medieval Casebooks, ed. Joyce E. Salisbury and Christopher Kleinhenz. New York and London: Garland.

Nirenberg, David, 1996. *Communities of Violence: Persecution of Minorities in the Middle Ages*. Princeton: Princeton University Press.

Noreen, E., 1932. "Ordet *bärsärk*." *Arkiv för nordisk filologi* 48: 242–54.

Oberman, Heiko Augustinus, 1963. *The Harvest of Medieval Theology: Gabriel Biel and Late Medieval Nominalism*. Cambridge, MA: Harvard University Press.

O'Donoghue, Heather, 2004. *Old Norse–Icelandic Literature: A Short Introduction*. Blackwell Introductions to Literature, 6. Malden, MA et al.: Blackwell.

Ohle, Karlheinz, 1978. *Das Ich und das Andere: Grundzüge einer Soziologie des Fremden*. Sozialwissenschaftliche Studien: Schriftenreihe des Seminars für Sozialwissenschaften der Universität Hamburg, 15, ed. Wilhelm Hennis et al. Stuttgart: Gustav Fischer Verlag.

Ólafur Halldórsson, 2001. "The Vínland Sagas," tr. Andrew Wawn. In Wawn and Þórunn Sigurðardóttir (2001), 39–51.

Olender, Maurice, 1990 [orig. 1985]. "Aspects of Baubo: Ancient Texts and Contexts," tr. Robert Lamberton. In *Before Sexuality: The Construction of Erotic Experience in the Ancient Greek World*, ed. David M. Halperin, John J. Winkler, and Froma I. Zeitlin, 83–113. Princeton: Princeton University Press.

Orthmann, Winfried, 1969–70. "Die säugende Göttin: Zu einem Relief aus Karatepe." *Istanbuler Mitteilungen* 19–20: 137–43.

Overing, Gillian R., 1999. "A Body in Question: Aging, Community, and Gender in Medieval Iceland." *Journal of Medieval and Early Modern Studies* 29: 211–25.

Packe, Michael, 1983. *King Edward III*, ed. L.C.B. Seaman. London et al.: Routledge & Kegan Paul.

Pagden, Anthony, 1982. *The Fall of Natural Man: The American Indian and the Origins of Comparative Ethnology*. Cambridge Iberian and Latin American Studies, ed. P.E. Russell. Cambridge et al.: Cambridge University Press.

Panofsky, Erwin, 1927. "'Imago Pietatis': Ein Beitrag zur Typengeschichte des 'Schmerzensmanns' und der 'Maria Mediatrix'." In *Festschrift für Max J. Friedländer zum 60. Geburtstage*, [ed. Gustav Kirstein], 261–308. Leipzig: E.A. Seemann.

Paris, Gaston, 1899. "Caradoc et le serpent." *Romania: Recueil trimestriel consacré a l'étude des langues et des littératures romanes* 28: 214–31.

Parks, Ward, 2000 [repr. 2002]. "Flyting [Fliting]." In *Medieval Folklore: A Guide to Myths, Legends, Tales, Beliefs, and Customs*, ed. Carl Lindahl, John

McNamara, and John Lindow, 137–38. Oxford et al.: Oxford University Press.

Parsons, John Carmi, 1992. "Ritual and Symbol in the English Medieval Queenship to 1500." In *Women and Sovereignty*, ed. Louise Olga Fradenburg, 60–77. Cosmos: The Yearbook of the Traditional Cosmology Society, 7, ed. Emily Lyle. Edinburgh: Edinburgh University Press.

———, 1995. "The Queen's Intercession in Thirteenth-Century England." In Carpenter & MacLean (1995), 147–77.

———, 1996. "The Pregnant Queen as Counsellor and the Medieval Construction of Motherhood." In *Medieval Mothering*, ed. John Carmi Parsons and Bonnie Wheeler, 39–61. New York and London: Garland.

———, 2004. "Violence, the Queen's Body and the Medieval Body Politic." In Meyerson et al. (2004), 241–67.

Patterson Corrington, Gail, 1989. "The Milk of Salvation: Redemption by the Mother in Late Antiquity and Early Christianity." *Harvard Theological Review* 82.4: 393–420.

Peckham, Morse, 1969. *Art and Pornography: An Experiment in Explanation*. New York: Basic Books.

Pedersen, Kirsten, 1989. "The Mälkĕ: An Ethiopian Prayer Form with Latin Origin?" In *Proceedings of the Eighth International Conference of Ethiopian Studies, University of Addis Ababa, 1984*, ed. Taddese Beyene, 2: 547–60. Addis Ababa: Institute of Ethiopian Studies.

Pederson, Kristen, 1997. "It Takes a Brave Man to Be a Woman: Seiðr and the Blurring of Gender Lines in Medieval Iceland." Paper presented at the 32nd International Congress on Medieval Studies, Kalamazoo, MI.

Pentikäinen, Juha, 2007. *Golden King of the Forest: The Lore of the Northern Bear*, ed. and tr. Clive Tolley. Helsinki: Etnika Oy.

Perdrizet, Paul, 1908. *La Vierge de Miséricorde: Étude d'un thème iconographique*. Bibliothèque des Écoles françaises d'Athènes et de Rome, 101. Paris: Albert Fontemoing.

Perkins, Richard, 2004. "Medieval Norse Visits to North America: Millennial Stocktaking." *Saga-Book* 28: 29–69.

———, 2011. *The Verses in Eric the Red's Saga. And again: Norse Visits to America*. The Dorothea Coke Memorial Lecture in Northern Studies delivered at University College London 5 March 2009. London: Viking Society for Northern Research.

Perron, Anthony, 2010. "Saxo Grammaticus's Heroic Chastity: A Model of Clerical Celibacy and Masculinity in Medieval Scandinavia." In *Negotiating Clerical Identities: Priests, Monks and Masculinity in the Middle Ages*, ed. Jennifer D. Thibodeaux, 113–35. Genders and Sexualities in History, ed. John H. Arnold, Joanna Bourke, and Sean Brady. Houndmills and New York: Palgrave Macmillan.

Phelpstead, Carl, 2003. "The Sexual Ideology of *Hrólfs saga kraka*." *Scandinavian Studies* 75.1: 1–24.

Pilkington, Ed, 2011. "SlutWalking Gets Rolling after Cop's Loose Talk about Provocative Clothing." *The Guardian*. Accessible at <http://www.guardian.co.uk/world/2011/may/06/slutwalking-policeman-talk-clothing> (originally posted 6 May 2011).

Pipping, Hugo, 1927. "Eddastudier III." *Studier i nordisk filologi* 18.4: 1–58.

———, 1930. "Hávamál 136." In *Studies in Honor of Hermann Collitz: Presented by a Group of his Pupils and Friends on the Occasion of his Seventy-Fifth Birthday, February 4, 1930*, 155–58. Baltimore: Johns Hopkins University Press.

Pohl, Frederick J., 1966. *The Viking Explorers*. New York: Thomas Y. Crowell Company.

———, 1972. *The Viking Settlements of North America*. New York: Clarkson N. Potter.

Poole, R.G., 1991. *Viking Poems on War and Peace: A Study in Skaldic Narrative*. Toronto Medieval Texts and Translations, 8. Toronto et al.: University of Toronto Press.

Præstgaard Andersen, Lise, 1982. *Skjoldmøer: En kvindemyte*. Viborg: Gyldendal.

———, 2002. "On Valkyries, Shield-Maidens and other Armed Women—in Old Norse Sources and Saxo Grammaticus." In *Mythological Women: Studies in Memory of Lotte Motz, 1922–1997*, ed. Rudolph Simek and Wilhelm Heizmann, 291–318. Studia Medievalia Septentrionalia, 7, ed. Rudolph Simek. Vienna: Fassbaender.

Price, Neil S., 2002. *The Viking Way: Religion and War in Late Iron Age Scandinavia*. AUN 31. Uppsala: Uppsala Univesitet.

Pulsiano, Phillip, et al. (eds.), 1993. *Medieval Scandinavia: An Encyclopedia*. New York and London: Garland Publishing.

Rabinowitz, Peter J., 1977. "Truth in Fiction: A Reexamination of Audiences." *Critical Inquiry* 4.1: 121–41.

Rayner, Steve, 1992. "Cultural Theory and Risk Analysis." In *Social Theories of Risk*, ed. Sheldon Krimsky and Dominic Golding, 83–115. Westport, CT and London: Praeger.

Reeves, Arthur Middleton (ed. and tr.), 1890. *The Finding of Wineland the Good: The History of the Icelandic Discovery of America*. London: Henry Frowde.

Remensnyder, Amy G., 2014. *La Conquistadora: The Virgin Mary at War and Peace in the Old and New Worlds*. Oxford: Oxford University Press.

Renard, Marcel, 1964. "Hercule allaité par Junon." In *Hommages à Jean Bayet*, ed. Marcel Renard and Robert Schilling, 611–18. Collection Latomus, 70. Brussels: Latomus.

Reventós, Domingo, 1869. "Lloch predestinat ó sia la Mare de Deu de la Bona Sort." *Lo Gay Saber* 1st ser. 2.33: 257–59.

[de Rey, G.,] 1885. *Les Saints de l'Église de Marseille.* Marseilles: Société anonyme de l'imprimerie marseillaise.

Rimmon-Kenan, Shlomith, 2002. *Narrative Fiction: Contemporary Poetics*, 2nd ed. New Accents, ed. Terence Hawkes. London and New York: Routledge.

Ronig, Franz J., 1974. "Zum theologischen Gehalt des Bilder der stillenden Muttergottes." In *Die Gottesmutter: Marienbild in Rheinland und in Westfalen*, ed. Leonhard Küppers, 2 vols., 1: 197–214. Recklinghausen: Aurel Bongers.

Roudinesco, Elisabeth, 1991 [orig. 1989]. *Théroigne de Méricourt: A Melancholic Woman during the French Revolution*, tr. Martin Thom. London and New York: Verso.

Rowe, Elizabeth A., 1995. "The Female Body Politic and the Miscarriage of Justice in *Athelston.*" *Studies in the Age of Chaucer* 17: 79–98.

Rozee, Patricia D., and Mary P. Koss, 2001. "Rape: A Century of Resistance." *Psychology of Women Quarterly* 25: 295–311.

Rubin, Miri, 2009a. *Mother of God: A History of the Virgin Mary.* New Haven and London: Yale University Press.

———, 2009b. *Emotion and Devotion: The Meaning of Mary in Medieval Religious Cultures.* The Natalie Zemon Davis Annual Lecture Series at Central European University, Budapest. Budapest and New York: Central European University Press.

Ryan, Salvador, 2002–3. "The Persuasive Power of a Mother's Breast: The Most Desperate Act of the Virgin Mary's Advocacy." *Studia Hibernica* 32: 59–74.

Salomons, Vera, 1972. *Charles Eisen: Eighteenth-Century French Book Illustrator and Engraver.* Foreword by Émile Bertaux. Scripta Artis Monographia, 17. Amsterdam: G.W. Hissink & Co.

Sandnes, Karl Olav, 2002. *Belly and Body in the Pauline Epistles.* Society for New Testament Studies Monograph Series, 120, ed. Richard Bauckham. Cambridge et al.: Cambridge University Press.

Sartori, Paul, 1935. "Ein apotropäischer Kriegsbrauch." *Archiv für Religionswissenschaft* 32.1–2: 191–92.

Sautman, Francesca Canadé, 2001. "What Can They Possibly Do Together? Queer Epic Performances in *Tristan de Nanteuil.*" In *Same Sex Love and Desire among Women in the Middle Ages*, ed. eadem and Pamela Sheingorn.

Schama, Simon, 1989. *Citizens: A Chronicle of the French Revolution.* New York: Alfred A. Knopf.

Schiller, Gertrud, 1968. "Die Fürbitte des Erlösers." In eadem, *Ikonographie der christlichen Kunst.* 5 vols., 2: 238–40. Gütersloh: Gerd Mohn. [references by column number]

Schledermann, Peter, 2000. "A.D. 1000: East Meets West." In Fitzhugh and Ward (2000), 189–92.

Schoolcraft, Henry Rowe, 1851–57. *Historical and Statistical Information respecting the History, Condition, and Prospects of the Indian Tribes of the United States*, 6 vols. Philadelphia: Lippincott and Grambo.

Schottmann, Hans, 1973. *Die isländische Mariendichtung: Untersuchungen zur volkssprachigen Mariendichtung des Mittelalters.* Münchner Germanistische Beiträge, 9, ed. Werner Betz and Hermann Kunisch. Munich: Wilhelm Fink.

Schrade, Hubert, 1930. "Beiträge zur Erklärung des Schmerzensmannbildes." In *Deutschkundliches: Friedrich Panzer zum 60. Geburtstage überreicht von Heidelberger Fachgenossen*, ed. Hans Teste, 164–82. Beiträge zur neueren Literaturgeschichte, n.s. 16, ed. Max Freiherr von Waldberg. Heidelberg: Carl Winters Universitätsbuchhandlung.

Schreiber, Georg, 1959. *Die Wochentage im Erlebnis der Ostkirche und des christlichen Abendlandes.* Wissenschaftliche Abhandlungen der Arbeitsgemeinschaft für Forschung des Landes Nordrhein-Westfalen, 11. Cologne and Opladen: Westdeutscher Verlag.

Schreiner, Klaus, 1994. *Maria: Jungfrau, Mutter, Herrscherin.* Munich and Vienna: Carl Hanser.

Schulenburg, Jane Tibbetts, 1986. "The Heroics of Virginity: Brides of Christ and Sacrificial Mutilation." In *Women in the Middle Ages and the Renaissance: Literary and Historical Perspectives*, ed. Mary Beth Rose, 29–72. Syracuse: Syracuse University Press.

———, 1998. *Forgetful of Their Sex: Female Sanctity and Society ca. 500–1100.* Chicago and London: University of Chicago Press.

Schwennicke, Detlev (ed.), 1980–2011. *Europäische Stammtafeln: Stammtafeln zur Geschichte der europäischen Staaten.* New ser., 28 vols [to date]. Marburg, Berlin, and Frankfurt a.M.: J.A. Stargardt and Vittorio Klostermann.

von See, Klaus, 1961. "Exkurs zum Haraldskvæði: Berserker." *Zeitschrift für deutsche Wortforschung* 17: 129–35.

Seidel, Max, 1977. "Ubera Matris: Die vielschichtige Bedeutung eines Symbols in der mitterlalterlichen Kunst." *Städel-Jahrbuch* n.s. 6: 41–98.

Seward, Desmond, 1978. *The Hundred Years War: The English in France, 1337–1453.* London: Constable.

Shahar, Shulamith, 1992 [orig. 1990]. *Childhood in the Middle Ages*, tr. Chaya Galai. London and New York: Routledge.

Sjoholm, Barbara, 2004. "Freydis: Heroine or Murderer?" In Linden (2004), 97.

Smith, Roger A., 1981. "Flyting: The Use of Abuse." MA Thesis, University of Nevada, Reno.

Somerville, Angus A., and R. Andrew McDonald (eds.), 2010. *The Viking Age: A Reader.* Readings in Medieval Civilizations and Cultures, 14, ed. Paul Edward Dutton. Toronto et al.: University of Toronto Press.

Sourvinou-Inwood, Christiane, 1991. *'Reading' Greek Culture: Texts and Images, Rituals and Myths.* Oxford: Clarendon Press.

Stallybrass, Peter, 1989. "'Drunk with the Cup of Liberty': Robin Hood, the Carnivalesque, and the Rhetoric of Violence in Early Modern England." In *The Violence of Representation: Literature and the History of Violence*, ed.

Nancy Armstrong and Leonard Tennenhouse, 45–76. Essays in Literature and Society, ed. iidem. London and New York: Routledge.

Stanford, W.B., 1970. "Towards a History of Classical Influences in Ireland." *Proceedings of the Royal Irish Academy, C: Archaeology, Celtic Studies,History, Linguistics, Literature* 70: 13–91.

Stange, Alfred, 1934–61 [repr. 1969]. *Deutsche Malerei der Gotik.* 11 vols. Berlin and Munich: Deutscher Kunstverlag.

Stannard, David E., 1992. *American Holocaust: Columbus and the Conquest of the New World.* New York and Oxford: Oxford University Press.

Stefán Einarsson, 1939. "The Freydís Incident in *Eiríks saga rauða*, Ch. 11." *Acta Philologica Scandinavica* 13.2: 246–56.

Steinberg, Leo, 1996. *The Sexuality of Christ in Renaissance Art and in Modern Oblivion*, 2nd ed. Chicago and London: University of Chicago Press.

Stevens, Edward B., 1942. "Comment and Conjecture on Ovid." *Classical Weekly* 35.20: 231.

Storm, Gustav, 1888. "Studies on the Vineland Voyages." *Mémoires de la Société royale des antiquaires du nord* n.s. [4]: 307–74.

Straub, Richard E.F., 1995. *David Aubert, escripvain et clerc.* Faux Titre: Etudes de langue et littérature françaises, 96, ed. Keith Busby et al. Amsterdam and Atlanta: Rodopi.

Strickland, Matthew, 1996. *War and Chivalry: The Conduct and Perception of War in England and Normandy, 1066–1217.* Cambridge: Cambridge University Press.

Strohm, Paul, 1992. "Queens as Intercessors." In idem, *Hochon's Arrow: The Social Imagination of Fourteenth-Century Texts*, 95–119. Princeton: Princeton University Press.

Sverrir Tómasson, 1988. *Formálar íslenskra sagnaritara á miðöldum.* Stofnun Árna Magnússonar á Íslandi, 33, ed. Sveinbjörn Rafnsson. Reykjavík: Stofnun Árna Magnússonar.

Swartling, Ingrid, 1963. "Maria såsom förebedjerska: Ett cisterciensiskt motiv i Årsunda kyrka." *Från Gästrikland*: 45–53.

Swenson, Karen, 1991. *Performing Definitions: Two Genres of Insult in Old Norse Literature.* Studies in Scandinavian Literature and Culture, 3. Columbia, SC: Camden House.

Taddesse Tamrat, 1972. *Church and State in Ethiopia, 1270–1527.* Oxford Studies in African Affairs, ed. John D. Hargreaves and George Shepperson. Oxford: Clarendon Press.

Thomas, Keith, 1971. *Religion and the Decline of Magic.* New York: Charles Scribner's Sons.

Thomas, R. George, 1946–53. "Some Exceptional Women in the Sagas." *Saga-Book* 13: 307–27.

Thompson, Stith, 1955–58. *Motif-Index of Folk-Literature*, rev. enl. ed., 6 vols. Bloomington: Indiana University Press.

Todorov, Tzvetan, 1984 [orig. 1982]. *The Conquest of America: The Question of the Other*, tr. Richard Howard. New York: Harper & Row.

Tolmie, Jane Marianna, 2001. *Persuasion: Blood-feud, Romance and the Disenfranchised*. Ph.D. Diss., Harvard University.

Townsend, David, 1995. "Sex and the Single Amazon in Twelfth-Century Latin Epic." *University of Toronto Quarterly* 64.2: 255–73.

Trouillas, Paul, 1988. *Le Complexe de Marianne*. Paris: Éditions du Seuil.

Tubach, Frederic C., 1969. *Index Exemplorum: A Handbook of Medieval Religious Tales*. Helsinki: Suomalianen tiedeakatemia.

Tulinius, Torfi H., 2005. "Sagas of Icelandic Prehistory (*fornaldarsögur*)." In McTurk (2005), 447–61.

Úlfar Bragason, 1986. *On the Poetics of Sturlunga*. PhD Diss., University of California at Berkeley.

———, 2010. *Ætt og saga: Um frásagnarfræði Sturlungu eða Íslendinga sögu hinnar miklu*. Reykjavík: Háskólaútgáfan.

Ullendorff, E., 1956. "Hebraic-Jewish Elements in Abyssinian (Monophysite) Christianity." *Journal of Semitic Studies* 1.3: 216–56.

Ullman, Sarah E., 1997. "Review and Critique of Empirical Studies of Rape Avoidance." *Criminal Justice and Behavior* 24.2: 177–204.

———, 2007. "A 10-Year Update of 'Review and Critique of Empirical Studies of Rape Avoidance.'" *Criminal Justice and Behavior* 34.3: 411–29.

Underhill, Evelyn, 1919. *Jacopone da Todi, Poet and Mystic — 1228–1306: A Spiritual Biography*. Verse translations by Mrs. Theodore Beck. London, Toronto and New York: J.M. Dent & Sons and E.P. Dutton.

Van den Bergen-Pantens, Christiane, and Michiel Verweij, 2009. "Cote — Signalement KBR 10432–35 (anc. 297)." In *La Librairie des ducs de Bourgogne: Manuscrits conservés à la Bibliothèque royale de Belgique*, ed. Bernard Bousmanne, Tania Van Hemelryck, and Céline Van Hoorebeeck, 4: 202–6. Turnhout: Brepols.

Van den Gheyn, J., et al. (ed.), 1901–48. *Catalogue des manuscrits de la Bibliothèque royale de Belgique*, 13 vols. Brussels and Renaix: Henri Lamertin and J. Leherte Courtin.

Vaughan, Richard, 1962. *Philip the Bold: The Formation of the Burgundian State*. London: Longmans.

Vésteinn Ólason, 2001. "Saga-tekstene — forskningsstatus." In *Leiv Eriksson, Helge Ingstad og Vinland: Kjelder og tradisjonar. innleg ved eit seminar i regi av Det Kongelige Norske Videnskabers Selskab 13–14 oktober 2000*, ed. Jan Ragnar Hagland and Steinar Supphellen, 41–64. Trondheim: Tapir Akademisk Forlag.

Villecourt, Louis, 1924. "Les Collections arabes des miracles de la Sainte Vierge." *Analecta Bollandiana* 42: 21–68.

Vinding, Niels, 1998. *Vinland 1000 år*. [Viborg:] Lindhardt og Ringhof.

Vinner, Max, 1993. "Vinland the Good — or the Lost." In Clausen (1993), 67–76.

Vollert, Konrad, 1912. *Zur Geschichte der lateinischen Facetiensammlungen des XV. und XVI. Jahrhunderts*. Palaestra: Untersuchungen und texte aus der deutschen und englischen Philologie, 113, ed. Alois Brandl, Gustav Roethe, and Erich Schmidt. Berlin: Mayer & Müller.

Vorwahl, H., 1933. "Ein apotropäischer Kriegsbrauch." *Archiv für Religionswissenschaft* 30.3–4: 395–97.

de Vries, Jan, 1962 [repr. 1977]. *Altnordischs etymologisches Wörterbuch*, 2nd ed. Leiden: E.J. Brill.

Wahlgren, Erik, 1938. *The Maiden King in Iceland*. Ph.D. Diss., University of Chicago.

———, 1969. "Fact and Fiction in the Vinland Sagas." In *Old Norse Literature and Mythology: A Symposium*, ed. Edgar C. Polomé, 19–80. Austin and London: University of Texas Press.

———, 1986. *The Vikings and America*. Ancient Peoples and Places, 102. London: Thames and Hudson.

———, 1993. "Vínland Sagas." In Pulsiano et al. (1993), 704–5.

Wakefield, Walter L., and Austin P. Evans (eds. and trs.), 1969 [repr. 1991]. *Heresies of the High Middle Ages*. Records of Western Civilization, ed. Malcolm Bean et al. New York: Columbia University Press.

Wallace, Birgitta Linderoth, 1993. "L'Anse aux Meadows, the Western Outpost." In Clausen (1993), 30–42.

———, 2000. "The Viking Settlement at L'Anse aux Meadows." In Fitzhugh and Ward (2000), 208–16.

———, 2003. "Vínland and the Death of Þorvaldr." In Lewis-Simpson (2003), 377–90.

———, 2006. *Westward Vikings: The Saga of L'Anse aux Meadows*. St. John's, NL: Historic Sites Association of Newfoundland and Labrador.

Walters, C.C., 1989. "Christian Paintings from Tebtunis." *Journal of Egyptian Archaeology* 75: 191–208, pll. XVI–XXIX.

Ward, H.L.D., 1883–93. *Catalogue of Romances in the Department of Manuscripts in the British Museum*, 2 vols. London: British Museum et al.

Warner, Marina, 1976. *Alone of All Her Sex: The Myth and the Cult of the Virgin Mary*. Dictionary of Moral Theology. London: Weidenfeld and Nicholson.

———, 1985. *Monuments & Maidens: The Allegory of the Female Form*. London: Weidenfeld and Nicolson.

Wawn, Andrew, and Þórunn Sigurðardóttir (eds.), 2001. *Approaches to Vínland: Proceedings of a Conference on the Written and Archaeological Sources for the Norse Settlements in the North-Atlantic Region and Exploration of America, The Nordic House, Reykjavík, 9–11 August 1999*. Sigurður Nordal Institute Studies 4. Reykjavík: Sigurður Nordal Institute.

Weber-Lehmann, Cornellia, 2000. "Anasyrma und Götterhochzeit: Ein orientalisches Bildmotiv im nacharchaischen Etrurien." In *Akten des Kolloquiums zum Thema Der Orient und Etrurien: Zum Phänomen des 'Orientalisierens' im westlichen Mittelmeerraum (10.-6. Jh. v. Chr.), Tübingen, 12–13. Juni 1997,* ed. Friedhelm Prayon and Wolfgang Röllig, 263–74 and Taf. 1. Istituto nazionale di studi etruschi ed italici, Biblioteca di "Studi Etruschi," 35. Rome: Istituti Editoriali e Poligrafici Internazionali.

Weir, Anthony, and James Jerman, 1986. *Images of Lust: Sexual Carvings on Medieval Churches.* London: B.T. Batsford.

Whatley, E. Gordon, 2011. "The Female Joseph? Sources of the Saint Eugenia Legend." Keynote address at the 21st Medieval Studies Student Colloquium, Cornell University, Ithaca, NY (19 February).

Wheeler, Bonnie (ed.), 2006. *Mindful Spirit in Late Medieval Literature: Essays in Honor of Elizabeth D. Kirk.* The New Middle Ages, ed. Bonnie Wheeler. New York and Houndmills: Palgrave Macmillan.

Widding, Ole, 1961. "Kilderne til den norrøne Nicolaus saga," *Opuscula 2 Bibliotheca Arnamagnæana* 25.1: 17–26.

———, and Hans Bekker-Nielsen, 1961. "The Virgin Bares her Breast: An Icelandic Version of a Miracle of the Blessed Virgin." *Opuscula 2, Bibliotheca Arnamagnæana* 25.1: 76–79.

Williams, Craig, 2012. "Perpetua's Gender: A Latinist Reads the *Passio Perpetuae et Felicitatis.*" In *Perpetua's Passions: Multidisciplinary Approaches to the Passio Perpetuae et Felicitatis,* ed. Jan N. Bremmer and Marco Formisano, 54–77. Oxford: Oxford University Press.

Williamsen, E.A., 2005. "Boundaries of Difference in the Vínland Sagas." *Scandinavian Studies* 77.4: 451–78.

Williamson, Beth, 2000. "The *Cloisters Double Intercession*: The Virgin as Co-Redemptrix." *Apollo: The International Magazine of the Arts* 152.465: 48–54.

Williamson, Marjorie, 1932. "Les yeux arrachés." *Philological Quarterly* 11.2: 149–62.

Winstead, Karen A., 1997. *Virgin Martyrs: Legends of Sainthood in Late Medieval England.* Ithaca and London: Cornell University Press.

Witkowski, G.-J., 1903. *Les Seins dans l'histoire.* Paris: Maloine.

Wolf, Kirsten, 1996. "Amazons in Vínland." *Journal of English and Germanic Philology* 95: 469–85.

———, 1997b. "The Severed Breast: A Topos in the Legends of Female Virgin Martyr Saints." *Arkiv for nordisk filologi* 112: 97–112.

———, 1997c. "Klæðskiptingar í Íslendingasögunum." *Skírnir* 171: 381–400.

Yalom, Marylin, 1997. *A History of the Breast.* New York: Alfred A. Knopf.